Cloud Native programming with Golang

Develop microservice-based high performance web apps for the cloud with Go

Mina Andrawos
Martin Helmich

BIRMINGHAM - MUMBAI

Cloud Native programming with Golang

First published: December 2017

Production reference: 1261217

Published by Packt Publishing Ltd.
Livery Place
35 Livery Street
Birmingham
B3 2PB, UK.

ISBN 978-1-78712-598-8

www.packtpub.com

Credits

Authors
Mina Andrawos
Martin Helmich

Copy Editor
Dhanya Baburaj

Reviewer
Jelmer Snoeck

Project Coordinator
Sheejal Shah

Commissioning Editor
Aaron Lazar

Proofreader
Safis Editing

Acquisition Editor
Nitin Dasan

Indexer
Francy Puthiry

Content Development Editor
Sreeja Nair

Graphics
Jason Monteiro

Technical Editor
Prashant Mishra

Production Coordinator
Arvindkumar Gupta

About the Authors

Mina Andrawos is an experienced engineer who has developed deep experience in Go from using it personally and professionally. He regularly authors articles and tutorials about the language, and also shares Go's open source projects. He has written numerous Go applications with varying degrees of complexity.
Other than Go, he has skills in Java, C#, Python, and C++. He has worked with various databases and software architectures. He is also skilled with the agile methodology for software development. Besides software development, he has working experience of scrum mastering, sales engineering, and software product management.

> *For Nabil, Mervat, Catherine, and Fady.*
> *Thanks to all my family for their amazing support, and continuous encouragement.*

Martin Helmich studied computer science at the University of Applied Sciences in Osnabrück and lives in Rahden, Germany. He works as a software architect, specializing in building distributed applications using web technologies and Microservice Architectures. Besides programming in Go, PHP, Python, and Node.js, he also builds infrastructures using configuration management tools such as SaltStack and container technologies such as Docker and Kubernetes.

He is an Open Source enthusiast and likes to make fun of people who are not using Linux. In his free time, you'll probably find him coding on one of his open source pet projects, listening to music, or reading science-fiction literature.

About the Reviewer

Jelmer Snoeck is a software engineer with a focus on performance, reliability, and scaling. He's very passionate about open source and maintains several open source projects. Jelmer comes from a Ruby background and has been working with the Go language since 2014. He's taken a special interest in containers and Kubernetes, and is currently working on several projects to help with the deployment flow for these tools. Jelmer understands how to operate and scale distributed systems and is excited to share his experience with the world.

www.PacktPub.com

For support files and downloads related to your book, please visit www.PacktPub.com.

Did you know that Packt offers eBook versions of every book published, with PDF and ePub files available? You can upgrade to the eBook version at www.PacktPub.com and as a print book customer, you are entitled to a discount on the eBook copy. Get in touch with us at service@packtpub.com for more details.

At www.PacktPub.com, you can also read a collection of free technical articles, sign up for a range of free newsletters and receive exclusive discounts and offers on Packt books and eBooks.

https://www.packtpub.com/mapt

Get the most in-demand software skills with Mapt. Mapt gives you full access to all Packt books and video courses, as well as industry-leading tools to help you plan your personal development and advance your career.

Why subscribe?

- Fully searchable across every book published by Packt
- Copy and paste, print, and bookmark content
- On demand and accessible via a web browser

Customer Feedback

Thanks for purchasing this Packt book. At Packt, quality is at the heart of our editorial process. To help us improve, please leave us an honest review on this book's Amazon page at https://www.amazon.com/dp/178712598X.

If you'd like to join our team of regular reviewers, you can e-mail us at customerreviews@packtpub.com. We award our regular reviewers with free eBooks and videos in exchange for their valuable feedback. Help us be relentless in improving our products!

Table of Contents

Preface   1

Chapter 1: Modern Microservice Architectures   9
  Why Go?   10
  Basic design goals   11
  Cloud service models   13
  Cloud application architecture patterns   14
    The twelve-factor app   15
    What are microservices?   17
    Deploying microservices   17
    REST web services and asynchronous messaging   18
  The MyEvents platform   20
  Summary   22

Chapter 2: Building Microservices Using Rest APIs   23
  The background   23
    So, what are microservices?   26
      Microservices internals   27
  RESTful Web APIs   28
    Gorilla web toolkit   32
    Implementing a Restful API   33
      Persistence layer   38
      MongoDB   39
      MongoDB and the Go language   45
    Implementing our RESTful APIs handler functions   52
  Summary   60

Chapter 3: Securing Microservices   61
  HTTPS   62
    Symmetric cryptography   62
      Symmetric-key algorithms in HTTPS   63
    Asymmetric cryptography   64
      Asymmetrical cryptography in HTTPS   66
  Secure web services in Go   68
    Obtaining a certificate   68
      OpenSSL   69
      generate_cert.go   70

Building an HTTPS server in Go   72
Summary   78
Chapter 4: Asynchronous Microservice Architectures Using Message Queues   79
The publish/subscribe pattern   80
Introducing the booking service   82
Event collaboration   83
Implementing publish/subscribe with RabbitMQ   85
The Advanced Message Queueing Protocol   85
RabbitMQ quickstart with Docker   87
Advanced RabbitMQ setups   89
Connecting RabbitMQ with Go   89
Publishing and subscribing to AMQP messages   91
Building an event emitter   94
Building an event subscriber   101
Building the booking service   105
Event sourcing   108
Implementing publish/subscribe and event sourcing with Apache Kafka   109
Kafka quickstart with Docker   110
Basic principles of Apache Kafka   110
Connecting to Kafka with Go   113
Publishing messages with Kafka   114
Consuming messages from Kafka   117
Summary   122
Chapter 5: Building a Frontend with React   123
Getting started with React   124
Setting up Node.js and TypeScript   124
Initializing the React project   124
Basic React principles   127
Kick-starting the MyEvents frontend   130
Implementing the event list   133
Bringing your own client   134
Building the event list components   134
Enabling CORS in the backend services   140
Testing the event list   142
Adding routing and navigation   142
Implementing the booking process   145

Summary	154
Chapter 6: Deploying Your Application in Containers	155
What are containers?	156
Introduction to Docker	157
Running simple containers	157
Building your own images	160
Networking containers	162
Working with volumes	164
Building containers	165
Building containers for the backend services	165
Using static compilation for smaller images	168
Building containers for the frontend	170
Deploying your application with Docker Compose	172
Publishing your images	177
Deploying your application to the cloud	178
Introduction to Kubernetes	179
Setting up a local Kubernetes with Minikube	180
Core concepts of Kubernetes	182
Services	186
Persistent volumes	188
Deploying MyEvents to Kubernetes	190
Creating the RabbitMQ broker	190
Creating the MongoDB containers	193
Making images available to Kubernetes	194
Deploying the MyEvents components	195
Configuring HTTP Ingress	198
Summary	200
Chapter 7: AWS I – Fundamentals, AWS SDK for Go, and EC2	201
AWS fundamentals	202
The AWS console	203
AWS command-line interface (CLI)	204
AWS regions and zones	204
AWS tags	205
AWS Elastic Beanstalk	205
AWS services	206
AWS SDK for Go	206
Configuring the AWS region	206
Configuring AWS SDK authentication	207
Creating IAM Users	207
Creating IAM Roles	212

The fundamentals of the AWS SDK for Go 215
Sessions 215
Service clients 216
Native datatypes 217
Shared configuration 218
Pagination methods 218
Waiters 220
Handling Errors 220
Elastic Compute Cloud (EC2) 221
Creating EC2 instances 222
Accessing EC2 instances 229
Accessing EC2 instances from a Linux or macOS machine 231
Accessing EC2 from Windows 233
Security groups 240
Summary 247

Chapter 8: AWS II – S3, SQS, API Gateway, and DynamoDB 249
Simple Storage Service (S3) 249
Configuring S3 249
Simple Queue Service (SQS) 252
AWS API gateway 265
DynamoDB 274
DynamoDB components 274
Attribute value data types 275
Primary keys 276
Secondary indexes 277
Creating tables 278
The Go language and DynamoDB 283
Summary 293

Chapter 9: Continuous Delivery 295
Setting up your project 296
Setting up version control 296
Vendoring your dependencies 298
Using Travis CI 302
Deploying to Kubernetes 310
Using GitLab 313
Setting up GitLab 313
Setting up GitLab CI 316
Summary 328

Chapter 10: Monitoring Your Application 329
Setting up Prometheus and Grafana 329

Prometheus's basics 330
Creating an initial Prometheus configuration file 331
Running Prometheus on Docker 332
Running Grafana on Docker 336
Exporting metrics 338
Using the Prometheus client in your Go application 338
Configuring Prometheus scrape targets 340
Exporting custom metrics 342
Running Prometheus on Kubernetes 346
Summary 350

Chapter 11: Migration 351
What is a monolithic application? 351
What are microservices? 352
Migrating from monolithic applications to microservices 353
Humans and technology 353
Cutting a monolithic application to pieces 354
How do we break the code? 356
Glue code 356
Microservices design patterns 357
Sacrificial architecture 357
A four-tier engagement platform 358
Bounded contexts in domain-driven designs 360
Data consistency 364
Event-driven architecture for data consistency 365
Events sourcing 367
CQRS 369
Summary 370

Chapter 12: Where to Go from Here? 371
Microservices communications 372
Protocol buffers 372
GRPC 374
More on AWS 374
DynamoDB streams 375
Autoscaling on AWS 375
Amazon Relational Database Service 376
Other cloud providers 377
Microsoft Azure 378
Google Cloud Platform 379

OpenStack   379
Running containers in the cloud   380
Serverless architectures   381
Summary   382

Index   383

Preface

Cloud computing and microservices are two very important concepts in modern software architecture. They represent key skills that ambitious software engineers need to acquire in order to design and build software applications capable of performing and scaling. Go is a modern cross-platform programming language that is very powerful yet simple; it is an excellent choice for microservices and cloud applications. Go is gaining increasing popularity and becoming a very attractive skill.

The book will take you on a journey into the world of microservices and cloud computing with the help of Go. It will start by covering the software architectural patterns of cloud applications as well as practical concepts regarding how to scale, distribute, and deploy those applications. From there, the book will dive deep into the techniques and design approaches that are needed for writing production-level microservices and their deployment into typical cloud environments.

After completing this book, you will have learned how to write effective production-grade microservices that are deployable to the cloud, practically understand the world of Amazon Web Services, and know how to build non-trivial Go applications.

What this book covers

Chapter 1, *Modern Microservice Architectures*, opens the book by describing typical features of cloud-based applications and microservice architectures. We will also establish requirements and a high-level architecture for a fictional application that will serve as a continuous example over the following chapters of this book.

Chapter 2, *Building Microservices Using REST APIs*, discusses how to build modern microservices with the Go language. We will cover important and non-trivial topics. By the end of this chapter, you will have enough knowledge to build microservices that can expose RESTFul APIs, support persistence, and can effectively communicate with other services.

Chapter 3, *Securing Microservices*, shows you how to secure your microservices. You will get to learn about how to handle certificates and HTTPS in the Go language.

`Chapter` 4, *Asynchronous Microservice Architectures*, presents how to implement an asynchronous microservice architecture using message queues. For this, we will give an overview on established message queuing software, such as RabbitMQ and Apache Kafka, and present Go libraries to integrate these components into your software. We will also discuss architectural patterns such as Event Collaboration and Event Sourcing that work well together with asynchronous architectures.

`Chapter` 5, *Building a Frontend with React*, takes a small detour from the Go world into the JavaScript world and shows you how to build a web frontend for the microservice-based project using the React framework. For this, we will give a short overview over the basic architectural principles of React and how to build a React-based frontend for existing REST APIs.

`Chapter` 6, *Deploying Your Application in Containers*, shows how to deploy Go applications in a portable and reproducible way using application containers. You will learn to install and using Docker and how to build custom Docker images for your own Go applications. Furthermore, we will describe how to use the Kubernetes orchestration engine to deploy containerized applications in large-scale cloud environments.

`Chapter` 7, *AWS – Fundamentals, AWS SDK for Go and AWS EC2*, is the first of two chapters to cover the AWS ecosystem. In this chapter, we will cover AWS in practical details. You will get exposed to several important concepts like how to setup AWS server instances , how to utilize the AWS API features, and how to write Go applications that are capable of interacting with AWS.

`Chapter` 8, *AWS – S3, SQS, API Gateway, and DynamoDB*, continues to cover the AWS ecosystem in more detail. You will dive deeper into popular services in the AWS world. By the end of this chapter, you will have enough knowledge to build non-trivial Go cloud applications using the powers of Amazon Web Services.

`Chapter` 9, *Continuous Delivery*, describes how to implement a basic Continuous Delivery pipeline for your Go applications. For this, we will describe the basic principles of CD and how to implement a simple pipeline using tools such as Travis CI and Gitlab. We will use Docker images as deployment artifacts and deploy these images into a Kubernetes cluster, thus building on the topics and skills covered in `Chapter` 4, *Asynchronous Microservice Architectures*.

Chapter 10, *Monitoring Your Application*, shows you how to monitor your microservice architecture using Prometheus and Grafana. We will cover the basic architecture of Prometheus and describe how to set up a Prometheus instance using Docker. Also, you will learn how to adjust your Go applications to expose metrics that can be scraped by Prometheus. We will also describe how to set up a graphical user interface for Prometheus using Grafana.

Chapter 11, *Migration*, covers practical factors and approaches to consider when migrating from legacy monolithic applications into modern microservices cloud-ready applications.

Chapter 12, *Where to Go from Here?*, shows you where to continue the learning journey from here. It will cover other modern cloud-related technologies that deserve to be explored, such as alternative communication protocols, other cloud providers, and new architectural paradigms that might be the next big thing.

What you need for this book

For this book, you should have some basic knowledge of the Go programming language (if you're still looking to get started with Go, we can recommend the book *Learning Go Programming* by Vladimir Vivien, also published by Packt). To run the code examples provided in this book, you will also need a working Go SDK on your local machine (Go 1.7 or newer). Head to `https://golang.org/dl/` for download and installation instructions.

For many of the practical examples in the book, you will need a working Docker installation (although previous experience in working with Docker is not required). Take a look at `https://www.docker.com/community-edition` for download and installation instructions.

For working with React in Chapter 5, *Building a Frontend With React*, you will also need some basic knowledge in JavaScript programming and a working Node.JS installation on your local machine. You can download the current release of Node.JS from `https://nodejs.org/en/#download`.

Who this book is for

This book is targeted at Go developers who want to build secure, resilient, robust, and scalable applications that are cloud native. Some knowledge of web services and web programming should be sufficient to get you through the book.

Conventions

In this book, you will find a number of text styles that distinguish between different kinds of information. Here are some examples of these styles and an explanation of their meaning.

Code words in text, database table names, folder names, filenames, file extensions, pathnames, dummy URLs, user input, and Twitter handles are shown as follows: "The `react-router-dom` package adds a few new components to our application."

A block of code is set as follows:

```
import * as React from "react";
import {Link} from "react-router-dom";

export interface NavigationProps {
  brandName: string;
}

export class Navigation extends React.Component<NavigationProps, {}> {
}
```

Any command-line input or output is written as follows:

```
$ npm install --save react-router-dom
$ npm install --save-dev @types/react-router-dom
```

New terms and **important words** are shown in bold. Words that you see on the screen, for example, in menus or dialog boxes, appear in the text like this: "For this, click on the **Create Repository** after logging in and choose a new name for your image."

Warnings or important notes appear in a box like this.

Tips and tricks appear like this.

Reader feedback

Feedback from our readers is always welcome. Let us know what you think about this book-what you liked or disliked. Reader feedback is important for us as it helps us develop titles that you will really get the most out of.

To send us general feedback, simply e-mail `feedback@packtpub.com`, and mention the book's title in the subject of your message.

If there is a topic that you have expertise in and you are interested in either writing or contributing to a book, see our author guide at `www.packtpub.com/authors`.

Customer support

Now that you are the proud owner of a Packt book, we have a number of things to help you to get the most from your purchase.

Downloading the example code

You can download the example code files for this book from your account at `http://www.packtpub.com`. If you purchased this book elsewhere, you can visit `http://www.packtpub.com/support` and register to have the files e-mailed directly to you.

You can download the code files by following these steps:

1. Log in or register to our website using your e-mail address and password.
2. Hover the mouse pointer on the **SUPPORT** tab at the top.
3. Click on **Code Downloads & Errata**.
4. Enter the name of the book in the **Search** box.
5. Select the book for which you're looking to download the code files.
6. Choose from the drop-down menu where you purchased this book from.
7. Click on **Code Download**.

You can also download the code files by clicking on the **Code Files** button on the book's webpage at the Packt Publishing website. This page can be accessed by entering the book's name in the **Search** box. Please note that you need to be logged in to your Packt account.

Once the file is downloaded, please make sure that you unzip or extract the folder using the latest version of:

- WinRAR / 7-Zip for Windows
- Zipeg / iZip / UnRarX for Mac
- 7-Zip / PeaZip for Linux

The code bundle for the book is also hosted on GitHub at `https://github.com/PacktPublishing/Cloud-Native-Programming-with-Golang`. We also have other code bundles from our rich catalog of books and videos available at `https://github.com/PacktPublishing/`. Check them out!

Downloading the color images of this book

We also provide you with a PDF file that has color images of the screenshots/diagrams used in this book. The color images will help you better understand the changes in the output. You can download this file from `https://www.packtpub.com/sites/default/files/downloads/CloudNativeprogrammingwithGolang_ColorImages.pdf`.

Errata

Although we have taken every care to ensure the accuracy of our content, mistakes do happen. If you find a mistake in one of our books-maybe a mistake in the text or the code-we would be grateful if you could report this to us. By doing so, you can save other readers from frustration and help us improve subsequent versions of this book. If you find any errata, please report them by visiting `http://www.packtpub.com/submit-errata`, selecting your book, clicking on the **Errata Submission Form** link, and entering the details of your errata. Once your errata are verified, your submission will be accepted and the errata will be uploaded to our website or added to any list of existing errata under the Errata section of that title.

To view the previously submitted errata, go to `https://www.packtpub.com/books/content/support` and enter the name of the book in the search field. The required information will appear under the **Errata** section.

Piracy

Piracy of copyrighted material on the Internet is an ongoing problem across all media. At Packt, we take the protection of our copyright and licenses very seriously. If you come across any illegal copies of our works in any form on the Internet, please provide us with the location address or website name immediately so that we can pursue a remedy.

Please contact us at `copyright@packtpub.com` with a link to the suspected pirated material.

We appreciate your help in protecting our authors and our ability to bring you valuable content.

Questions

If you have a problem with any aspect of this book, you can contact us at `questions@packtpub.com`, and we will do our best to address the problem.

1
Modern Microservice Architectures

In the world of computing and software, we hear about many cool new technologies and frameworks almost every week. Some of them stay and persist, whereas others fail the test of time and disappear. Needless to say, cloud computing sits very comfortably in the former category. We live in a world where cloud computing powers almost everything that needs serious backend computing power, from **Internet of Things** (**IOT**) devices that check the temperature on a refrigerator to video games that show you real-time stats for your scores compared to your peers in multiplayer games.

Cloud computing benefits huge enterprises with offices all over the world, as well as minimal start-ups of two people writing code in a coffee shop. There is tons of material that cover why cloud computing is so important for modern information technologies. For the sake of efficiency, we'll provide a straightforward answer to this question, without going into long bullet points, graphs, and lengthy paragraphs. For businesses, it's all about making money and saving costs. Cloud computing drives costs down significantly for most organizations. That's because cloud computing saves you the cost of building your own data center. No expensive hardware needs to be bought, and no expensive buildings with fancy air-conditioning systems need to be commissioned. Additionally, almost all cloud computing offerings give you the ability to pay for only what you use and no more. Cloud computing also offers massive flexibility for software engineers and IT administrators to do their jobs quickly and efficiently, thus achieving developer happiness and increased productivity.

In this chapter, we will cover the following topics:

- Design goals of cloud-native applications, especially scalability
- Different cloud service models
- The twelve-factor app
- Microservice architectures
- Communication patterns, especially synchronous versus asynchronous communication

Why Go?

Go (or Golang) is a relatively new programming language that is taking the software development world by storm. It was developed by Google to facilitate the construction of its backend software services. However, it's now being used by numerous enterprises and start-ups to write powerful applications. What sets Go apart is the fact that it was built from the ground up to provide performance that is destined to compete with very powerful languages, such as C/C++, while supporting a relatively simple syntax that resembles dynamic languages such as JavaScript. The Go runtime offers garbage collection; however, it does not rely on virtual machines to achieve that. Go programs are compiled into native machine code. When invoking the Go compiler, you simply choose the type of platform (Windows, Mac, and so on) that you'd like the binary to run on when you build. The compiler will then produce a single binary that works on that platform. This makes Go capable of cross-compiling and producing native binaries.

Go is perfect for microservice architectures, which we will be seeing a lot of in the future. A microservice architecture is an architecture where you divide the responsibilities of your application between smaller services that only focus on specific tasks. These services can then communicate among themselves to obtain the information they need to produce results.

Go is a fresh programming language, developed in the age of cloud computing, and with modern software technologies in mind. Go is optimized for portable microservice architectures due to the fact that a Go program mostly compiles to a single binary, making the need for dependencies and virtual machines in production environments almost non-existent. Go is also a pioneer in container technologies. **Docker**, the top name in software containers, is written in none other than Go. Due to Go's popularity, there is work being done by major cloud providers, as well as third-party contributors, to ensure that Go gets the API support it needs for different cloud platforms.

The goal of this book is to build the knowledge bridge between the Go programming language and the cloud technologies of modern computing. In this book, you will gain practical knowledge of Go microservice architectures, message queues, containers, cloud platform Go APIs, SaaS applications design, monitoring cloud applications, and more.

Basic design goals

In order to fully benefit from the advantages of modern cloud platforms, we need to consider their characteristic properties when developing applications that should run on these platforms.

One of the main design goals of cloud applications is **scalability.** On the one hand, this means growing your application's resources as needed in order to efficiently serve all your users. On the other hand, it also means shrinking your resources back to an appropriate level when you do not need them anymore. This allows you to run your application in a cost-efficient manner without having to constantly overprovision for peak workloads.

In order to achieve this, typical cloud deployments often use small virtual machine instances that host an application and scale by adding (or removing) more of these instances. This method of scaling is called **horizontal scaling** or **scale out**—as opposed to **vertical scaling** or **scale up**, where you would not increase the number of instances, but provision more resources to your existing instances. Horizontal scaling is often preferred to vertical scaling for several reasons. First, horizontal scaling promises unlimited linear scalability. On the other hand, vertical scaling has its limits due to the fact that the number of resources that you can add to an existing server cannot grow infinitely. Secondly, horizontal scaling is often more cost-efficient since you can use cheap commodity hardware (or, in cloud environments, smaller instance types), whereas larger servers often grow exponentially more expensive.

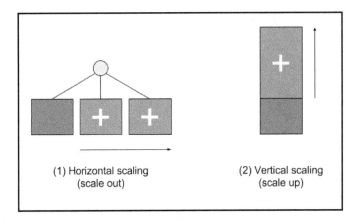

(1) Horizontal scaling
(scale out)

(2) Vertical scaling
(scale up)

Horizontal scaling versus vertical scaling; the first works by adding more instances and load-balancing the workload across them, whereas the latter works by adding more resources to existing instances

All major cloud providers offer the ability to perform horizontal scaling automatically, depending on your application's current resource utilization. This feature is called **auto-scaling**. Unfortunately, you do not get horizontal scalability for free. In order to be able to scale out, your application needs to adhere to some very important design goals that often need to be considered from the start, as follows:

- **Statelessness**: Each instance of a cloud application should not have any kind of internal state (meaning that any kind of data is saved for later use, either in-memory or on the filesystem). In a scale-out scenario, subsequent requests might be served by another instance of the application and, for this reason, must not rely on any kind of state being present from previous requests. In order to achieve this, it is usually necessary to externalize any kind of persistent storage, such as databases and filesystems. Both database services and file storage are often offered as managed services by the cloud provider that you use in your application.

Of course, this does not mean that you cannot deploy stateful applications to the cloud. They will just be considerably harder to scale out, hindering you from using cloud computing environments to their full potential.

- **Ease of deployment**: When scaling out, you will need to deploy new instances of your application quickly. Creating a new instance should not require any kind of manual setup, but should be automated as much as possible (ideally completely).
- **Resiliency:** In a cloud environment, especially when using auto-scaling, instances may be shut down at a moment's notice. Also, most cloud providers do not guarantee an extremely high availability on individual instances (and suggest scaling out instead, optionally across multiple availability zones). For this reason, termination and sudden death (either intentionally, in case of auto-scaling, or unintentionally, in case of failure) is something that we always need to expect in a cloud environment, and the application must handle it accordingly.

Achieving these design goals is not always easy. Cloud providers often support you in this task by offering managed services (for example, highly scalable database services of distributed file storage) that otherwise you would have to worry about yourself. Concerning your actual application, there is the **twelve-factor app** methodology (which we will cover in more detail in a later section), which describes a set of rules for building scalable and resilient applications.

Cloud service models

When it comes to cloud computing offerings, there are three main service models to consider for your project:

- **IaaS** (**Infrastructure as a Service**): This is the model where the cloud service provider gives you access to infrastructure on the cloud, such as servers (virtual and bare metal), networks, firewalls, and storage devices. You use IaaS when all that you need is for the cloud provider to manage the infrastructure for you and take the hassle and the cost of maintaining it out of your hands. IaaS is used by start-ups and organizations that want full control over their application's layer. Most IaaS offerings come with a dynamic or elastic scaling option, which would scale your infrastructure based on your consumption. This, in effect, saves organizations costs since they only pay for what they use.

- **PaaS** (**Platform as a Service**): This is the next layer up from IaaS. PaaS provides the computing platform you need to run your application. PaaS typically includes the operating systems you need to develop your applications, the databases, the web layer (if needed), and the programming language execution environment. With PaaS, you don't have to worry about updates and patches for your application environment; it gets taken care of by the cloud provider. Let's say you wrote a powerful .NET application that you want to see running in the cloud. A PaaS solution will provide the .NET environment you need to run your application, combined with the Windows server operating systems and the IIS web servers. It will also take care of load-balancing and scale for larger applications. Imagine the amount of money and effort you could save by adopting a PaaS platform instead of doing the effort in-house.
- **SaaS** (**Software as a Service**): This is the highest layer offering you can obtain as a cloud solution. A SaaS solution is when a fully functional piece of software is delivered over the web. You access SaaS solutions from a web browser. SaaS solutions are typically used by regular users of the software, as opposed to programmers or software professionals. A very famous example of a SaaS platform is Netflix—a complex piece of software hosted in the cloud, which is available to you via the web. Another popular example is Salesforce. Salesforce solutions get delivered to customers through web browsers with speed and efficiency.

Cloud application architecture patterns

Usually, developing applications that run in a cloud environment is not that different from regular application development. However, there are a few architectural patterns that are particularly common when targeting a cloud environment, which you will learn in the following section.

The twelve-factor app

The twelve-factor app methodology is a set of rules for building scalable and resilient cloud applications. It was published by Heroku, one of the dominant PaaS providers. However, it can be applied to all kinds of cloud applications, independent of concrete infrastructure or platform providers. It is also independent of programming languages and persistence services and can equally be applied to Go programming and, for example, Node.js programming. The twelve-factor app methodology describes (unsurprisingly) twelve factors that you should consider in your application for it to be easily scalable, resilient, and platform independent. You can read up on the full description on each factor on `https://12factor.net`. For the purpose of this book, we will highlight some factors that we deem especially important:

- **Factor II: Dependencies—Explicitly declare and isolate dependencies**: This factor deserves special mention because it is actually not as important in Go programming as in other languages. Typically, a cloud application should never rely on any required library or external tool being already present on a system. Dependencies should be explicitly declared (for example, using an npm `package.json` file for a Node.js application) so that a package manager can pull all these dependencies when deploying a new instance of the application. In Go, an application is typically deployed as a statically compiled binary that already contains all required libraries. However, even a Go application can be dependent on external system tools (for example, it can fork out to tools such as **ImageMagick**) or on existing C libraries. Ideally, you should deploy tools like these alongside your application. This is where container engines, such as Docker, shine.

- **Factor III: Config—Store config in the environment**: Configuration is any kind of data that might vary for different deployment, for example, connection data and credentials for external services and databases. These kinds of data should be passed to the application via environment variables. In a Go application, retrieving these is then as easy as calling `os.Getenv ("VARIABLE_NAME")`. In more complex cases (for example, when you have many configuration variables), you can also resort to libraries such as `github.com/tomazk/envcfg` or `github.com/caarlos0/env`. For heavy lifting, you can use the `github.com/spf13/viper` library.

- **Factor IV: Backing Services—Treat backing services as attached resources**: Ensure that services that your app depends on (such as databases, messaging systems, or external APIs) are easily swappable by configuration. For example, your app could accept an environment variable, such as `DATABASE_URL`, that might contain `mysql://root:root@localhost/test` for a local development deployment and `mysql://root:XXX@prod.XXXX.eu-central-1.rds.amazonaws.com` in your production setup.

- **Factor VI: Processes—Execute the app as one or more stateless processes**: Running application instances should be stateless; any kind of data that should persist beyond a single request/transaction needs to be stored in an external persistence service.
  One important case to keep in mind is user sessions in web applications. Often, user session data is stored in the process's memory (or is persisted to the local filesystem) in the expectancy that subsequent requests of the same user will be served by the same instance of your application. Instead, try to keep user sessions stateless or move the session state into an external data store, such as **Redis** or **Memcached**.

- **Factor IX: Disposability—Maximize robustness with fast startup and graceful shutdown**: In a cloud environment, sudden termination (both intentional, for example, in case of downscaling, and unintentional, in case of failures) needs to be expected. A twelve-factor app should have fast startup times (typically in the range of a few seconds), allowing it to rapidly deploy new instances. Besides, fast startup and graceful termination is another requirement. When a server shut down, the operating system will typically tell your application to shut down by sending a **SIGTERM** signal that the application can catch and react to accordingly (for example, by stopping to listen on the service port, finishing requests that are currently being processed, and then exiting).

- **Factor XI: Logs—Treat logs as event streams:** Log data is often useful for debugging and monitoring your application's behavior. However, a twelve-factor app should not concern itself with the routing or storage of its own log data. The easiest and simplest solution is to simply write your log stream to the process's standard output stream (for example, just using `fmt.Println(...)`). Streaming events to `stdout` allows a developer to simply watch the event stream on their console when developing the application. In production setups, you can configure the execution environment to catch the process output and send the log stream to a place where it can be processed (the possibilities here are endless—you could store them in your server's **journald**, send them to a syslog server, store your logs in an ELK setup, or send them to an external cloud service).

What are microservices?

When an application is maintained by many different developers over a longer period of time, it tends to get more and more complex. Bug fixes, new or changing requirements, and constant technological changes result in your software continually growing and changing. When left unchecked, this software evolution will lead to your application getting more complex and increasingly difficult to maintain.

Preventing this kind of software erosion is the objective of the microservice architecture paradigm that has emerged over the past few years. In a microservice architecture, a software system is split into a set of (potentially a lot of) independent and isolated services. These run as separate processes and communicate using network protocols (of course, each of these services should in itself be a twelve-factor app). For a more thorough introduction to the topic, we can recommend the original article on the microservice architecture by Lewis and Fowler at https://martinfowler.com/articles/microservices.html.

In contrast to traditional **Service-Oriented Architectures** (**SOA**), which have been around for quite a while, microservice architectures focus on simplicity. Complex infrastructure components such as ESBs are avoided at all costs, and instead of complicated communication protocols such as SOAP, simpler means of communication such as REST web services (about which you will learn more in Chapter 2, *Building Microservices Using Rest APIs*) or AMQP messaging (refer to Chapter 4, *Asynchronous Microservice Architectures Using Message Queues*) are preferred.

Splitting complex software into separate components has several benefits. For instance, different services can be built on different technology stacks. For one service, using Go as runtime and MongoDB as persistence layer may be the optimal choice, whereas a Node.js runtime with a MySQL persistence might be a better choice for other components. Encapsulating functionality in separate services allows developer teams to choose the right tool for the right job. Other advantages of microservices on an organizational level are that each microservice can be owned by different teams within an organization. Each team can develop, deploy, and operate their services independently, allowing them to adjust their software in a very flexible way.

Deploying microservices

With their focus on statelessness and horizontal scaling, microservices work well with modern cloud environments. Nevertheless, when choosing a microservice architecture, deploying your application will tend to get more complex overall, as you will need to deploy more, different applications (all the more reason to stick with the twelve-factor app methodology).

However, each individual service will be easier to deploy than a big monolithic application. Depending on the service's size, it will also be easier to upgrade a service to a new runtime or to replace it with a new implementation entirely. Also, you can scale each microservice individually. This allows you to scale out heavily used parts of your application while keeping less utilized components cost-efficient. Of course, this requires each service to support horizontal scaling.

Deploying microservices gets (potentially) more complex when different services use different technologies. A possible solution for this problem is offered by modern container runtimes such as Docker or RKT. Using containers, you can package an application with all its dependencies into a container image and then use that image to quickly spawn a container running your application on any server that can run Docker (or RKT) containers. (Let's return to the twelve-factor app—deploying applications in containers is one of the most thorough interpretations of dependency isolation as prescribed by **Factor II**.)

Running container workloads is a service offered by many major cloud providers (such as AWS' **Elastic Container Service**, the **Azure Container Service**, or the **Google Container Engine**). Apart from that, there are also container orchestration engines such as **Docker Swarm**, **Kubernetes**, or **Apache Mesos** that you can roll out on IaaS cloud platforms or your own hardware. These orchestration engines offer the possibility to distribute container workloads over entire server clusters, and offer a very high degree of automation. For example, the cluster manager will take care of deploying containers across any number of servers, automatically distributing them according to their resource requirements and usages. Many orchestration engines also offer auto-scaling features and are often tightly integrated with cloud environments.

You will learn more about deploying microservices with Docker and Kubernetes in Chapter 6, *Deploying Your Application in Containers*.

REST web services and asynchronous messaging

When building a microservice architecture, your individual services need to communicate with one another. One widely accepted de facto standard for microservice communication is RESTful web services (about which you will learn more in Chapter 2, *Building Microservices Using Rest APIs*, and Chapter 3, *Securing Microservices*). These are usually built on top of HTTP (although the REST architectural style itself is more or less protocol independent) and follow the client/server model with a request/reply communication model.

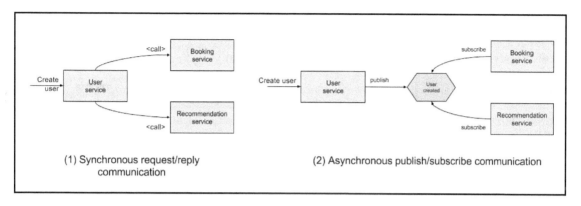

(1) Synchronous request/reply communication

(2) Asynchronous publish/subscribe communication

Synchronous versus Asynchronous communication model

This architecture is typically easy to implement and to maintain. It works well for many use cases. However, the synchronous request/reply pattern may hit its limits when you are implementing a system with complex processes that span many services. Consider the first part of the preceding diagram. Here, we have a user service that manages an application's user database. Whenever a new user is created, we will need to make sure that other services in the system are also made aware of this new user. Using RESTful HTTP, the user service needs to notify these other services by REST calls. This means that the user service needs to know all other services that are in some way affected by the user management domain. This leads to a tight coupling between the components, which is something you'd generally like to avoid.

An alternative communication pattern that can solve these issues is the publish/subscribe pattern. Here, services emit events that other services can listen on. The service emitting the event does not need to know which other services are actually listening to these events. Again, consider the second part of the preceding diagram—here, the user service publishes an event stating that a new user has just been created. Other services can now subscribe to this event and are notified whenever a new user has been created. These architectures usually require the use of a special infrastructure component: the message broker. This component accepts published messages and routes them to their subscribers (typically using a queue as intermediate storage).

The publish/subscribe pattern is a very good method to decouple services from one another—when a service publishes events, it does not need to concern itself with where they will go, and when another service subscribes to events, it also does not know where they came from. Furthermore, asynchronous architectures tend to scale better than ones with synchronous communication. Horizontal scaling and load balancing are easily accomplished by distributing messages to multiple subscribers.

Unfortunately, there is no such thing as a free lunch; this flexibility and scalability are paid for with additional complexity. Also, it becomes hard to debug single transactions across multiple services. Whether this trade-off is acceptable for you needs to be assessed on a case-by-case basis.

In Chapter 4, *Asynchronous Microservice Architectures Using Message Queues,* you will learn more about asynchronous communication patterns and message brokers.

The MyEvents platform

Throughout this book, we will build a useful SaaS application called *MyEvents*. MyEvents will utilize the technologies that you'll be learning in order to become a modern, scalable, cloud-native, and snappy application. MyEvents is an event management platform that allows users to book tickets for events all over the world. With MyEvents, you will be able to book tickets for yourself and your peers for concerts, carnivals, circuses, and more. MyEvents will keep a record of the bookings, the users, and the different locations where the events are taking place. It will manage your reservations efficiently.

We will make use of microservices, message queues, ReactJS, MongoDB, AWS, and more to construct MyEvents. In order to understand the application better, let's take a look at the logical entities that our overall application will be managing. They will be managed by multiple microservices in order to establish a clear separation of concerns and to achieve the flexibility and scalability that we need:

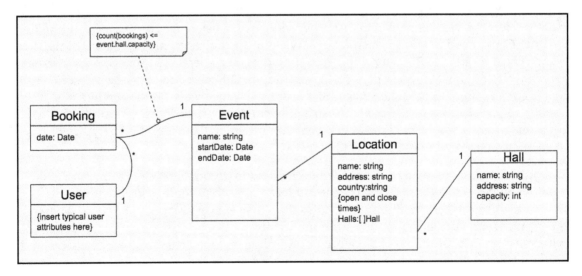

We will have multiple users; each **User** can have multiple bookings for events, and each **Booking** will correspond to a single **Event**. For each one of our events, there will be a **Location** where the event is taking place. Inside the **Location**, we will need to identify the **Hall** or room where the event is taking place.

Now, let's take a look at the microservice architecture and the different components that make our application:

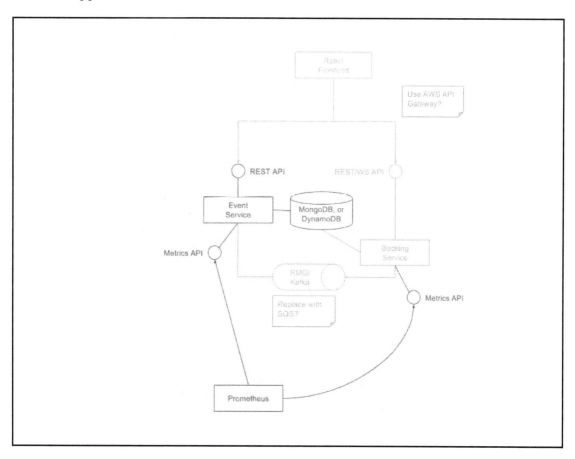

Microservice architecture

We will use a ReactJS frontend to interface with the users of our applications. The ReactJS UI will use an API gateway (AWS or local) to communicate with the different microservices that form the body of our application. There are two main microservices that represent the logic of MyEvents:

- **Event Service**: This is the service that handles the events, their locations, and changes that happen to them
- **Booking Service**: This service handles bookings made by users

All our services will be integrated using a publish/subscribe architecture based on message queues. Since we aim to provide you with practical knowledge in the world of microservices and cloud computing, we will support multiple types of message queues. We will support **Kafka**, **RabbitMQ**, and **SQS** from AWS.

The persistence layer will support multiple database technologies as well, in order to expose you to various practical database engines that empower your projects. We will support **MongoDB**, and **DynamoDB**.

All of our services will support metrics APIs, which will allow us to monitor the statistics of our services via **Prometheus**.

The MyEvents platform is designed in a way that will build strong foundations of knowledge and exposure to the powerful world of microservices and cloud computing.

Summary

In this introductory chapter, you learned about the basic design principles of cloud-native application development. This includes design goals, such as supporting (horizontal) scalability and resilience, and also architectural patterns, such as the twelve-factor app and microservice architectures.

Over the course of the following chapters, you will learn to apply many of these principles while building the MyEvents application. In Chapter 2, *Building Microservices Using Rest APIs*, you will learn how to implement a small microservice that offers a RESTful web service using the Go programming language. In the next chapters, you will continue to extend this small application and learn how to handle the deployment and operate on of this application in various cloud environments.

2
Building Microservices Using Rest APIs

In this chapter, we'll go on a journey to learn about the world of microservices. We'll learn about how they are structured, how they communicate, and how they persist data. The concept of microservices is a key concept to cover due to the fact that most of the modern cloud applications in production today rely on microservices to achieve resiliency and scalability.

In this chapter, we will cover the following topics :

- Deep diving into the microservices architecture
- RESTful web APIs
- Building RESTful APIs in the Go language

The background

We provided a practical definition for microservices in the first chapter. In this chapter, let's define microservices a bit more.

To fully appreciate microservices, let's start by telling the story of their rise. Before the idea of microservices became popular, most applications used to be monolithic. A monolithic application is a single application that tries to get numerous tasks accomplished at once. Then, as new features are needed, the application will get bigger and bulkier. This, in effect, produced unmaintainable applications in the long run. With the emergence of cloud computing, and distributed applications with massive loads, the need for a more flexible application architecture became obvious.

In Chapter 1, *Modern Microservice Architectures*, we provided an introduction to the MyEvents application, which we will be expecting to build in this book. The MyEvents application is used to manage event bookings for concerts, plays, and so on. The main tasks for the application include the following:

- **Process bookings**: For example, a user makes a booking for a concert next month. We will need to store this reservation, ensure that there are seats available for this event, and confirm no prior reservations were made with the same name, among other things.
- **Handle events**: Our application needs to be aware of all the concerts, plays, and other types of events that we're expecting to support. We need to know the event addresses, the total number of seats, their duration, and so on.
- **Handle search**: Our application needs to be capable of performing efficient searches to retrieve our bookings and events.

The following image shows how a monolithic application design for MyEvents would look like:

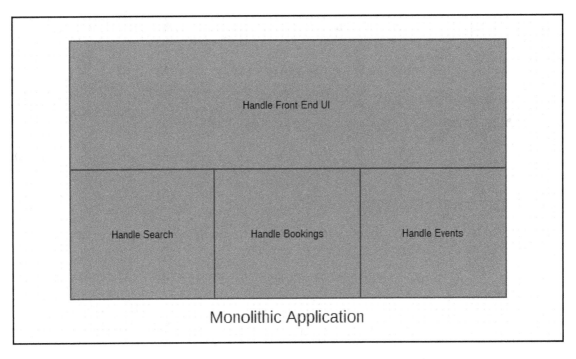

Monolithic application

We'll build multiple software layers within the application to handle each distinct task needed. Our application will become a program with a large code base. Since the code is all connected, there will always be a risk of change in one layer affecting code on the other layers.

Since it's a single program, it won't be easy to write some of the software layers in different programming languages. This is typically a very good option to have when you know there is a really good library in language X to support feature Y, however, language X is not good for feature Z.

Also, as you add new features or layers, your single program will keep growing with no good scalability options. Wouldn't it be better to be able to run different software layers on different servers so that you can control your application load without throwing more hardware on one or two servers?

Software engineers have tried to solve the monolithic application's dilemma for a long time. Microservices is one approach to address the issues that come with monolithic applications. Before the term microservices became popular, there was the concept of SOA, which was similar in principle to microservices.

Before we dive more into microservices, it is worth mentioning that monolithic applications are not always bad. It all depends on what you are trying to achieve. If you are trying to build an application that is expected to have a limited set of tasks, and not expected to grow by much, then a single well-built application might be all you need. If on the other hand, you are looking to build a complex application that is expected to perform numerous independent tasks, being maintained by multiple people, while handling massive data loads, then the microservices architecture is your friend.

So, what are microservices?

Simply put, microservices is the idea that instead of putting all of your code in one basket (monolithic application), you write multiple small software services or *microservices*. Each service is expected to focus on one task and perform it well. The accumulation of those services will make up your application.

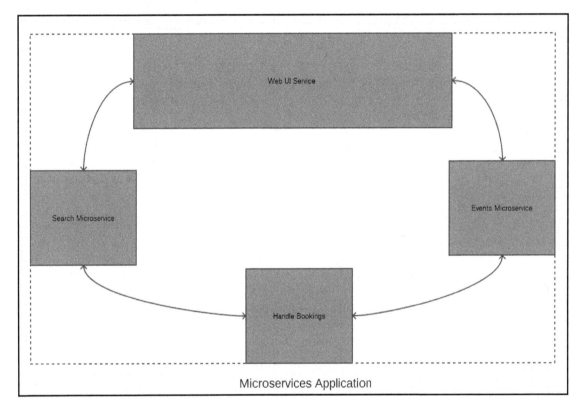

Microservices application

For the MyEvents application, each software layer from the monolithic application will translate into a software service. This will then communicate together to form our application. Each one of those software services will be, in effect, a microservice.

Since those services collaborate to build a complex application, they need to be able to communicate via protocols that they all understand. Microservices that use web Restful APIs for communication make use of the HTTP protocol extensively. We'll cover Restful APIs in more detail in this chapter.

Microservices internals

To build proper microservices, there are several components we would need to consider. To understand the five components, let's discuss the main tasks a microservice is expected to undertake:

- The microservice will need to be able to send and receive messages with other services and the outside world so that tasks can be carried out in harmony. The communication aspect of a microservice takes different forms. Restful APIs are very popular when interacting with the outside world, and message queues are very helpful when communicating with other services. There are other popular techniques that are also popular such as **gRPC**.

- The microservice will need a configuration layer; this could be via environmental variables, a file or database. This configuration layer will tell the microservice how to operate. For example, let's assume that our service needs to listen on a TCP address and a port number to be able to receive messages; the TCP address and the port number will be part of the configuration that gets fed to our service when it starts up.

- The microservice will need to log events that happen to it so that we can troubleshoot issues and understand behaviors. For example, if a communication issue occurs while sending a message to another service, we'll need the error to be logged somewhere in order for us to be able to identify the problem.

- The microservice will need to be able to persist data by storing it in a database or other forms of data stores; we'll also need to be able to retrieve data at a later time. For example, in case of the MyEvents application, our microservices will need to store and retrieve data related to the users, the bookings, and the events.

- Finally, there is the core, the most important piece of our microservice. The core is the code responsible for the task that our microservice is expected to do. For example, if our microservice is responsible for handling user bookings, then the microservice core is where we write the code that would perform the task of handling the user's bookings.

So, based on the previous five points, the building blocks of a microservice should look like this:

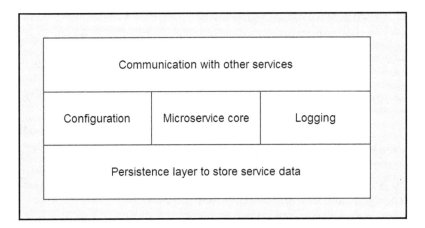

Building blocks of a microservice

Those building blocks provide a good foundation to build efficient microservices. The rules are not set in stone. You can make your microservice either simpler or more complex, depending on the application you are trying to build.

RESTful Web APIs

REST stands for **Representational State Transfer**. REST is simply a way for different services to communicate and exchange data. The core of the REST architecture consists of a client and a server. The server listens for incoming messages, then replies to it, whereas the client starts the connection, then sends messages to the server.

In the modern web programming world, RESTful web applications use the HTTP protocol for communication. The RESTful client would be an HTTP client, and the RESTful server would be the HTTP server. The HTTP protocol is the key application layer communication protocol that powers the internet, which is why RESTful applications can also be called web applications. The communication layer of the RESTful applications is often simply referred as RESTful APIs.

REST APIs allow applications developed in various types of platforms to communicate. This includes other microservices in your application that run on other operating systems, as well as client applications running on other devices. For example, a smartphone can communicate with your web services reliably via REST.

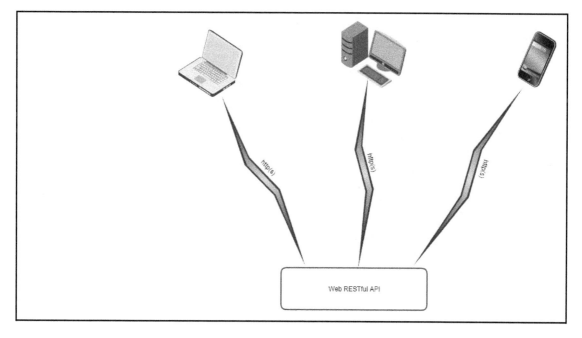

Web RESTful API

To understand how RESTful applications work, we will first need to gain a decent understanding of how the HTTP protocol works. HTTP is an application-level protocol used for data communications all over the web, the clouds, and the world of modern microservices.

HTTP is a client-server, request-response protocol. This means that the data flow works as follows:

- An HTTP client sends a request to an HTTP server
- The HTTP server listens to incoming requests, then responds to them as they come

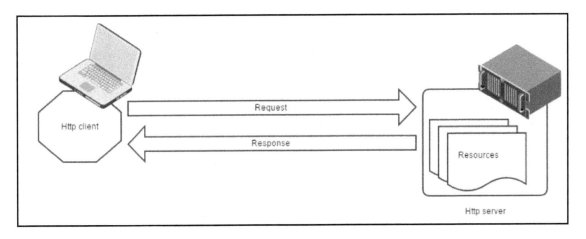

Requests and response

An HTTP client request is typically one of two things:

- The client is requesting a resource from the server
- The client is requesting to add/edit a resource on the server

The nature of the resource depends on your application. For example, if your client is a web browser trying to access a web page, then your client will send a request to the server asking for an HTML web page. The HTML page would be the resource returned within the response of the HTTP web server to the client.

In the world of communicating microservices, REST applications usually use the HTTP protocol in combination with the JSON data format in order to exchange data messages.

Consider the following scenario: In our MyEvents application, one of our microservices needs to obtain the information of an event (duration, start date, end date, and location) from another microservice. The microservice in need of the information will be our client, whereas the microservice providing the information will be our server. Let's assume that our client microservice has the event ID, but needs the server microservice to provide the information of the event that belongs to that ID.

The client will send a request inquiring about the event information via the event ID; the server will respond with the information enclosed in the JSON format, as follows:

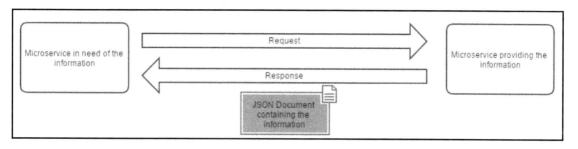

JSON document with response

This description sounds simple; however, it doesn't deliver the full picture. The inquiring part of the client needs more elaboration in order for us to understand how REST APIs really work.

There are two primary pieces of information that a REST API client request needs to specify in order to declare its intent—the *request URL* and the *request method*.

The request URL is the address of the resource at the server that the client seeks. An URL is a web address, an example of a REST API URL would be `http://quotes.rest/qod.json`, which is an API service that returns a quote for the day.

In our scenario, the MyEvents client microservice can send an HTTP request to the `http://10.12.13.14:5500/events/id/1345` URL to inquire about event ID `1345`.

The request method is basically the type of operation that we would like to execute. That could range from a request to obtain a resource to a request to edit a resource, add a resource, or even delete a resource. In the HTTP protocol, there are multiple types of methods that need to be part of the client request; the following are some of the most common methods:

- `GET`: A very common HTTP method in web applications; this is how we request a resource from our HTTP web servers; this is the request type we would use in our scenario to request the data of event ID `1345`.
- `POST`: The HTTP method we would use to update or create a resource.

  Let's assume that we would like to update a piece of information that belongs to event ID 1345 using `POST`, then we'd send a `POST` request to relative URL `../events/id/1345` with new event information in the request body.

If on the other hand, we would like to create a new event that has an ID of 1346, we shouldn't send a POST request to `../events/id/1346` with the new event information because the ID doesn't yet exist. What we should do is just send a POST request to `.../events` and attach all the new event information in the request body.

- PUT: The HTTP method to create or overwrite a resource.

  Unlike POST, the PUT request can be used to create a new resource by sending a request to a resource ID that didn't exist from before. So, for example, if we want to create a new event with an ID 1346, we can send a PUT request to `../events/id/1346`, and the web server should create the resource for us.

  PUT can also be used to fully overwrite an existing resource. So, unlike POST, we shouldn't use PUT to just update a single piece of information of a resource.

- DELETE: It is used to delete a resource. For example, if we send a delete request to the relative URL `../events/id/1345` of the web server, the web server will then delete the resource from the database.

Gorilla web toolkit

Now that we have covered how web Restful APIs work, it's time to understand how to best implement them in Go. The Go language comes with a very powerful web package in the standard library; Go also enjoys the support of numerous third-party packages. In this book, we will use a very popular Go web third-party toolkit called Gorilla web toolkit. The Gorilla web toolkit consists of a collection of Go packages that together helps build powerful web applications quickly and efficiently.

The key package in the Gorilla web toolkit ecosystem is called `gorilla/mux`. The mux package is described in the package documentation as *a request router and dispatcher*. This is basically a software component that accepts an incoming HTTP request, then decides what to do based on the nature of the request. For example, let's assume that a client sends an HTTP request to our web server. The HTTP router dispatcher component in our web server can then detect that the incoming request includes a GET method with a relative URL of `../events/id/1345`. It will then retrieve the information of the event ID 1345 and send it back to the client.

Implementing a Restful API

The first step to utilize the package is to make use of the `go get` command in order to obtain the package to our development environment:

```
$ go get github.com/gorilla/mux
```

With that, the `mux` package will be ready to use. In our code, we can now `import` the `mux` package to our web server code:

```
import "github.com/gorilla/mux"
```

Inside our code, we now need to create a router using the Gorilla `mux` package. This is accomplished via the following code:

```
r := mux.NewRouter()
```

With this, we will get a router object called `r`, to help us define our routes and link them with actions to execute.

From this point forward, the code will differ based on the microservice in question since different services will support different routes and actions. Earlier in this chapter, we covered the following four different types of services to use in our MyEvents application—Web UI service, search microservice, bookings microservice, and events microservice. Let's focus on the events microservice.

The events microservice will need to support a RESTFul API interface that is capable of doing the following:

- Searching for events via an ID or event name
- Retrieving all events at once
- Creating a new event

Let's focus on each one of those tasks. Since we are in the process of designing a web RESTful API for the microservice, each task will need to translate into an HTTP method combined with a URL and an HTTP body if need be.

The following is the break down:

- Searching for events via:
    - ID: Relative URL is `/events/id/3434`, method is `GET`, and no data is expected in the HTTP body
    - Name: Relative URL is `/events/name/jazz_concert`, method is `GET`, and no data is expected in the HTTP body
- Retrieving all events at once: Relative URL is `/events`, method is `GET`, and no data is expected in the HTTP body
- Creating a new event: Relative URL is `/events`, the method is `POST`, and expected data in the HTTP body needs to be the JSON representation of the new event we would like to add. Let's say we would like to add the event of `opera aida` that would play in the U.S., then the HTTP body would look like this:

```
{
    name: "opera aida",
    startdate: 768346784368,
    enddate: 43988943,
    duration: 120, //in minutes
    location:{
        id : 3 , //=>assign as an index
        name: "West Street Opera House",
        address: "11 west street, AZ 73646",
        country: "U.S.A",
        opentime: 7,
        clostime: 20
        Hall: {
            name : "Cesar hall",
            location : "second floor, room 2210",
            capacity: 10
        }
    }
}
```

Now, if you look at the HTTP translations of each task, you will notice that their relative URLs all share a common property, which is the fact that it starts with `/events`. In the Gorilla web toolkit, we can create a subrouter for the `/events`—relative URL. A subrouter is basically an object that will be in charge of any incoming HTTP request directed towards a relative URL that starts with `/events`.

To create a subrouter for URLs prefixed with /events, the following code is needed:

```
eventsrouter := r.PathPrefix("/events").Subrouter()
```

The preceding code makes use of the router object we created earlier, then calls the PathPrefix method, which is used to capture any URL path that starts with /events. Then, finally, we call the Subrouter() method, which will create a new router object for us to use from now on to handle any incoming requests to URLs that start with /events. The new router is called eventsrouter.

Next, the eventsrouter object can be used to define what to do with the rest of the URLs that share the /events prefix. So, let's revisit the list of HTTP translations for our tasks and explore the code needed to get them done:

1. **Task:** Searching for events via:
   - id: Relative URL is /events/id/3434, the method is GET, and no data is expected in the HTTP body
   - name: Relative URL is /events/name/jazz_concert, the method is GET, and no data is expected in the HTTP body:

   ```
   eventsrouter.Methods("GET").Path("/{SearchCriteria}/{search}").
   HandlerFunc(handler.findEventHandler)
   ```

   The handler object in the preceding code is basically the object that implements the methods that represent the functionality that we expect to be mapped to the incoming HTTP request. More on that later.

2. **Task:** Retrieving all events at once—Relative URL is /events, the method is GET, and no data is expected in the HTTP body:

   ```
   eventsrouter.Methods("GET").Path("").HandlerFunc(handler.allEve
   ntHandler)
   ```

3. **Task:** Creating a new event—Relative URL is /events, the method is POST, and expected data in the HTTP body needs to be the JSON representation of the new event we would like to add:

   ```
   eventsrouter.Methods("POST").Path("").HandlerFunc(handler.newEv
   entHandler)
   ```

For tasks 2 and 3, the code is self-explanatory. The Gorilla `mux` package allows us access to Go methods that eloquently define the properties of the incoming HTTP request that we would like to capture. The package also allows us to chain the calls together in a line to efficiently structure our code. The `Methods()` call defined the expected HTTP method, the `Path()` call defined the expected relative URL path (note that we placed the call on the `eventsrouter` object, which would append `/events` to the relative path defined in the `Path()` call), and finally comes the `HandlerFunc()` method.

The `HandlerFunc()` method is how we will link the captured incoming HTTP request with an action. `HandlerFunc()` takes an argument of the `func(http.ResponseWriter, *http.Request)` type. This argument is basically a function with two important arguments—an HTTP response object that we need to fill with our response to the incoming request and an HTTP request object, which will contain all the information about the incoming HTTP request.

The functions we pass to `HandlerFunc()` in the preceding code is `handler.findEventHandler`, `handler.allEventHandler`, and `handler.newEventHandler`—all support the `func(http.ResponseWriter, *http.Request)` signature. `handler` is a Go struct object, created to host all those functions. The `handler` object belongs to a custom Go struct type called `eventServiceHandler`.

In order for the `eventServiceHandler` type to support the HTTP handlers for tasks 1, 2, and 3, it needs to be defined like this:

```
type eventServiceHandler struct {}

func (eh *eventServiceHandler) findEventHandler(w http.ResponseWriter, r
*http.Request) {

}

func (eh *eventServiceHandler) allEventHandler(w http.ResponseWriter, r
*http.Request) {

}

func (eh *eventServiceHandler) newEventHandler(w http.ResponseWriter, r
*http.Request) {

}
```

In the preceding code, we created `eventServiceHandler` as a struct type with no fields, then, we attached three empty methods to it. Each one of the handler methods supports the function signature needed to become an argument for the Gorilla `mux` package `HandlerFunc()` method. The detailed implementation of each one of the `eventServiceHandler` methods will be discussed in more detail in this chapter when we cover the persistence layer of our microservice.

Now, let's go back to task 1. The `/{SearchCriteria}/{search}` path in our code represents the equivalent of the `/id/2323` path to search for the event ID `2323`, or the path `/name/opera aida` to search for an event with name `opera aida`. The curly braces in our path alert the Gorilla `mux` package that `SearchCriteria` and `search` are basically variables expected to be substituted in the real-incoming HTTP request URL with other things.

The Gorilla `mux` package enjoys powerful support for URL path variables. It also supports pattern-matching via regular expressions. So, for example, if I use a path that looks like `/{search:[0-9]+}`, it will provide me a variable called `search` that hosts a number.

After we finish defining our routers, paths, and handlers, we will need to specify the local TCP address where our web server will listen for incoming HTTP requests. For this, we need Go's `net/http` package; here's what the code would look like:

```
http.ListenAndServe(":8181", r)
```

In this single line of code, we created a web server. It will listen for incoming HTTP requests on local port `8181` and will use the `r` object as the router for the requests. We created the `r` object earlier using the `mux` package.

It's now time to put all the code we covered up to this point together. Let's assume that the code lives inside a function called `ServeAPI()` that is responsible for activating the Restful API logic for our microservice.

```
func ServeAPI(endpoint string) error {
  handler := &eventservicehandler{}
  r := mux.NewRouter()
  eventsrouter := r.PathPrefix("/events").Subrouter()
eventsrouter.Methods("GET").Path("/{SearchCriteria}/{search}").HandlerFunc(
handler.FindEventHandler)
  eventsrouter.Methods("GET").Path("").HandlerFunc(handler.AllEventHandler)
eventsrouter.Methods("POST").Path("").HandlerFunc(handler.NewEventHandler)
  return http.ListenAndServe(endpoint, r)
}
```

We defined the `eventServiceHandler` object to look like this:

```
type eventServiceHandler struct {}

func (eh *eventServiceHandler) findEventHandler(w http.ResponseWriter, r
*http.Request) {}

func (eh *eventServiceHandler) allEventHandler(w http.ResponseWriter, r
*http.Request) {}

func (eh *eventServiceHandler) newEventHandler(w http.ResponseWriter, r
*http.Request) {}
```

Obviously, the next step will be to fill in the empty methods of the `eventServiceHandler` type. We have the `findEventHandler()`, `allEventHandler()`, and `newEventHandler()` methods. Each one of them needs a persistence layer to carry out their tasks. That is because they either retrieve stored data or add new data to a store.

As mentioned earlier in this section, the persistence layer is the component of a microservice that is tasked with storing data in databases or retrieving data from databases. We arrived to the point where we need to cover the persistence layer in much more detail.

Persistence layer

The first decision that needs to be made when designing a persistence layer is to decide on the type of the data store. The data store could be a relational SQL database such as Microsoft SQL or MySQL, among others. Alternatively, it can be a NoSQL store, such as MongoDB, or Apache Cassandra, among others.

In an efficient and complex production environment, the code needs to be capable of switching from one data store to another without too much refactoring. Consider the following example—you build a number of microservices for a start-up that relies on MongoDB as the data store; then, as the organization changes, you decide that AWS cloud-based DynamoDB would make a better data store for the microservices. If the code doesn't allow easily unplugging MySQL, then plugging a MongoDB layer in its place, tons of code refactoring will be needed in our microservices. In Go, we will achieve that flexible design using interfaces.

It is worth mentioning that in microservices architectures, different services can require different types of datastores, so it is normal for one microservice to use MongoDB, whereas another service would use MySQL.

Let's assume that we are building a persistence layer for the events microservice. Based on what we have covered so far, the events microservice persistence layer would primarily care about three things:

- Adding a new event to the databases
- Finding an event by ID
- Finding an event by name

To achieve flexible code design, we would need the preceding three functionalities to be defined in an interface. It would look like this:

```
type DatabaseHandler interface {
    AddEvent(Event) ([]byte, error)
    FindEvent([]byte) (Event, error)
    FindEventByName(string) (Event, error)
    FindAllAvailableEvents() ([]Event, error)
}
```

The `Event` datatype is a struct type that represents the data of an event, such as the event name, location, time, among other things. For now, let's focus on the `DatabaseHandler` interface. It supports four methods that represent the required tasks from the events service persistence layer. We can then create numerous concrete implementations from this interface. One implementation can support MongoDB, while another can support the cloud-native AWS DynamoDB database.

We'll cover AWS DynamoDB in a later chapter. In this chapter, the focus will be on MongoDB.

MongoDB

If you are not already familiar with the MongoDB NoSQL database engine, this section will be very useful for you.

MongoDB is a NoSQL document store database engine. The two keywords to understand MongoDB are *NoSQL* and *document store*.

NoSQL is a relatively recent keyword in the software industry that is used to indicate that a database engine does not deeply rely on relational data. Relational data is the idea that there are webs of relations between different pieces of data in your database, following the relations between your data will build a full picture of what the data represents.

Take MySQL as an example of a relational database. Data gets stored in numerous tables, then, primary and foreign keys are used to define the relations between the different tables. MongoDB doesn't work this way, which is why MySQL is considered as a SQL database, whereas MongoDB is considered NoSQL.

If you are not yet familiar with Mongodb, or don't have a local installation you can test with. Go to `https://docs.mongodb.com/manual/installation/`, where you find a list of helpful links to guide through the process of installing and running the database in your operating system of choice. Generally, when installed, Mongodb provides two key binaries: `mongod` and `mongo`. The `mongod` command is what you need to execute, in order to run your database. Any software you then write will communicate with `mongod` to access Mongodb's data. The `mongo` command, on the other hand, is basically a client tool you can use to test the data on Mongodb, the `mongo` command communicates with `mongod`, similarly to any application you write that accesses the database.

There are two flavors of MongoDB: the community edition, and the enterprise edition. Obviously, the enterprise edition targets larger enterprise installations, whereas the community edition is what you'd use for your testing and smaller scale deployments. Here are the links for the community edition guides covering the three major operating systems:

- For linux Mongodb installation and deployment: `https://docs.mongodb.com/manual/administration/install-on-linux/`
- For Windows Mongodb installation and deployment: `https://docs.mongodb.com/manual/tutorial/install-mongodb-on-windows/`
- For OS X Mongodb installation and deployment: `https://docs.mongodb.com/manual/tutorial/install-mongodb-on-os-x/`

Overall, there are three main steps you need to consider when deploying a Mongodb instance:

1. Install Mongodb for your operating system, the download page can be found here: `https://www.mongodb.com/download-center`
2. Ensure MongoDB's key binaries are defined in your environmental path, so that you can run them from the terminal no matter what your current directory is. The key binaries are `mongod` and `mongo`. Another binary worth mentioning is `mongos`, which is important if you are planning to utilize clustering

3. Run the `mongod` command with no arguments, and this will run Mongodb with all your default settings. Alternatively, you can use it with different configuration. You can either use a configuration file or just runtime parameters. You can find information about the configuration file here: `https://docs.mongodb.com/manual/reference/configuration-options/#configuration-file`. To start `mongod` with a custom configuration file, you can use the `--config` option, here is an example: `mongod --config /etc/mongod.conf`. On the other hand, for runtime parameters, you can just use `--option` to change an option when running `mongod`, for example you can type `mongod --port 5454` to start `mongod` on a different port than the default

There are different types of NoSQL databases. One of these types is the *document store* database. The idea of a document store is that data gets stored in numerous document files stacked together to represent what we are trying to store. Let's take the data store needed for the event's microservice as an example. If we are using a document store in the microservice persistence layer, each event will be stored in a separate document with a unique ID. Say that we have an Opera Aida event, a Coldplay concert event, and a ballet performance event. In MongoDB, we would create a collection of documents called *events*, which will contain three documents—one for the Opera, one for Coldplay, and one for the ballet performance.

So, to solidify our understanding of how MongoDB would represent this data, here is a diagram of the events collection:

Events collection

Collections and documents are important concepts in MongoDB. A production MongoDB environment typically consists of multiple collections; each collection would represent a different piece of our data. So, for example, our MyEvents application consists of a number of microservices, each microservice cares about a distinctive piece of data. The bookings microservice would store data in a bookings collection, and the events microservices would store data in an events collection. We'd also need the user's data to be stored separately in order to manage the users of our applications independently. Here is what this would end up looking like:

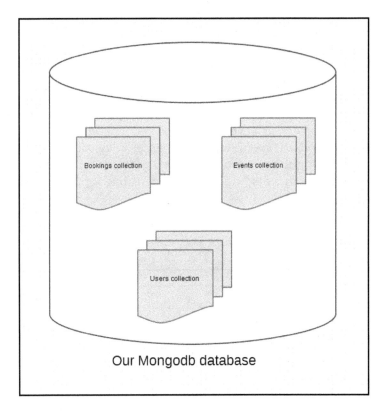

Our MongoDB database

You can download this file from `https://www.packtpub.com/sites/default/files/downloads/CloudNativeprogrammingwithGolang_ColorImages.pdf`.
The code bundle for the book is also hosted on GitHub at `https://github.com/PacktPublishing/Cloud-Native-Programming-with-Golang`.

Since we have focused so far on the events microservice as a showcase on how to build a microservice, let's dive deeper into the events collection, which would be used by the event's microservice:

Events collection

Each document in the events collection needs to include all the information necessary to represent a single event. Here's how an event document should look like:

```
//events
{
    name: "opera aida",
    startdate: 768346784368,
    enddate: 43988943,
    duration: 120, //in minutes
    location:{
        id : 3 , //=>assign as an index
        name: "West Street Opera House",
        address: "11 west street, AZ 73646",
        country: "U.S.A",
        opentime: 7,
        clostime: 20
        Hall: {
            name : "Cesar hall",
            location : "second floor, room 2210",
            capacity: 10
        }
    }
}
```

If you haven't noticed already, the preceding JSON document is the same as the HTTP body document that we presented as an example of what the add event API HTTP POST request body looks like.

In order to write software that can work with this data, we need to create models. Models are basically data structures containing fields that match the data we are expecting from the database. In the case of Go, we'd use struct types to create our models. Here is what a model for an event should look like:

```
type Event struct {
    ID bson.ObjectId `bson:"_id"`
    Name string
    Duration int
    StartDate int64
    EndDate int64
    Location Location
}
type Location struct {
    Name string
    Address string
    Country string
    OpenTime int
    CloseTime int
    Halls []Hall
}
type Hall struct {
    Name string `json:"name"`
    Location string `json:"location,omitempty"`
    Capacity int `json:"capacity"`
}
```

The `Event struct` is the data structure or model for our event document. It contains the ID, event name, event duration, event start date, event end date, and event location. Since the event location needs to hold more information than just a single field, we will create a struct type called location to model a location. The `Location struct` type contains the location's name, address, country, open time and close time, and the halls in that area. A hall is basically the room inside the location where the event is taking place.

So, for example, Mountain View, Opera house in downtown Mountain View would be the location, whereas the silicon valley room on the east side would be the hall.

In turn, the hall cannot be represented by a single field since we need to know its name, its location in the building (south-east, west, and so forth), and its capacity (the number of people it can host).

The `bson.ObjectId` type in the event struct is a special type that represents MongoDB document ID. The `bson` package can be found in the `mgo` adapter, which is the Go third part framework of choice to communicate with MongoDB. The `bson.ObjectId` type also provides some helpful methods that we can use later in our code to verify the validity of the ID.

Before we start covering `mgo`, let's take a moment to explain what `bson` means. `bson` is a data format used by MongoDB to represent data in stored documents. It could be simply considered as binary JSON because it is a binary-encoded serialization of JSON-like documents. The specification can be found at: `http://bsonspec.org/`.

Now, let's cover `mgo`.

MongoDB and the Go language

`mgo` is a popular MongoDB driver written in the Go language. The package page can be found at: `http://labix.org/mgo`. The driver is nothing more than a number of Go packages that facilitate writing Go programs capable of working with MongoDB.

In order to make use of `mgo`, the first step is to make use of the `go get` command to retrieve the package:

```
go get gopkg.in/mgo.v2
```

With the preceding command executed, we get the ability to use `mgo` in our code. We'd need to import the `mgo` package and the `bson` package that we discussed earlier. The package name we use to host our MongoDB persistence layer is called `mongolayer`.

Let's have a look at the `mongolayer` package:

```
package mongolayer
import (
    mgo "gopkg.in/mgo.v2"
    "gopkg.in/mgo.v2/bson"
)
```

Next, let's create some constants to represent the name of our database and the names of the collections involved in our persistence layer. The database name in MongoDB would be myevents. The collection names we'll use are users for the users collection, and events for the collection of events in our database:

```
const (
    DB = "myevents"
    USERS = "users"
    EVENTS = "events"
)
```

In order to expose the features of the mgo package, we will need to utilize a database session object that belongs to the mgo package, the session object type is called *mgo.session. To make use of *mgo.session inside our code, we will wrap it with a struct type called MongoDBLayer, as follows:

```
type MongoDBLayer struct {
    session *mgo.Session
}
```

It is now time to implement the DatabaseHandler interface that we covered earlier in order to construct the concrete persistence layer of our application. In the Go language, it is typically preferred to use a pointer type when implementing an interface because pointers preserve references to the original memory addresses of the underlying objects as opposed to copying the entire object around when we make use of it. In other words, the implementer object type for the DatabaseHandler interface needs to be a pointer to a MongoDBLayer struct object, or just simply *MongoDBLayer.

However, before we start implementing the interface, we will first need to create a constructor function that returns an object of the *MongoDBLayer type. This is idiomatic in Go in order for us to be able to execute any necessary initialization code while creating a new object of the *MongoDBLayer type. In our cases, the initialization code is basically to obtain a connection session handler to the desired MongoDB database address. The following is what the constructor code will look like:

```
func NewMongoDBLayer(connection string) (*MongoDBLayer, error) {
    s, err := mgo.Dial(connection)
    if err!= nil{
        return nil,err
    }
    return &MongoDBLayer{
        session: s,
    }, err
}
```

In the preceding code, we created a constructor function called `NewMongoDBLayer`, which requires a single argument of type string. The argument represents the connection string with the information needed to establish the connection to the MongoDB database. According to `mgo` documentation at `https://godoc.org/gopkg.in/mgo.v2#Dial`, the format of the connection string needs to look like this:

```
[mongodb://][user:pass@]host1[:port1][,host2[:port2],...][/database][?options]
```

If it is just a localhost connection, the connection string will look as follows: `mongodb://127.0.0.1`

If a port number is not provided in the connection string, the port defaults to `27017`.

Now, let's look at the code inside our constructor function. In the first line, we call `mgo.Dial()` with the connection string as an argument. The `mgo.Dial()` is the function in the `mgo` package, which will return a MongoDB connection session for us to use later in our code. It returns two results—the `*mgo.Session` object and an error object. We use struct literals at the end to return a fresh object of type pointer to `MongoDBLayer`, which hosts the newly created `*mgo.Session` object. We also return the error object so that we communicate to the caller any errors that would have occurred during the initialization process.

Now, with the constructor out of the way, it's time to implement the methods of the `DatabaseHandler` interface. So far, we have four methods—`AddEvent(Event)`, `FindEvent([]byte)`, `FindEventByName(string)`, and `FindAllAvailableEvents()`.

Here is what the code for the `AddEvent(Event)` method will look like:

```go
func (mgoLayer *MongoDBLayer) AddEvent(e persistence.Event) ([]byte, error)
{
    s := mgoLayer.getFreshSession()
    defer s.Close()
    if !e.ID.Valid() {
        e.ID = bson.NewObjectId()
    }
    //let's assume the method below checks if the ID is valid for the
location object of the event
    if !e.Location.ID.Valid() {
        e.Location.ID = bson.NewObjectId()
    }
    return []byte(e.ID), s.DB(DB).C(EVENTS).Insert(e)
}
```

The method takes an argument of type `persistence.Event,` which models the information expected from an event as we covered earlier. It returns a slice of bytes, which represents the event ID, and an error object, which will be nil if no errors are found.

In the first line, we call a `getFreshSession()` method—this is a helper method implemented in our code to help retrieve a fresh database session from the connection pool. Here is what the method code looks like:

```
func (mgoLayer *MongoDBLayer) getFreshSession() *mgo.Session {
    return mgoLayer.session.Copy()
}
```

The `session.Copy()` is the method that is called whenever we are requesting a new session from the `mgo` package connection pool. `mgoLayer.session` here is basically the `*mgo.Session` object we have hosted inside the `MongoDBLayer` struct. It is idiomatic to call `session.Copy()` at the beginning of any method or function that is about to issue queries or commands to MongoDB via the `mgo` package. The `getFreshSession()` method is just a helper method that calls `session.Copy()` for us and returns the resulting session.

Now, let's return to the `AddEvent()` method. We now have a working `*mgo.Session` object from the database connection pool to use in our code. The first thing to do is to call defer `s.Close()` to ensure that this session gets returned back to the `mgo` database connection pool after the `AddEvent()` method exits.

Next, we check whether the event ID supplied by the `Event` argument object is valid and whether the ID field of the `Event` object is of the `bson.ObjectID` type as we covered earlier. `bson.ObjectID` supports a `Valid()` method, which we can use to detect whether the ID is a valid MongoDB document ID or not. If the supplied event ID is not valid, we will create one of our own using the `bson.NewObjectID()` function call. We will then repeat the same pattern with the location-embedded object inside the event.

Finally, at the end, we will return two results—the first result is the event ID of the added event, and a second result is an error object representing the result of the event insertion operation. In order to insert the event object to the MongoDB database, we will use the session object in the `s` variable, then call `s.DB(DB).C(EVENTS)` to obtain an object that represents our events collection in the database. The object will be of the `*mgo.Collection` type. The `DB()` method helps us access the database; we will give it the `DB` constant as an argument, which has our database name. The `C()` method helps us access the collection; we will give it the `EVENTS` constant, which has the name of our events collection.

The DB and EVENTS constants were defined earlier in our code. Then, finally, we will call the Insert() method of the collection object, with the Event object as an argument, which is why the code ends up looking like this—s.DB(DB).C(EVENTS).Insert(e). This line is what we need in order to insert a new document into a MongoDB database collection that utilizes Go objects and the mgo package.

Now, let's look at the code for FindEvent(), which we use to retrieve the information of a certain event from the database from its ID. The code will look as follows:

```
func (mgoLayer *MongoDBLayer) FindEvent(id []byte) (persistence.Event,
error) {
    s := mgoLayer.getFreshSession()
    defer s.Close()
    e := persistence.Event{}
    err := s.DB(DB).C(EVENTS).FindId(bson.ObjectId(id)).One(&e)
    return e, err
}
```

Note how the ID is passed as a slice of bytes instead of a bson.ObjectId type. We do this to ensure that the FindEvent() method in the DatabaseHandler interface stays as generic as possible. For example, we know that in the world of MongoDB, the ID will be of the bson.ObjectId type, but what if we now want to implement a MySQL database layer? It would not make sense to have the ID argument type passed to FindEvent() as bson.ObjectId. So, that's why we picked the []byte type to represent our ID argument. In theory, we should be able to convert a slice of bytes to any other type that can represent an id.

 An important remark is that we could also have picked the empty interface type (interface{}), which in Go can be converted to any other type.

In the first line of the FindEvent() method, we obtained a fresh session from the connection pool using the mgoLayer.getFreshSession() as before. We then call defer s.Close() to ensure that the session goes back to the connection pool after we are done.

Next, we created an empty event object e using the code e := persistence.Event{}. We then use s.DB(DB).C(EVENTS) to access the events collection in MongoDB. There is a method called FindId(), which is supported by *mgoCollection objects of mgo. The method takes an object of the bson.ObjectId type as an argument then searches for the document with the desired ID.

`FindId()` returns an object of the `*mgo.Query` type, which is a common type in `mgo` that we can use to retrieve results of queries. In order to feed the retrieved document data to the `e` object we created earlier, we will need to call the `One()` method, which belongs to the `*mgo.Query` type, and pass a reference to `e` as an argument. By doing this, `e` will obtain the data of the retrieved document with the desired ID. If the operation fails, the `One()` method will return an error object containing the error information, otherwise `One()` will return nil.

At the end of the `FindEvent()` method, we will return the event object and the error object.

Now, let's look at the implementation of the `FindEventByName()` method, which retrieves an event by its name from the MongoDB database. Here is what the code looks like:

```
func (mgoLayer *MongoDBLayer) FindEventByName(name string)
(persistence.Event, error) {
    s := mgoLayer.getFreshSession()
    defer s.Close()
    e := persistence.Event{}
    err := s.DB(DB).C(EVENTS).Find(bson.M{"name": name}).One(&e)
    return e, err
}
```

The method is very similar to the `FindEvent()` method, except for two things. The first difference is the fact that `FindEvent()` takes a string as an argument, which represents the event name that we would like to find.

The second difference is that we query for an event name instead of an event ID. The code line where we query the document uses a method called `Find()` instead of `FindId()`, which makes the code look like this:

```
err := s.DB(DB).C(EVENTS).Find(bson.M{"name":name}).One(&e)
```

The `Find()` method takes an argument that represents the query we would like to pass along to MongoDB. The `bson` package provides a nice type called `bson.M`, which is basically a map we can use to represent the query parameters that we would like to look for. In our case, we are looking for the name that got passed as an argument to `FindEventByName`. The name field in the event collection in our database is simply coded as `name`, whereas the variable that got passed to us as an argument and has the name is called `name`. Hence, our query ends up as `bson.M{"name":name}`.

Last but not least is our `FindAllAvailableEvents()` method. The method returns all available events in our database. In other words, it returns the entire events collection from our MongoDB database. Here is what the code looks like:

```
func (mgoLayer *MongoDBLayer) FindAllAvailableEvents()
([]persistence.Event, error) {
    s := mgoLayer.getFreshSession()
    defer s.Close()
    events := []persistence.Event{}
    err := s.DB(DB).C(EVENTS).Find(nil).All(&events)
    return events, err
}
```

The code is almost the same as `FindEventByName()`, except for three simple differences. The first difference is obviously the fact that `FindAllAvailableEvents()` doesn't take any arguments.

The second difference is the fact that we need the query results to be fed to a slice of the event's objects instead of a single event object. This is why the return type is `[]persistence.Event`, instead of just `persistence.Event`.

The third difference is that the `Find()` method will take an argument of nil instead of a `bson.M` object. This will cause the code to look like this:

```
err := s.DB(DB).C(EVENTS).Find(nil).All(&events)
```

When the `Find()` method gets a nil argument, it will return everything found in the associated MongoDB collection. Also, note that we used `All()` instead of `One()` after `Find()`. That is because we expect multiple results and not just one.

With this, we finish covering our persistence layer.

Implementing our RESTful APIs handler functions

So, now that have covered our persistence layer, it's time to return to our RESTful API handlers and cover their implementation. Earlier in this chapter, we defined the `eventServiceHandler` struct type to look like this:

```
type eventServiceHandler struct {}
func (eh *eventServiceHandler) findEventHandler(w http.ResponseWriter, r
*http.Request) {}
func (eh *eventServiceHandler) allEventHandler(w http.ResponseWriter, r
*http.Request) {}
func (eh *eventServiceHandler) newEventHandler(w http.ResponseWriter, r
*http.Request) {}
```

The `eventServiceHandler` type now needs to support the `DatabaseHandler` interface type we created earlier in the chapter in order to be capable of performing database operations. This will make the struct look like this:

```
type eventServiceHandler struct {
    dbhandler persistence.DatabaseHandler
}
```

Next, we will need to write a constructor to initialize the `eventServiceHandler` object; it will look as follows:

```
func newEventHandler(databasehandler persistence.DatabaseHandler)
*eventServiceHandler {
    return &eventServiceHandler{
        dbhandler: databasehandler,
    }
}
```

However, we left the three methods of the `eventServiceHandler` struct type empty. Let's go through them one by one.

The first method `findEventHandler()` is responsible for handling HTTP requests used to query events stored in our database. We can query events via their IDs or names. As mentioned earlier in the chapter, when searching for an ID, the request URL will resemble `/events/id/3434` and will be of the GET type. On the other hand, when searching by name, the request will resemble `/events/name/jazz_concert` and be of the GET type. As a reminder, the following is how we defined the path and linked it to the handler:

```
eventsrouter := r.PathPrefix("/events").Subrouter()
eventsrouter.Methods("GET").Path("/{SearchCriteria}/{search}").HandlerFunc(
handler.findEventHandler)
```

`{SearchCriteria}` and `{Search}` are two variables in our path. `{SearchCriteria}` can be replaced with `id` or `name`.

Here is what the code for the `findEventHandler` method will look like:

```
func (eh *eventServiceHandler) findEventHandler(w http.ResponseWriter, r
*http.Request) {
    vars := mux.Vars(r)
    criteria, ok := vars["SearchCriteria"]
    if !ok {
        w.WriteHeader(400)
        fmt.Fprint(w, `{error: No search criteria found, you can either
search by id via /id/4
                    to search by name via /name/coldplayconcert}`)
        return
    }
    searchkey, ok := vars["search"]
    if !ok {
        w.WriteHeader(400)
        fmt.Fprint(w, `{error: No search keys found, you can either search
by id via /id/4
                    to search by name via /name/coldplayconcert}`)
        return
    }
    var event persistence.Event
    var err error
    switch strings.ToLower(criteria) {
        case "name":
        event, err = eh.dbhandler.FindEventByName(searchkey)
        case "id":
        id, err := hex.DecodeString(searchkey)
        if err == nil {
            event, err = eh.dbhandler.FindEvent(id)
        }
    }
    if err != nil {
        fmt.Fprintf(w, "{error %s}", err)
        return
    }
    w.Header().Set("Content-Type", "application/json;charset=utf8")
    json.NewEncoder(w).Encode(&event)
}
```

The method takes two arguments: an object of the `http.ResponseWriter` type, which represents the HTTP response we need to fill, whereas the second argument is of the `*http.Request` type, which represents the HTTP request that we received. In the first line, we use `mux.Vars()` with the request object as an argument; this will return a map of keys and values, which will represent our request URL variables and their values. So, for example, if the request URL looks like `/events/name/jazz_concert`, we will have two key-value pairs in our resulting map—the first key is `"SearchCriteria"` with a value of `"name"`, whereas the second key is `"search"` with a value of `jazz_concert`. The resulting map is stored in the vars variable.

We then obtain the criteria from our map in the next line:

```
criteria, ok := vars["SearchCriteria"]
```

So, the criteria variable will now have either `name` or `id` if the user sent the correct request URL. The `ok` variable is of the boolean type; if `ok` is true, then we will find a key called `SearchCriteria` in our `vars` map. If it is false, then we know that the request URL we received is not valid.

Next, we check whether we retrieved the search criteria; if we didn't, then we report the error and then exit. Notice here how we report the error in a JSON like format? That is because it is typically preferred for RESTful APIs with JSON body formats to return everything in JSON form, including errors. Another way to do this is to create a JSONError type and feed it our error strings; however, I will just spell out the JSON string here in the code for simplicity:

```
if !ok {
    fmt.Fprint(w, `{error: No search criteria found, you can either search
by id via /id/4 to search by name via /name/coldplayconcert}`)
    return
}
```

`fmt.Fprint` allows us to write the error message directly to the `w` variable, which contains our HTTP response writer. The `http.responseWriter` object type supports Go's `io.Writer` interface, which can be used with `fmt.Fprint()`.

Now, we will need to do the same with the `{search}` variable:

```
searchkey, ok := vars["search"]
if !ok {
    fmt.Fprint(w, `{error: No search keys found, you can either search by
id via /id/4
            to search by name via /name/coldplayconcert}`)
    return
}
```

It's time to extract the information from the database based on the provided request URL variables; here is how we do it:

```
var event persistence.Event
var err error
switch strings.ToLower(criteria) {
    case "name":
    event, err = eh.dbhandler.FindEventByName(searchkey)
    case "id":
    id, err := hex.DecodeString(searchkey)
    if nil == err {
        event, err = eh.dbhandler.FindEvent(id)
    }
}
```

In case of the name search criteria, we will use the `FindEventByName()` database handler method to search by name. In case of the ID search criteria, we will convert the search key to a slice of bytes using `hex.DecodeString()`—if we successfully obtain the slice of bytes, we will call `FindEvent()` with the obtained ID.

We then check whether any errors occurred during the database operations by checking the err object. If we find errors, we write a `404` error header in our response, then print the error in the HTTP response body:

```
if err != nil {
    w.WriteHeader(404)
    fmt.Fprintf(w, "Error occured %s", err)
    return
}
```

The last thing we need to do is to convert the response to a JSON format, so we change the HTTP `content-type` header to `application/json`; then, we use the powerful Go JSON package to convert the results obtained from our database calls to the JSON format:

```
w.Header().Set("Content-Type", "application/json;charset=utf8")
json.NewEncoder(w).Encode(&event)
```

Now, let's look at the code for the `allEventHandler()` method, which will return all the available events in the HTTP response:

```
func (eh *eventServiceHandler) allEventHandler(w http.ResponseWriter, r
*http.Request) {
    events, err := eh.dbhandler.FindAllAvailableEvents()
    if err != nil {
        w.WriteHeader(500)
        fmt.Fprintf(w, "{error: Error occured while trying to find all
available events %s}", err)
        return
    }
    w.Header().Set("Content-Type", "application/json;charset=utf8")
    err = json.NewEncoder(w).Encode(&events)
    if err != nil {
        w.WriteHeader(500)
        fmt.Fprintf(w, "{error: Error occured while trying encode events to
JSON %s}", err)
    }
}
```

We start by calling the `FindAllAvailableEvents()` that belongs to the database handler in order to obtain all events from the database. We then check whether any errors occurred. If any found, we write an error header, print the error to the HTTP response, and then return from the function.

If no errors have occurred, we write `application/json` to the `Content-Type` header of the HTTP response. We then encode the events to the JSON format and send them to the HTTP response writer object. Again, if any errors occur, we will log them and then exit.

Now, let's discuss the `newEventHandler()` handler method, which will add a new event to our database using the data retrieved from incoming HTTP requests. We expect the event data in the incoming HTTP request to be in the JSON format. Here is what the code will look like:

```
func (eh *eventServiceHandler) newEventHandler(w http.ResponseWriter, r
*http.Request) {
    event := persistence.Event{}
    err := json.NewDecoder(r.Body).Decode(&event)
    if err != nil {
        w.WriteHeader(500)
        fmt.Fprintf(w, "{error: error occured while decoding event data
%s}", err)
        return
    }
    id, err := eh.dbhandler.AddEvent(event)
```

```
    if nil != err {
        w.WriteHeader(500)
        fmt.Fprintf(w, "{error: error occured while persisting event %d
%s}",id, err)
        return
    }
```

In the first line, we create a new object of the `persistence.Event` type, which we will use to hold the data we are expecting to parse out from the incoming HTTP request.

In the second line, we use Go's JSON package to take the body of the incoming HTTP request (which we obtain by calling `r.Body`). We then decode the JSON data embedded in it and feed it to the new event object, as follows:

```
    err := json.NewDecoder(r.Body).Decode(&event)
```

We then check our errors as usual. If no errors are observed, we call the `AddEvent()` method of our database handler and pass the event object as the argument. This in effect will add the event object we obtained from the incoming HTTP request to the database. We then check errors again as usual and exit.

To put the final touches on our events microservice, we will need to do three things. The first is to allow the `ServeAPI()` function we covered earlier in this chapter, which define the HTTP routes and handlers, to call the `eventServiceHandler` constructor. The code will end up looking like this:

```
func ServeAPI(endpoint string, dbHandler persistence.DatabaseHandler) error
{
    handler := newEventHandler(dbHandler)
    r := mux.NewRouter()
    eventsrouter := r.PathPrefix("/events").Subrouter()
eventsrouter.Methods("GET").Path("/{SearchCriteria}/{search}").HandlerFunc(
handler.findEventHandler)
eventsrouter.Methods("GET").Path("").HandlerFunc(handler.allEventHandler)
eventsrouter.Methods("POST").Path("").HandlerFunc(handler.newEventHandler)
    return http.ListenAndServe(endpoint, r)
}
```

The second final touch we need to do is to write a configuration layer for our microservice. As mentioned earlier in the chapter, a well-designed microservice needs a configuration layer which reads from a file, a database, an environmental variable, or a similar medium. There are three main parameters we need to support for now for our configuration—the database type used by our microservice (MongoDB is our default), the database connection string (default is `mongodb://127.0.0.1` for a local connection), and the Restful API endpoint. Here is what our configuration layer will end up looking like:

```
package configuration
var (
    DBTypeDefault = dblayer.DBTYPE("mongodb")
    DBConnectionDefault = "mongodb://127.0.0.1"
    RestfulEPDefault = "localhost:8181"
)
type ServiceConfig struct {
    Databasetype dblayer.DBTYPE `json:"databasetype"`
    DBConnection string `json:"dbconnection"`
    RestfulEndpoint string `json:"restfulapi_endpoint"`
}
func ExtractConfiguration(filename string) (ServiceConfig, error) {
    conf := ServiceConfig{
        DBTypeDefault,
        DBConnectionDefault,
        RestfulEPDefault,
    }
    file, err := os.Open(filename)
    if err != nil {
        fmt.Println("Configuration file not found. Continuing with default
values.")
        return conf, err
    }
    err = json.NewDecoder(file).Decode(&conf)
    return conf,err
}
```

The third touch is to build a database layer package that acts as the gateway to the persistence layer in our microservice. The package will utilize the factory design pattern by implementing a factory function. A factory function will manufacture our database handler. This is done by taking the name of the database that we would like to connect to, as well as the connection string, then returning a database handler object which we can use for database related tasks from this point forward. We currently only support MongoDB, so here is how this would look like:

```
package dblayer

import (
```

```
    "gocloudprogramming/chapter2/myevents/src/lib/persistence"
    "gocloudprogramming/chapter2/myevents/src/lib/persistence/mongolayer"
)

type DBTYPE string

const (
  MONGODB DBTYPE = "mongodb"
  DYNAMODB DBTYPE = "dynamodb"
)

func NewPersistenceLayer(options DBTYPE, connection string)
(persistence.DatabaseHandler, error) {

  switch options {
  case MONGODB:
    return mongolayer.NewMongoDBLayer(connection)
  }
  return nil, nil
}
```

The fourth and final touch is our `main` package. We will write the main function that makes use of the `flag` package to take the location of the configuration file from the user and then use the configuration file to initialize the database connection and the HTTP server. The following is the resultant code:

```
package main
func main(){
    confPath := flag.String("conf", `.\configuration\config.json`, "flag to
set
                            the path to the configuration json file")
    flag.Parse()
    //extract configuration
    config, _ := configuration.ExtractConfiguration(*confPath)
    fmt.Println("Connecting to database")
    dbhandler, _ := dblayer.NewPersistenceLayer(config.Databasetype,
config.DBConnection)
    //RESTful API start
    log.Fatal(rest.ServeAPI(config.RestfulEndpoint, dbhandler,
eventEmitter))
}
```

With this piece of code, we come to the conclusion of this chapter. In the next chapter, we will discuss how to secure our microservice.

Summary

In this chapter, we covered a wide range of topics regarding designing and building modern microservices. You now should have practical knowledge regarding RESTful web APIs, NoSQL data stores like MongoDB, and proper Go design patterns for scalable code.

3
Securing Microservices

Welcome to the third chapter in our journey to learn modern Go cloud programming. In this chapter, we will secure the restful API service that was authored in the preceding chapter.

Before we start diving into the code we need to write, there are some key concepts that we have to cover in order to provide a decent knowledge foundation.

As we covered in the preceding chapter, web applications need to make use of HTTP (which is an application-level protocol) in order to communicate. HTTP by itself is not secure, which means that it sends data over plain text. Obviously, if we are trying to send credit card information or sensitive personal data, we would never want to send it as a clear text. Fortunately, HTTP communications can be secured via a protocol known as **TLS** (**Transport Layer Security**). The combination of HTTP and TLS is known as HTTPS.

In this chapter, we will cover the following topics:

- The internal workings of HTTPS
- Securing microservices in Go

HTTPS

To practically understand HTTPS, we will need to first talk about the TLS protocol. TLS is a protocol that can be utilized to encrypt data communicated over a computer network. TLS relies on two types of cryptography algorithms to achieve its goals—**symmetric cryptography** and **public-key cryptography**.

 Public-key cryptography is also known as asymmetrical cryptography. We will cover where the name came from shortly. On the other hand, symmetric cryptography can also be called symmetric-key algorithms.

Symmetric cryptography

The core idea of data encryption is the use of complex mathematical equations to encode (or cipher) data, which in effect will make this data unreadable to humans. In the world of secure software communication, the encrypted data can then be sent to the intended receiver, which will be expected to decrypt the data back to its original human-readable form.

In almost all cases, to encrypt a piece of data, you will need an **encryption key**. Encryption keys are simply a piece of the complex mathematical equations used to encode the data. In some encryption algorithms, you can use the same encryption key to decrypt your data back to its original form. In others, a **decryption key** that is different than the encryption key is needed to perform the decryption.

Symmetric cryptography or symmetric-key algorithms are the algorithms that make use of the same key to encrypt and decrypt the data, which is why they are called **symmetric**. The following diagram shows where an encryption key is utilized to encrypt the word **Hello** into an encoded form, then the same key is used with the encoded data to decrypt it back to the word **Hello**.

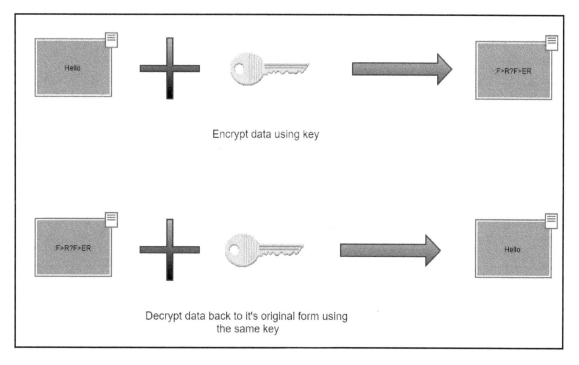

Symmetric cryptography

Symmetric-key algorithms in HTTPS

Now, let's return to the world of web applications and HTTP. In general, web applications are just different pieces of software that communicate using the HTTP protocol. As mentioned earlier in the chapter, to secure HTTP and transform it to HTTPS, we will combine it with another protocol called TLS. The TLS protocol makes use of symmetric-key algorithms to encrypt HTTP data between a client and a server. In other words, the web client and the web server start their communication by agreeing on a shared encryption key (some call it a shared secret), which is then used to protect the data going back and forth between them.

The sender application uses the key to encrypt the data before sending it to the recipient application, which in turn utilizes a copy of the same key to decrypt this data. This process is the symmetric-key algorithm part of the TLS protocol.

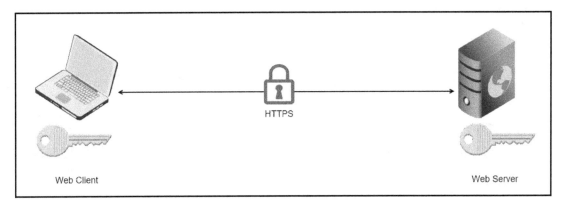

Symmetric-key algorithms in HTTPS

This sounds all good and well, but how exactly would a web client and web server securely agree on the same encryption key before starting to use it to send encrypted data? Obviously, the web client can't just send the key in plain text to the web server and not expect the key to being captured by an unauthorized third party that can then simply decrypt any secure communication via the stolen key. The answer to that question as we mentioned earlier is that the TLS protocol relies on not one, but two types of cryptography algorithms to secure HTTP. The symmetric-key algorithms, which we have covered so far, are utilized to secure most of the communication; however, the public-key algorithms are used for the initial handshake. This is where the client and the server say hi and identify each other, then agree on an encryption key to use thereafter.

Asymmetric cryptography

Unlike symmetric-key algorithms, asymmetric cryptography or public-key algorithms that utilize two keys for protection of data. One key to encrypt the data is known as the public key, and it can be shared safely with other parties. Another key to decrypt the data is known as the private key, and it must not be shared.

The public key can be used by any person to encrypt data. However, only the person with the private key that corresponds to the public key can decrypt the data back to its original human-readable form. The public and private keys are generated using complex computational algorithms.

In a typical scenario, a person who owns a pair of public and private keys would share the public key with other people that they want to communicate with. The other people would then use the public key to encrypt the data being sent to the key owner. The key owner, in turn, can use their private key to decrypt this data back to its original content.

Consider a good example—courtesy of Wikipedia—that showcases the idea. Let's say Alice want to communicate with her friends securely over the internet. For that, she uses an application that generates a pair of public-private keys.

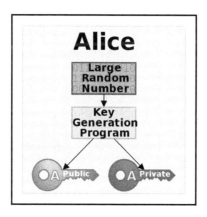

Alice's public-private key

Now, a friend of Alice called Bob would like to send her a secure message over the internet. The message is simply **Hello Alice!** Alice first needs to send Bob a copy of her public key so that Bob can use it to encrypt his message before sending it to Alice. Then, when Alice receives the message, she can use her private key, which is not shared with anyone, to decrypt the message back to the human-readable text and see that Bob said hello.

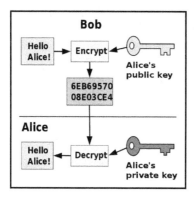

Asymmetric cryptography between Alice and Bob

With this, you should have enough practical understanding of public-key algorithms. However, how is this utilized in the HTTPS protocol?

Asymmetrical cryptography in HTTPS

As mentioned earlier in this chapter, asymmetrical cryptography is utilized between a web client and web server to agree on a shared encryption key (also known as shared secret or session key) that is then used in symmetrical cryptography. In other words, the key is used by both the web client and web server to encrypt mutual HTTP communications. We have already covered the symmetrical cryptography part of this interaction, so now let's dive a bit deeper into how the asymmetrical cryptography part is carried out.

A **handshake** occurs between the web client and web server, where the client indicates its intention to start a secure communication session to the server. Typically, this entails agreeing on some mathematical details on how the encryption occurs.

The server then replies with a **digital certificate**. If you are not familiar with the concept of digital certificates, then now is the time to shed some light on what it is. A digital certificate (or a public-key certificate) is an electronic document that proves the ownership of a public key. To understand the importance of digital certificates, let's take a couple of steps back to remember what a public key is.

As covered earlier, a public key is an encryption key used in asymmetric cryptography (or public-key algorithms); the key can only encrypt data but can never decrypt it back, and it can be shared with anyone who we wish to communicate with. The issuer of the public key always holds a corresponding key called the private key, which can decrypt the data encrypted by the public key.

This sounds great, but what happens if a client requests a public key to communicate with a server, then a bad agent intercepts this request and replies with its own public key (this is known as a man-in-the-middle attack)? The client will then keep communicating with this bad agent thinking that it is the legitimate server; the client may then send sensitive information, such as credit card numbers or personal data, to the bad agent. Obviously, if we seek true protection and security, we want to avoid this scenario at all costs, hence comes the need for certificates.

A digital certificate is a digital document that gets issued by a trusted third-party entity. The document contains a public encryption key, the server name that the key belongs to, and the name of the trusted third-party entity who verifies that the information is correct and that the public key belongs to the expected key owner (also called the issuer of the certificate). The trusted third-party entity who issues the certificate is known as a **CA (certificate authority)**. There are multiple known CA who issue a certificate and verify identities for businesses and organizations. They typically charge a fee for their service. For larger organizations or government bodies, they issue their own certificates; this process is known as **self-signing**, and hence, their certificates are known as self-signed certificates. Certificates can have expiry dates by which the certificates will need to be renewed; this is for extra protection to protect in case the entity that owned the certificate in the past had changed.

A web client typically contains a list of certificate authorities that it knows of. So, when the client attempts to connect to a web server, the web server responds with a digital certificate. The web client looks for the issuer of the certificate and compares the issuer with the list of certificate authorities that it knows. If the web client knows and trusts the certificate issuer, then it will continue with the connection to that server and make use of the public key in the certificate.

The public key obtained from the server will then be used to encrypt communications in order to securely negotiate a shared encryption key (or session key or shared secret) to then be used in symmetrical cryptography communications between the web client and web server. There is a number of algorithms that can be used to generate this session key, but they are beyond the scope of this chapter. What we need to know is that once a session key is agreed on, the initial handshake between the web client and web server will conclude, allowing the actual communication session to proceed securely under the protection of the shared session key.

With this, we now have sufficient practical understanding of how web communications are secured. This is used for secure Restful web APIs and secure web page loads. One more important remark to add is that the URL utilized for secure web communications starts with `https://` instead of `http://`. This is obvious because secure web communications utilize HTTPS instead of just HTTP.

Secure web services in Go

Now it's time to find out how to write secure web services in the Go language. Fortunately, Go was built from the grounds up with modern software architectures in mind, which includes secure web applications. Go comes with a powerful standard library that allows a smooth transition from HTTP servers to HTTPS servers. Before we start looking into the code, let's answer the simple question of how to obtain a digital certificate to use in our web server.

Obtaining a certificate

The default method to obtain a digital certificate for your organization, start-up, or website is to buy the service of verifying your identity and issuing a certificate from a certificate authority provider. As we mentioned earlier, there are multiple certificate authority providers. A list of the most popular providers can be found in Wikipedia at: `https://en.wikipedia.org/wiki/Certificate_authority#Providers`

There are also certificate authorities who provide the service for free. For example, in 2016, the **Mozilla Foundation** along with the **Electronic Frontier Foundation** and the **University of Michigan** collaborated to found a certificate authority called *Let's Encrypt*, which can be found at: `https://letsencrypt.org/`. *Let's Encrypt* is a free service that performs the validation, signing, and issuing of certificates in an automated fashion.

That sounds great. However, what if we just want to test some local web application such as the event's microservice we built in the preceding chapter? In this case, we will need a more straightforward way to generate certificates that we can work and test with. Then, after that, when we deploy to production, we can use a trusted certificate authority to issue certificates for us that will be respected by web browsers and clients connected to the internet.

The straightforward approach to generating certificates for our testing, in this case, would be to manually create our own certificates and self-sign them. The advantage of this is that we can generate numerous certificates to use in our internal testing without getting through a verification process. The disadvantage, however, is the fact that any third-party web clients, such as web browsers, that would try to connect to our web applications via our self-signed certificates would not identify the issuer of those certificates and hence will generate a lot of warnings before allowing us to proceed.

To generate our newly minted self-signed digital certificates, we will need to use specialized tools that understand the algorithms enough to create the necessary outputs. Remember that in order to initiate an HTTPS session, we need the following:

- A digital certificate which will contain the following:
    - A public key that can be shared with other parties.
    - The server name or domain name who owns the certificate.
    - The issuer of the certificate. In case of a self-signed certificate, the issuer would just be us. In case of a certificate issued by a trusted certificate authority, the issuer will be the CA.
- A private key that we need to keep a secret and not share with anyone

OpenSSL

One of such specialized tools that can generate a TLS digital certificate and is very popular is called **OpenSSL**. OpenSSL can be found at: `https://www.openssl.org/`. OpenSSL is an open source commercial grade TLS toolkit that can be used to perform a variety of tasks; among them is to generate self-signed digital certificates. The OpenSSL organization by itself does not provide prebuilt binaries for the tool. However, there is a wiki page that lists third-party places where a binary can be downloaded for the tool. The wiki page can be found at: `https://wiki.openssl.org/index.php/Binaries`. Once you have the tool downloaded, here is an example of how to make use of it to generate a digital certificate in addition to its private key:

```
openssl req -x509 -newkey rsa:2048 -keyout key.pem -out cert.pem -days 365
```

The first word in the preceding code is obviously the name of the binary. Let's cover the arguments one by one:

- `req`: Stands for the request; it indicates that we request a certificate.
- `-x509`: This will indicate that we want to output a self-signed certificate. In the world of cryptography, the notion `X.509` is a standard that defines the format of public key certificates. Digital certificates used in many internet protocols utilize this standard.
- `-newkey`: This option indicates that we would like a new certificate with a paired private key. As mentioned before, a certificate is nothing but a public key combined with a bunch of identifiers. So, to perform asymmetric cryptography, we will need a private key paired with this public key.

- `rsa:2048`: This is an argument to the `-newkey` option, indicating the type of encryption algorithm that we would like to use for generating the key.
- `-keyout`: This option provides the filename to write the newly created private key to.
- `key.pem`: This is the argument to the `-keyout` option. It indicates that we would like the private key to be stored in a file called `key.pem`. This key needs to be kept private and not shared with anyone, as mentioned earlier.
- `-out`: This option provides the filename to write the newly created self-signed certificate to.
- `cert.pem`: This is the argument to the `-out` option; it indicates that we would like to save the certificate in a file called `cert.pem`. This certificate can then be shared with web clients attempting to communicate securely with our web server in order to invoke HTTPS.
- `-days`: The number of days that the certificate should be valid for.
- `365`: This is the argument for the `-days` option. It is simply us saying that we would like the certificate to be valid for 365 days, or simply one year.

generate_cert.go

In the world of the Go language, there is another approach besides OpenSSL to generate self-signed certificates to utilize in our testing. If you go to the GOROOT folder, which is where the Go language is installed and then head to the `/src/crypto/tls` folder, you will find a file called `generate_cert.go`. This file is nothing but a simple tool that can easily and efficiently generate certificates for our testing pleasure. In my computer, the GOROOT folder is located at `C:\Go`. The following is a screenshot of the `generate_cert.go` file on my machine:

Name	Date modified	Type	Size
testdata	3/10/2017 2:00 AM	File folder	
alert.go	2/16/2017 7:23 PM	GO File	3 KB
cipher_suites.go	2/16/2017 7:23 PM	GO File	14 KB
common.go	2/16/2017 7:23 PM	GO File	33 KB
conn.go	2/16/2017 7:23 PM	GO File	39 KB
conn_test.go	2/16/2017 7:23 PM	GO File	10 KB
example_test.go	2/16/2017 7:23 PM	GO File	4 KB
generate_cert.go	2/16/2017 7:23 PM	GO File	5 KB
handshake_client.go	2/16/2017 7:23 PM	GO File	24 KB
handshake_client_test.go	2/16/2017 7:23 PM	GO File	43 KB
handshake_messages.go	2/16/2017 7:23 PM	GO File	33 KB
handshake_messages_test.go	2/16/2017 7:23 PM	GO File	9 KB
handshake_server.go	2/16/2017 7:23 PM	GO File	24 KB
handshake_server_test.go	2/16/2017 7:23 PM	GO File	45 KB
handshake_test.go	2/16/2017 7:23 PM	GO File	6 KB
key_agreement.go	2/16/2017 7:23 PM	GO File	15 KB
prf.go	2/16/2017 7:23 PM	GO File	11 KB
prf_test.go	2/16/2017 7:23 PM	GO File	6 KB

generate_cert.go file

The `generate_cert.go` is a self-contained Go program that can run simply via the `go run` command. Once you run it, it will create a certificate and private key files for you and place them in your current folder. The tool supports a number of arguments, but typically the most commonly used argument is `--host`, which indicates the name of the web server that we would like to generate the certificate and the key for. The following is how we would run the tool via the `go run` command:

```
go run %GOROOT%/src/crypto/tls/generate_cert.go --host=localhost
```

The preceding command was executed on the Windows operating system, which is why it represents the `GOROOT` environmental path variable as `%GOROOT%`. How the environmental variable is represented differs from one operating system to another. In the case of Linux, for example, the environmental variable would be represented as `$GOROOT`.

We will now instruct the command to build a certificate and a private key for a server called `localhost`. The command will generate the certificate and the key for us, then place them in the current folder, as mentioned earlier. Here is a screenshot showing a successful execution of the command:

```
C:\>go run %GOROOT%/src/crypto/tls/generate_cert.go --host=localhost
2017/08/12 20:25:02 written cert.pem
2017/08/12 20:25:02 written key.pem
```

generate_cert.go command

The `generate_cert` tool supports other options besides `--host`. It is worth it to cover some of them:

- `--start-date`: This option indicates the start validation date of the certificate. The argument to this option needs to be formatted as Jan 1 15:04:05 2011, for example.
- `--duration`: This option indicates the duration that the certificate is valid for in hours. The default value is a year.
- `--rsa-bits`: This option indicates the number of bits to be utilized in the rsa encryption of the keys. The default value is 2,048.
- `--help`: This provides a list of supported options with their descriptions.

Once the certificate and key files are generated, we can obtain and use them in our web server application in order to support HTTPS. We'll see how to do just that in the next section.

Building an HTTPS server in Go

It's finally time to dig into some code. Since Go is very well-suited for building modern web software, writing an HTTPS web server is easy. Let's begin by reviewing the piece of code we wrote in the preceding chapter to establish an HTTP web server:

```
http.ListenAndServe(endpoint, r)
```

It was a single line of code, a function called `ListenAndServe()`, which belongs to the HTTP Go package in the standard library. The first argument to `ListenAndServe()` was the endpoint to which we would like our web server to listen to. So, for example, if we would like our web server to listen to local port 8181, the endpoint would be `:8181` or `localhost:8181`. The second argument is the object that describes the HTTP routes and their handlers—this object was created by the Gorilla `mux` package. The code to create it from the preceding chapter is as follows:

```
r := mux.NewRouter()
```

To convert the web server from the preceding chapter from HTTP to HTTPS, we will need to perform one simple change—instead of calling the `http.ListenAndServer()` function, we'll utilize instead another function called `http.ListenAndServeTLS()`. The code will look as follows:

```
http.ListenAndServeTLS(endpoint, "cert.pem", "key.pem", r)
```

As shown in the preceding code, the `http.ListenAndServeTLS()` function takes more arguments than the `original http.ListenAndServe()` function. The extra arguments are the second and third arguments. They are simply the digital certificate filename and the private key filename. The first argument is still the web server listening endpoint, whereas the last argument is still the handler object (which, in our case, is a Gorilla `*Router` object). We have already generated the certificate and private key files from the preceding step, so all we need to do here is to ensure that the second and third arguments point to the correct files.

That's it. This is all what we need to do in order to create an HTTPS web server in Go; the Go HTTP standard package will then take the certificate and private key and utilize them as required by the TLS protocol.

However, what if we would like to support both HTTP and HTTPS in our microservice? For this, we will need to get a little creative. The first logical step would be to run both the `http.ListenAndServe()` and the `http.ListenAndServeTLS()` functions in our code, but then we come across an obvious challenge: how would both functions listen on the same local port? We simply solve this by picking a listening port for HTTPS that is different than the listening port of HTTP. In the preceding chapter, we used a variable called **endpoint** to hold the value of the local HTTP server listening address. For HTTPS, let's assume that the local listening address is stored in a variable called `tlsendpoint`. With this, the code will look as follows:

```
http.ListenAndServeTLS(tlsendpoint, "cert.pem", "key.pem", r)
```

That sounds great, but now we are faced with another hurdle, both of `http.ListenAndServeTLS()` and the `http.ListenAndServe()` are blocking functions. This means that whenever we call them, they block the current goroutine indefinitely until an error occurs. This means that we can't call both functions on the same goroutine.

 A goroutine is a vital language component in Go. It can be considered as a lightweight thread. Go developers make use of goroutines everywhere to achieve efficient concurrency. To communicate information between multiple goroutines, we use another Go language components called Go channels.

So, the solution for this is simple. We call one of the functions in a different goroutine. This can be simply achieved by placing the word go before the function name. Let's run the `http.ListenAndServe()` function in a different goroutine. Here is what the code would look like:

```
go http.ListenAndServe(endpoint,r)
http.ListenAndServeTLS(tlsendpoint, "cert.pem", "key.pem", r)
```

Perfect! With this, our web server can function as an HTTP server for clients who would like to use HTTP or an HTTPS server for clients who prefer to use HTTPS. Now, let's address another question: both of the `http.ListenAndServe()` and the `http.ListenAndServeTLS()` functions return error objects to report any issues in case of failure; so, can we capture errors produced from either function in case of failure, even though they run on different goroutines? For this, we'll need to make use of Go channels, which is the Go idiomatic way to communicate between two goroutines. Here is how the code will look like:

```
httpErrChan := make(chan error)
httptlsErrChan := make(chan error)
go func() { httptlsErrChan <- http.ListenAndServeTLS(tlsendpoint,
"cert.pem", "key.pem", r) }()
go func() { httpErrChan <- http.ListenAndServe(endpoint, r) }()
```

In the preceding code, we create two Go channels, one called `httpErrChan` and the other one called `httptlsErrChan`. The channels will hold an object of type error. One of the channels will report errors observed from the `http.ListenAndServe()` function, whereas the other will report errors returned from the `http.ListenAndServeTLS()` function. We then use two goroutines with anonymous functions in order to run the two `ListenAndServe` functions and push their results into the corresponding channels. We use anonymous functions here because our code entails more than just calling the `http.ListenAndServe()` or the `http.ListenAndServeTLS()` functions.

You may note that we now run both of the `ListenAndServe` functions in goroutines instead of just one. The reason we do that is to prevent either of them from blocking the code, which will allow us to return both of the `httpErrChan` and the `httptlsErrChan` channels to the caller code. The caller code, which is the main function in our case, can then handle the errors as it pleases if any errors occur.

In the preceding chapter, we placed this code in a function called `ServeAPI()`; let's now look at the completed code of this function after our changes:

```
func ServeAPI(endpoint, tlsendpoint string, databasehandler
persistence.DatabaseHandler) (chan error, chan error) {
    handler := newEventHandler(databaseHandler)
    r := mux.NewRouter()
    eventsrouter := r.PathPrefix("/events").Subrouter()
eventsrouter.Methods("GET").Path("/{SearchCriteria}/{search}").HandlerFunc(
handler.FindEventHandler)
eventsrouter.Methods("GET").Path("").HandlerFunc(handler.AllEventHandler)
eventsrouter.Methods("POST").Path("").HandlerFunc(handler.NewEventHandler)
    httpErrChan := make(chan error)
    httptlsErrChan := make(chan error)
    go func() { httptlsErrChan <- http.ListenAndServeTLS(tlsendpoint,
"cert.pem", "key.pem", r) }()
    go func() { httpErrChan <- http.ListenAndServe(endpoint, r) }()
    return httpErrChan, httptlsErrChan
}
```

The function now takes a new string argument called `tlsendpoint`, which will hold the HTTPS server listening address. The function will also return two error channels. The function code then proceeds to define the HTTP routes that our REST API supports. From there, it will create the error channels we discussed, call the HTTP package `ListenAndServe` functions in two separate goroutines, and return the error channels. The next logical step for us is to cover the code that will call the `ServeAPI()` function and see how it handles the error channels.

As discussed earlier, our main function is what calls the `ServeAPI()` function, so this will put the burden of handling the returned error channels on the main function as well. Here is what the code in the main function will look like:

```
//RESTful API start
httpErrChan, httptlsErrChan := rest.ServeAPI(config.RestfulEndpoint,
config.RestfulTLSEndPint, dbhandler)
select {
case err := <-httpErrChan:
    log.Fatal("HTTP Error: ", err)
case err := <-httptlsErrChan:
```

```
        log.Fatal("HTTPS Error: ", err)
    }
```

The code will call the `ServeAPI()` function, which will then capture the two returned error channels into two variables. We will then use the power of the Go's `select` statement to handle those channels. A `select` statement in Go can block the current goroutine to wait for multiple channels; whatever channel returns first will invoke the `select` case that corresponds to it. In other words, if `httpErrChan` returns, the first case will be invoked, which will print a statement in the standard output reporting that an HTTP error occurred with the error found. Otherwise, the second case will be invoked. Blocking the main goroutine is important, because if we don't block it then the program will just exit, which is something we don't want happening if there are no failures. In the past, the `http.ListenAndServe()` function used to block our main goroutine and prevent our program from exiting if no errors occurred. However, since we now have run both of the `ListenAndServe` functions on separate goroutines, we needed another mechanism to ensure that our program does not exit unless we want it to.

In general, whenever you try to receive a value from a channel or send a value to a channel, the goroutine will be blocked till a value is passed. This means that if no errors are returned from the `ListenAndServe` functions, then no value will pass through the channels, which will block the main goroutine till an error happens.

 There is another type of channels in Go beside regular channels called buffered channels, which can allow you to pass values without blocking your current goroutine. However, in our case here, we use regular channels.

The last piece of code we need to cover here is to update the configuration. Remember—in the previous chapter—that we used a configuration object in order to process configuration information for our microservice. The configuration information entailed database addresses, HTTP endpoints, and so on. Since we now also need an HTTPS endpoint, we need to add it to the configuration. The configuration code existed in the `./lib/configuration.go` file. Here is what it should now look like:

```
package configuration

import (
        "encoding/json" "fmt"
        "gocloudprogramming/chapter3/myevents/src/lib/persistence/dblayer"
        "os"
)

var (
```

```go
        DBTypeDefault        = dblayer.DBTYPE("mongodb")
        DBConnectionDefault  = "mongodb://127.0.0.1"
        RestfulEPDefault     = "localhost:8181"
        RestfulTLSEPDefault  = "localhost:9191"
    )

type ServiceConfig struct {
    Databasetype       dblayer.DBTYPE `json:"databasetype"`
    DBConnection       string         `json:"dbconnection"`
    RestfulEndpoint    string         `json:"restfulapi_endpoint"`
    RestfulTLSEndPint  string         `json:"restfulapi-tlsendpoint"`
}

func ExtractConfiguration(filename string) (ServiceConfig, error) {
    conf := ServiceConfig{
                DBTypeDefault,
                DBConnectionDefault,
                RestfulEPDefault,
                RestfulTLSEPDefault,
                }
    file, err := os.Open(filename)
    if err != nil {
        fmt.Println("Configuration file not found. Continuing with default
values.")
        return conf, err
    }
    err = json.NewDecoder(file).Decode(&conf)
    return conf, err
}
```

In the preceding code, we did three main things from the last chapter:

- We added a constant called `RestfulTLSEPDefault`, which will default to
  `localhost:9191`.
- We added a new field to the `ServiceConfig` struct. The field is
  called `RestfulTLSEndPint`; it will be expected to correspond to a JSON field
  called `restfulapi-tlsendpoint`.
- In the `ExtractConfiguration()` function, we set the default value of the
  `RestfulTLSEndPint` field of the initialized `ServiceConfig` struct object
  to `RestfulTLSEPDefault`.

With those three changes, our configuration layer will be able to read the HTTPS endpoint value from a configuration JSON file if a configuration override exists. If either no configuration file exists, or no `restfulapi-tlsendpoint` JSON field is set in the configuration file, then we will take the default value, which is `localhost:9191`.

Any code that will call the `ExtractConfiguration()` function will get access to this functionality and be able to obtain either a default or a configured value for the HTTPS endpoint. In our code, the main function will call the `ExtractConfiguration()` function and will obtain the necessary information to call the `ServeAPI()` function, which will run our RESTful API.

Perfect! With this last piece, we conclude our chapter.

Summary

In this chapter, we took a deep dive into the world of secure web software and how it works internally. We explored HTTPS, symmetric and asymmetric cryptography, and how to secure web services in the Go language.

In the next chapter, we will cover a key topic in the world of distributed microservices architectures: message queues.

4
Asynchronous Microservice Architectures Using Message Queues

In the past two chapters, you learned how to build REST-based microservices with the Go programming language. The REST architectural style is both simple and flexible at the same time, which makes it an excellent choice for many use cases. However, being built on top of HTTP, all communication in a REST architecture will follow the client/server model with request/reply transactions. In some use cases, this might be restrictive and other communication models might be better suited.

In this chapter, we will introduce the publish/subscribe communication model, along with the technologies that you need to implement it. Typically, publish/subscribe architectures require a central infrastructure component—the message broker. In the open source world, there are many different implementations of message brokers; so, in this chapter, we will introduce two different message brokers that we feel to be among the most important ones—**RabbitMQ** and **Apache Kafka**. Both are suited for specific use cases; you will learn how to set up each of these two message brokers, how to connect your Go application, and when you should use one or the other.

We will then show you how to use this knowledge in order to extend the event management microservice that you have worked in the previous chapters to publish an event whenever something important happens. This allows us to implement a second microservice that listens on those events. You will also learn about advanced architectural patterns that usually work well alongside asynchronous communication, such as *event collaboration* and *event sourcing*, and how (and when) to use them in your application.

In this chapter, we will cover the following topics:

- The publish/subscribe architectural pattern
- Event collaboration
- Event sourcing
- AMQP with RabbitMQ
- Apache Kafka

The publish/subscribe pattern

The publish/subscribe pattern is a communication pattern alternative to the well-known request/reply pattern. Instead of a client (issuing a request) and a server (replying with a response to that request), a publish/subscribe architecture consists of publishers and subscribers.

Each publisher can emit messages. It is of no concern to the publisher who actually gets these messages. This is the concern of the subscribers; each subscriber can subscribe to a certain type of message and be notified whenever a publisher publishes a given type of message. In reverse, each subscriber does not concern itself with where a message actually came from.

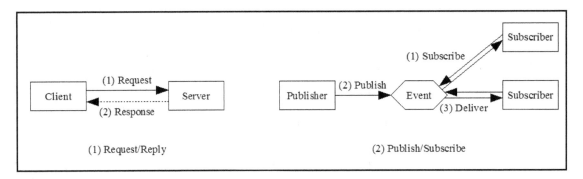

The request/reply and the publish/subscribe communication patterns

In practice, many publish/subscribe architectures require a central infrastructure component—the message broker. Publishers publish messages at the message broker, and subscribers subscribe to messages at the message broker. One of the broker's main tasks then is to route published messages to the subscribers that have expressed interest in them.

Typically, messages will be routed **topic-based**. This means that each publisher specified a topic for a published message (a topic usually just being a string identifier, for example, user.created). Each subscriber will also subscribe to a certain topic. Often, a broker will also allow a subscriber to subscribe to an entire set of topic using wildcard expressions such as user.*.

In contrast to request/reply, the publish/subscribe pattern brings some clear advantages:

- Publishers and subscribers are very loosely coupled. This goes to the extent that they do not even know about one another.
- A pub/sub architecture is very flexible. It is possible to add new subscribers (and, therefore, extend existing processes) without having to modify the publisher. The inverse also applies; you can add new publishers without having to modify the subscribers.
- In case the messages are routed by a message broker, you also gain resiliency. Usually, the message broker stores all messages in a queue, in which they are kept until they have been processed by a subscriber. If a subscriber becomes unavailable (for example, due to a failure or an intentional shutdown), the messages that should have been routed to that subscriber will become queued until the subscriber is available again.
- Often, you will also get some kind of reliability guaranteed by the message broker on a protocol level. For example, RabbitMQ guarantees *reliable delivery* by requiring each subscriber to acknowledge a received message. Only when the message has been acknowledged, the broker will remove the message from the queue. If the subscriber should fail (for example, by disconnection) when a message had already been delivered, but not yet acknowledged, the message will be put back into the message queue. If another subscriber listens on the same message queue, the message might be routed to that subscriber; otherwise, it will remain in the queue until the subscriber is available again.
- You can easily scale out. In case that too many messages are published for a single subscriber to efficiently handle them, you can add more subscribers and have the message broker load-balance the messages sent to these subscribers.

Of course, introducing a central infrastructure component such as a message broker brings its own risk. When not done right, your message broker might become a single point of failure, taking your entire application down with it in case it fails. When introducing a message broker in a production environment, you should take appropriate measures to ensure high-availability (usually by clustering and automatic failover).

In case your application is run in a cloud environment, you may also take advantage of one of the managed message queuing and delivery services that are offered by the cloud providers, for example, AWS **Simple Queue Service (SQS)** or the Azure Service Bus.

In this chapter, you will learn how to use two of the most popular open source message brokers—RabbitMQ and Apache Kafka. In Chapter 8, *AWS Part II - S3, SQS, API Gateway, and DynamoDB*, you will learn about AWS SQS.

Introducing the booking service

In this section, we will start by implementing a publish/subscribe architecture using RabbitMQ. For this, we will need new microservices to our architecture—the booking service will handle bookings for events. Its responsibilities will include making sure that events are not overbooked. For this, it will need to know about existing events and locations. In order to achieve this, we will modify the **EventService** to emit events whenever a location or an event was created (yes, the terminology is confusing—make sure not to mistake the *notification that something has happened* kind-of-event with the *Metallica is playing here* kind-of-event). The **BookingService** can then listen to these events and emit events itself whenever someone books a ticket for one of these events.

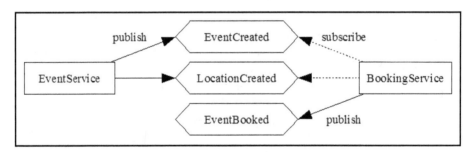

An overview of our microservices and the events that they will be publishing and subscribing to

Event collaboration

Event collaboration describes an architectural principle that works well together with an event-driven publish/subscribe architecture.

Consider the following example that uses the regular request/reply communication pattern—a user requests the booking service to book a ticket for a certain event. Since the events are managed by another microservice (the **EventService**), the **BookingService** will need to request information on both the event and its location from the **EventService.** Only then can the **BookingService** check whether there are still seats available and save the user's booking in its own database. The requests and responses required for this transaction are illustrated in the following diagram:

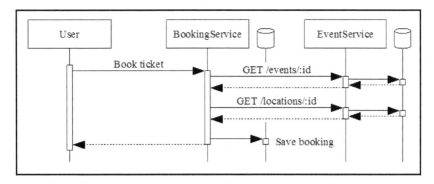

requests and responses

Now, consider the same scenario in a publish/subscribe architecture, in which the **BookingService** and **EventService** are integrated using events: every time data changes in the **EventService**, it emits an event (for example, *a new location was created, a new event was created, an event was updated,* and so on).

Now, the **BookingService** can listen to these events. It can build its own database of all currently existing locations and events. Now, if a user requests a new booking for a given event, the **BookingService** can simply use the data from its own local database, without having to request this data from another service. Refer to the following diagram for another illustration of this principle:

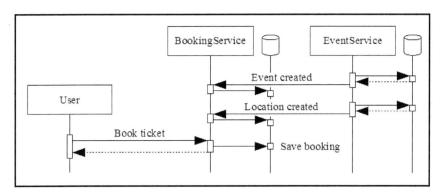

BookingService using the data from its own local database

This is the key point of an event collaboration architecture. In the preceding diagram, a service almost never needs to query another service for data, because it already knows everything it needs to know by listening to the events emitted by other services.

Obviously, this architectural pattern works extremely well together with publish/subscribe. In the preceding example, the **EventService** would be the publisher and the **BookingService** (potentially, among others) the subscriber. Of course, one might flinch at the fact that this principle will inevitably lead to redundant data being stored by the two services. However, this is not necessarily a bad thing—since every service constantly listens to events emitted by the other services, the entire dataset can be kept (eventually) consistent. Also, this increases the system's overall resiliency; for example, if the event service suffers a sudden failure, the **BookingService** would stay operational since it does not rely on the event service to be working anymore.

Implementing publish/subscribe with RabbitMQ

In the following section, you will learn how to implement a basic publish/subscribe architecture. For this, we will take a look at the **Advanced Message Queueing Protocol** (**AMQP**) and one of its most popular implementations, RabbitMQ.

The Advanced Message Queueing Protocol

On a protocol level, RabbitMQ implements the AMQP. Before getting started with RabbitMQ, let's get started by taking a look at the basic protocol semantics of AMQP.

An AMQP message broker manages two basic kinds of resources—**Exchanges** and **Queues**. Each publisher publishes its messages into an exchange. Each subscriber consumes a queue. The AMQP broker is responsible for putting the messages that are published in an exchange into the respective queue. Where messages go after they have been published to an exchange depends on the **exchange type** and the routing rules called **bindings**. AMQP knows three different types of exchanges:

- **Direct exchanges**: Messages are published with a given topic (called **routing key** in AMQP) that is a simple string value. Bindings between a direct exchange and queue can be defined to match exactly that topic.
- **Fanout exchanges**: Messages are routed to all queues that are connected to a fanout exchange via a binding. Messages can have a routing key, but it will be ignored. Every bound queue will receive all messages that are published in the fanout exchange.
- **Topic exchanges**: This works similar to direct exchanges. However, queues are now bound to the exchange using patterns that the message's routing key must match. Topic exchanges usually assume routing keys to be segmented with the dot character '.'. As an example, your routing keys could follow the `"<entityname>.<state-change>.<location>"` pattern (for example, `"event.created.europe"`). You can now create queue bindings that may contain wildcards using the '*' or '#' characters. * will match any single routing key segment, whereas # will match any number of segments. So, for the preceding example, valid bindings might be as follows:
  - `event.created.europe` (obviously)
  - `event.created.*` (listen to whenever an event is created anywhere in the world)

- `event.#` (listen to whenever any change is made to an event anywhere in the world)
- `event.*.europe` (listen to whenever any change is made to an event in Europe)

One possible example exchange and queue topology are shown in the next diagram. In this case, we have one service that publishes messages, the **EventService**. We have two queues in which messages will be routed. The first queue, **evts_booking**, will receive any and all messages that are related to any kind of change made to an event. The second queue, **evts_search**, will receive messages only regarding the creation of new events. Note that the **evts_booking** queue has two subscribers. When two or more subscribers subscribe to the same queue, the message broker will dispatch messages to one of the subscribers on a rotating basis.

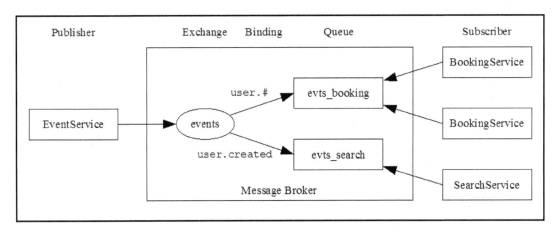

Message broker displaying messages to one of the subscribers on a rotating basis

It is important to note that the entire AMQP topology (meaning all the exchanges and queues and how they are bound to one another) is not defined by the broker, but by the publishers and consumers themselves. AMQP specifies several methods that clients can use to declare the exchanges and queues they need. For example, a publisher would typically use the `exchange.declare` method to assert that the exchange it wants to publish actually exists (the broker will then create it if it did not exist before). On the other hand, a subscriber might use the `queue.declare` and `queue.bind` methods to declare a queue that it wants to subscribe and bind it to an exchange.

There are multiple open source message brokers that implement AMQP. One of the most popular ones (and also the one that we will be working within this chapter) is the RabbitMQ broker, an open source AMQP broker developed by **Pivotal** and made available under the **Mozilla Public License**. Other message brokers that implement AMQP are **Apache QPID** (`https://qpid.apache.org`) and **Apache ActiveMQ** (`http://activemq.apache.org`).

> Although we will use RabbitMQ in this example, the code written in this chapter should work will all kinds of AMQP implementations.

RabbitMQ quickstart with Docker

Before building our publish/subscribe architecture, you will need to set up a running RabbitMQ message broker in your development environment. The easiest way to get started with RabbitMQ is by using the official Docker images.

> For this example, we will assume that you have a working Docker installation on your local machine. Take a look at the official installation instructions to learn how you can install Docker on your operating system at: `https://docs.docker.com/engine/installation`.

You can start a new RabbitMQ broker using the following command on your command line:

```
$ docker run --detach \
    --name rabbitmq \
    -p 5672:5672 \
    -p 15672:15672 \
    rabbitmq:3-management
```

The preceding command will create a new container named `rabbitmq` on your machine. For this, Docker will use the `rabbitmq:3-management` image. This image contains the latest release of RabbitMQ 3 (at the time of writing, 3.6.6) and the management UI. The `-p 5672:5672` flag will instruct Docker to map the TCP port `5672` (which is the IANA-assigned port number for AMQP) to your `localhost` address. The `-p 15672:15672` flag will do the same for the management user interface.

After starting the container, you will be able to open an AMQP connection to `amqp://localhost:5672` and open the management UI in your browser at `http://localhost:15672`.

When you are using Docker on Windows, you will need to substitute localhost with the IP address of your local Docker virtual machine. You can determine this IP address using the following command on the command line: `$ docker-machine ip default`.

Regardless whether you are using docker-machine or a local Docker installation, the RabbitMQ user interface should look very much like it does in the following screenshot:

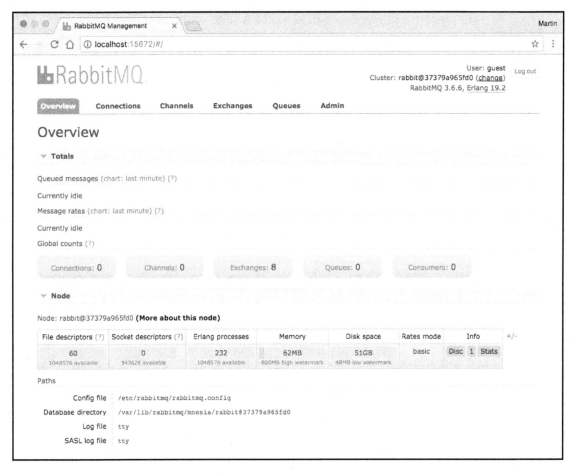

RabbitMQ's management user interface

Open the management interface in your browser (`http://localhost:15672` or your docker-machine IP address). The RabbitMQ image ships a default guest user whose password is also `guest`. When running RabbitMQ in production, this is, of course, the first thing that you should change. For development purposes, it will do fine.

Advanced RabbitMQ setups

The Docker-based setup described in the preceding section allows you to get started quickly and are also (with a few adjustments) suitable for production setups. If you do not want to use Docker for your message broker, you can also install RabbitMQ on most common Linux distribution from package repositories. For example, on Ubuntu and Debian, you can install RabbitMQ using the following commands:

```
$ echo 'deb http://www.rabbitmq.com/debian/ testing main' | \
    sudo tee /etc/apt/sources.list.d/rabbitmq.list
$ wget -O- https://www.rabbitmq.com/rabbitmq-release-signing-key.asc | \
    sudo apt-key add -
$ apt-get update
$ apt-get install -y rabbitmq-server
```

Similar commands also work on **CentOS** and **RHEL**:

```
$ rpm --import https://www.rabbitmq.com/rabbitmq-release-signing-key.asc
$ yum install rabbitmq-server-3.6.6-1.noarch.rpm
```

For a production setup, you might want to consider setting up RabbitMQ as a cluster to ensure high availability. Take a look at the official documentation at `http://www.rabbitmq.com/clustering.html` for more information on how to set up a RabbitMQ cluster.

Connecting RabbitMQ with Go

For connecting to a RabbitMQ broker (or any AMQP broker, for that matter), we recommend that you use the `github.com/streadway/amqp` library (which is the de facto standard Go library for AMQP). Let's start by installing the library:

```
$ go get -u github.com/streadway/amqp
```

You can then start by importing the library into your code. Open a new connection using the amqp.Dial method:

```
import "github.com/streadway/amqp"

func main() {
  connection, err := amqp.Dial("amqp://guest:guest@localhost:5672")
  if err != nil {
    panic("could not establish AMQP connection: " + err.Error())
  }

  defer connection.Close()
}
```

In this case, "amqp://guest:guest@localhost:5672" is the URL of your AMQP broker. Note that the user credentials are embedded into the URL. The amqp.Dial method returns a connection object on success, or nil and an error, otherwise (as usual in Go, make sure that you actually check for this error). Also, do not forget to close the connection using the Close() method when you do not need it anymore.

Of course, it is usually not a good practice to hardcode connection details such as these (much fewer credentials) into your application. Remember what you learned about twelve-factor applications, and let's introduce an environment variable AMQP_URL that we can use to dynamically configure the AMQP broker:

```
import "github.com/streadway/amqp"
import "os"

func main() {
  amqpURL := os.Getenv("AMQP_URL");
  if amqpURL == "" {
    amqpURL = "amqp://guest:guest@localhost:5672"
  }

  connection, err := amqp.Dial(amqpURL)
  // ...
}
```

In AMQP, most operations are done not directly on the connection, but on channels. Channels are used to *multiplex* several virtual connections over one actual TCP connection.

Channels themselves are not thread-safe. In Go, we will need to keep this in mind and pay attention to not access the same channel from multiple goroutines. However, using multiple channels, with each channel being accessed by only one thread, is completely safe. So, when in doubt, it is best to create a new channel.

Continue by creating a new channel on the existing connection:

```
connection, err := amqp.Dial(amqpURL)
if err != nil {
  panic("could not establish AMQP connection: " + err.Error())
}

channel, err := connection.Channel()
if err != nil {
  panic("could not open channel: " + err.Error())
}
```

We can now use this channel object for some actual AMQP operations, for example, publishing messages and subscribing to messages.

Publishing and subscribing to AMQP messages

Before diving back into the MyEvents microservice architecture, let's take a look at the basic AMQP methods that we can use. For this, we will start by building a small example program that is capable of publishing messages to an exchange.

After opening a channel, a message publisher should declare the exchange into which it intends to publish messages. For this, you can use the `ExchangeDeclare()` method on the channel object:

```
err = channel.ExchangeDeclare("events", "topic", true, false, false, false,
nil)
if err != nil {
  panic(err)
}
```

As you can see, `ExchangeDeclare` takes quite a number of parameters. These are as follows:

- The exchange name
- The exchange type (remember that AMQP knows `direct`, `fanout`, and `topic` exchanges)
- The `durable` flag will cause the exchange to remain declared when the broker restarts
- The `autoDelete` flag will cause the exchange to be deleted as soon as the channel that declared it is closed
- The `internal` flag will prevent publishers from publishing messages into this queue
- The `noWait` flag will instruct the `ExchangeDeclare` method not to wait for a successful response from the broker
- The `args` argument may contain a map with additional configuration parameters

After having declared an exchange, you can now publish a message. For this, you can use the channel's `Publish()` method. The emitted message will be an instance of the `amqp.Publishing` struct that you need to instantiate at first:

```
message := amqp.Publishing {
  Body: []byte("Hello World"),
}
```

Then, use the `Publish()` method to publish your message:

```
err = channel.Publish("events", "some-routing-key", false, false, message)
if err != nil {
  panic("error while publishing message: " + err.Error())
}
```

The `Publish()` method takes the following parameters:

- The name of the exchange to publish to
- The message's routing key
- The `mandatory` flag will instruct the broker to make sure that the message is actually routed into at least one queue
- The `immediate` flag will instruct the broker to make sure that the message is actually delivered to at least one subscriber
- The `msg` argument contains the actual message that is to be published

For a publish/subscribe architecture, in which a publisher does not need to know about who is subscribing its published messages, the mandatory and immediate flags are obviously unsuited, so we simply set them to false in this example (and all following ones).

You can now run this program, and it will connect to your local AMQP broker, declare an exchange, and publish a message. Of course, this message will not be routed anywhere and vanish. In order to actually process it, you will need a subscriber.

Continue by creating a second Go program in which you connect to the AMQP broker and create a new channel just like in the previous section. However, now, instead of declaring an exchange and publishing a message, let's declare a queue and bind it to that exchange:

```
_, err = channel.QueueDeclare("my_queue", true, false, false, false, nil)
if err != nil {
  panic("error while declaring the queue: " + err.Error())
}

err = channel.QueueBind("my_queue", "#", "events", false, nil)
if err != nil {
  panic("error while binding the queue: " + err.Error())
}
```

After having declared and bound a queue, you can now start consuming this queue. For this, use the channel's Consume() function:

```
msgs, err := channel.Consume("my_queue", "", false, false, false, false, nil)
if err != nil {
  panic("error while consuming the queue: " + err.Error())
}
```

The Consume() method takes the following parameters:

- The name of the queue to be consumed.
- A string that uniquely identifies this consumer. When left empty (like in this case), a unique identifier will be automatically generated.
- When the autoAck flag is set, received messages will be acknowledged automatically. When it is not set, you will need to explicitly acknowledge messages after processing them using the received message's Ack() method (see the following code example).
- When the exclusive flag is set, this consumer will be the only one allowed to consume this queue. When not set, other consumers might listen on the same queue.

- The `noLocal` flag indicated to the broker that this consumer should not be delivered messages that were published on the same channel.
- The `noWait` flag instructs the library not to wait for confirmation from the broker.
- The `args` argument may contain a map with additional configuration parameters.

In this example, `msgs` will be a channel (this time, meaning an actual Go channel, not an AMQP channel) of `amqp.Delivery` structs. In order to receive messages from the queue, we can simply read values from that channel. If you want to read messages continuously, the easiest way to do this is using a `range` loop:

```
for msg := range msgs {
  fmt.Println("message received: " + string(msg.Body))
  msg.Ack(false)
}
```

Note that we explicitly acknowledge the message using the `msg.Ack` function in the preceding code. This is necessary because we have set the `Consume()` function's `autoAck` parameter to false, earlier.

Explicitly acknowledging a message serves an important purpose—if your consumer fails for whatever reason between receiving and acknowledging the message, the message will be put back into the queue, and then redelivered to another consumer (or stay in the queue, if there are no other consumers). For this reason, a consumer should only acknowledge a message when it has finished processing it. If a message is acknowledged before it was actually processed by the consumer (which is what the `autoAck` parameter would cause), and the consumer then unexpectedly dies, the message will be lost forever. For this reason, explicitly acknowledging messages is an important step in making your system resilient and failure-tolerant.

Building an event emitter

In the preceding example, we used AMQP channels to send simple string messages from publisher to subscriber. In order to use AMQP to build an actual publish/subscribe architecture, we will need to transmit more complex messages with structured data. In general, each AMQP message is simply a string of bytes. To submit structured data, we can use serialization formats, such as JSON or XML. Also, since AMQP is not limited to ASCII messages, we could also use binary serialization protocols such as `MessagePack` or `ProtocolBuffers`.

For whichever serialization format you decide, you need to make sure that both publisher and subscriber understand both the serialization format and the actual internal structure of the messages.

Regarding the serialization format, we will take the easy choice in this chapter and use the JSON serialization format. It is widely adopted; serializing and unserializing messages are easily done using Go standard libraries and also in other programming languages (which is important—although in this book we have committed ourselves exclusively to Go, it is common in microservice architectures to have lots of different application runtimes).

We also need to make sure that both publisher and subscribers know how the messages will be structured. For example, a `LocationCreated` event might have a `name` property and an `address` property. To solve this issue, we will introduce a shared library that will contain struct definitions for all possible events, together with instructions for the JSON (un)serialization. This library can then be shared between the publisher and all subscribers.

Start by creating the `todo.com/myevents/contracts` directory in your GOPATH. The first event type that we will describe is the `EventCreatedEvent` event. This message will later be published by the event service when a new event is created. Let's define this event as a struct in the `event_created.go` file in the newly created package:

```
package contracts

import "time"

type EventCreatedEvent struct {
    ID          string      `json:"id"`
    Name        string      `json:"id"`
    LocationID  string      `json:"id"`
    Start       time.Time   `json:"start_time"`
    End         time.Time   `json:"end_time"`
}
```

Also, we need a possibility to generate a topic name for each event (in RabbitMQ, the topic name will also be used as a routing key for the messages). For this, add a new method—`EventName()`—to your newly defined struct:

```
func (e *EventCreatedEvent) EventName() string {
    return "event.created"
}
```

We can now use a Go interface to define a generic event type. This type can be used to enforce that each event type actually implements an `EventName()` method. Since both event publisher and event subscriber will also later be used across multiple services, we will put the event interface code into the `todo.com/myevents/lib/msgqueue` package. Start by creating the package directory and a new file, `event.go`, within that package:

```
package msgqueue

type Event interface {
  EventName() string
}
```

 Of course, our example application uses more events than just the `EventCreatedEvent`. For example, we also have a `LocationCreatedEvent` and an `EventBookedEvent`. Since showing all their implementations in print would be fairly repetitive, we would like to refer to the example files for this chapter.

Let's now continue by building an event emitter that can actually publish these messages to an AMQP broker. Since we will also explore other message brokers in later sections of this chapter, we will start by defining the interface that any event emitter should fulfil. For this, create a `emitter.go` file in the `msgqueue` package that was created before with the following contents:

```
package msgqueue

type EventEmitter interface {
  Emit(event Event) error
}
```

This interface describes the methods (actually, just one method) that all event emitter implementations need to fulfil. Let's now continue by creating a `todo.com/myevents/lib/msgqueue/amqp` subpackage with a `emitter.go` file. This file will contain a struct definition for the `AMQPEventEmitter`.

Consider the following code example:

```
package amqp

import "github.com/streadway/amqp"

type amqpEventEmitter struct {
  connection *amqp.Connection
}
```

Note how the `amqpEventEmitter` type is declared package-private, as it is declared with a lowercase name. This will prevent users from instantiating the `amqpEventEmitter` type directly. For a proper instantiation, we will provide a constructor method, instead.

Next, let's add a `setup` method that we can use to declare the exchange that this publisher is going to publish into:

```go
func (a *amqpEventEmitter) setup() error {
    channel, err := a.connection.Channel()
    if err != nil {
        return err
    }

    defer channel.Close()

    return channel.ExchangeDeclare("events", "topic", true, false, false,
false, nil)
}
```

You might be wondering why we created a new AMQP channel in this method and closed it immediately after declaring the exchange. After all, we could reuse this same channel for publishing messages later. We will get to that in a moment.

Continue by adding a constructor function—`NewAMQPEventEmitter`—for building new instances of this struct:

```go
func NewAMQPEventEmitter(conn *amqp.Connection) (EventEmitter, error) {
    emitter := &amqpEventEmitter{
        connection: conn,
    }

    err := emitter.setup()
    if err != nil {
        return nil, err
    }

    return emitter, nil
}
```

Now, to the actual heart of the `amqpEventEmitter` event—the `Emit` method. First, we will need to transform the event that has been passed into the method as a parameter into a JSON document:

```
import "encoding/json"

// ...

func (a *amqpEventEmitter) Emit(event Event) error {
  jsonDoc, err := json.Marshal(event)
  if err != nil {
    return err
  }
}
```

Next, we can create a new AMQP channel and publish our message to the events exchange:

```
func (a *amqpEventEmitter) Emit(event Event) error {
  // ...

  chan, err := a.connection.Channel();
  if err != nil {
    return err
  }

  defer chan.Close()

  msg := amqp.Publishing{
    Headers:     amqpTable{"x-event-name": event.EventName()},
    Body:        jsonDoc,
    ContentType: "application/json",
  }

  return chan.Publish(
    "events",
    event.EventName(),
    false,
    false,
    msg
  )
}
```

Note that we used the `Headers` field of `amqp.Publishing` to add the event name in a special message header. This will make it easier for us to implement the event listener later.

Also, note that we are creating a new channel for each published message within this code. While it is, in theory, possible to reuse the same channel for publishing multiple messages, we need to keep in mind that a single AMQP channel is not thread-safe. This means that calling the event emitter's `Emit()` method from multiple go-routines might lead to strange and unpredictable results. This is exactly the problem that AMQP channels are there to solve; using multiple channels, multiple threads can use the same AMQP connection.

Next, we can integrate our new event emitter into the existing event service that you have already built in `Chapter 2`, *Building Microservices Using Rest APIs*, and `Chapter 3`, *Securing Microservices*. Start by adding a configuration option for the AMQP broker in the `ServiceConfig` struct:

```
type ServiceConfig struct {
  // ...
  AMQPMessageBroker string `json:"amqp_message_broker"`
}
```

This allows you to specify the AMQP broker via the JSON configuration file. In the `ExtractConfiguration()` function, we can also add a fallback that optionally extracts this value from an environment variable, if set:

```
func ExtractConfiguration(filename string) ServiceConfig {
  // ...

  json.NewDecoder(file).Decode(&conf)
  if broker := os.Getenv("AMQP_URL"); broker != "" {
    conf.AMQPMessageBroker = broker
  }

  return conf
}
```

We can now use this configuration option to construct a new event emitter in the event service's `main` function:

```
package main

// ...
import "github.com/streadway/amqp"
import msgqueue_amqp "todo.com/myevents/lib/msgqueue/amqp"

func main() {
  // ...

  config := configuration.ExtractConfiguration(*confPath)
  conn, err := amqp.Dial(config.AMQPMessageBroker)
```

```
    if err != nil {
      panic(err)
    }

    emitter, err := msgqueue_amqp.NewAMQPEventEmitter(conn)
    if err != nil {
      panic(err)
    }

    // ...
  }
```

We can now pass this event emitter into the `rest.ServeAPI` function, which can, in turn, pass it into the `newEventHandler` function:

```
func ServeAPI(endpoint string, dbHandler persistence.DatabaseHandler,
eventEmitter msgqueue.EventEmitter) error {
  handler := newEventHandler(dbHandler, eventEmitter)
  // ...
}
```

The event emitter can then be stored as a field in the `eventServiceHandler` struct:

```
type eventServiceHandler struct {
  dbhandler persistence.DatabaseHandler
  eventEmitter msgqueue.EventEmitter
}

func newEventHandler(dbhandler persistence.DatabaseHandler, eventEmitter
msgqueue.EventEmitter) *eventServiceHandler {
  return &eventServiceHandler{
    dbhandler: dbhandler,
    eventEmitter: eventEmitter,
  }
}
```

Now, the `eventServiceHandler` holds a reference to the event emitter that you can use in the actual REST handlers. This allows you, for example, to emit an `EventCreatedEvent` whenever a new event is created via the API. For this, modify the `newEventHandler` method of `eventServiceHandler`, as follows:

```
func (eh *eventServiceHandler) newEventHandler(w http.ResponseWriter, r
*http.Request) {
  id, err := eh.dbhandler.AddEvent(event)
  if err != nil {
    // ...
  }
```

```
msg := contracts.EventCreatedEvent{
    ID: hex.EncodeToString(id),
    Name: event.Name,
    LocationID: event.Location.ID,
    Start: time.Unix(event.StartDate, 0),
    End: time.Unix(event.EndDate, 0),
}
eh.eventEmitter.emit(&msg)

// ...
}
```

Building an event subscriber

Now that we can publish events on a `RabbitMQ` broker using the `EventEmitter`, we also
need a possibility to listen to these events. This will be the purpose of the `EventListener`,
which we will build in this section.

Like before, let's start by defining the interface that all event listeners (the AMQP event
listener being one of them) should fulfil. For this, create the `listener.go` file in
the `todo.com/myevents/lib/msgqueue` package:

```
package msgqueue

type EventListener interface {
    Listen(eventNames ...string) (<-chan Event, <-chan error, error)
}
```

This interface looks quite different than the event emitter's interface. This is because each
call to the event emitter's `Emit()` method simply publishes one message immediately.
However, an event listener is typically active for a long time and needs to react to incoming
messages whenever they may be received. This reflects in the design of our `Listen()`
method: first of all, it will accept a list of event names for which the event listener should
listen. It will then return two Go channels: the first will be used to stream any events that
were received by the event listener. The second will contain any errors that occurred while
receiving those events.

Start with building the AMQP implementation by creating a new `listener.go` file in the
`todo.com/myevents/lib/msgqueue/amqp` package:

```
package amqp

import "github.com/streadway/amqp"
```

```
type amqpEventListener struct {
  connection *amqp.Connection
  queue       string
}
```

Similar to the event emitter, continue by adding a `setup` method. In this method, we will need to declare the AMQP queue that the listener will be consuming:

```
func (a *ampqEventListener) setup() error {
  channel, err := a.connection.Channel()
  if err != nil {
    return nil
  }

  defer channel.Close()

  _, err := channel.QueueDeclare(a.queue, true, false, false, false, nil)
  return err
}
```

Note that the name of the queue that the listener will consume is configurable using the `amqpEventListener` struct's `queue` field. This is because later, multiple services will use the event listener to listen to their events, and each service will require its own AMQP queue for this.

You may have noticed that we did not yet actually bind the newly declared queue to the events exchange. This is because we do not know yet which events we actually have to listen for (remember the `Listen` method's `events` parameter?).

Finally, let's add a constructor function to create new AMQP event listeners:

```
func NewAMQPEventListener(conn *amqp.Connection, queue string)
(msgqueue.EventListener, error) {
  listener := &amqpEventListener{
    connection: conn,
    queue:      queue,
  }

  err := listener.setup()
  if err != nil {
    return nil, err
  }

  return listener, nil
}
```

With the possibility to construct new AMQP event listeners, let's implement the actual `Listen()` method. The first thing to do is use the `eventNames` parameter and bind the event queue accordingly:

```
func (a *amqpEventListener) Listen(eventNames ...string) (<-chan
msgqueue.Event, <-chan error, error) {
  channel, err := a.connection.Channel()
  if err != nil {
    return nil, nil, err
  }

  defer channel.Close()

  for _, eventName := range eventNames {
    if err := channel.QueueBind(a.queue, eventName, "events", false, nil);
err != nil {
      return nil, nil, err
    }
  }
}
```

Next, we can use the channel's `Consume()` method to receive messages from the queue:

```
func (a *amqpEventListener) Listen(eventNames ...string) (<-chan
msgqueue.Event, <-chan error, error) {
  // ...

  msgs, err := channel.Consume(a.queue, "", false, false, false, false,
nil)
  if err != nil {
    return nil, nil, err
  }
}
```

The `msgs` variable now holds a channel of `amqp.Delivery` structs. However, our event listener is supposed to return a channel of `msgqueue.Event`. This can be solved by consuming the `msgs` channel in our own goroutine, build the respective event structs, and then publish these in another channel that we return from this function:

```
func (a *amqpEventListener) Listen(eventNames ...string) (<-chan
msgqueue.Event, <-chan error, error) {
  // ...

  events := make(chan msgqueue.Event)
  errors := make(errors)

  go func() {
```

```
        for msg := range msgs {
          // todo: Map message to actual event struct
        }
      }()

    return events, errors, nil
  }
```

The tricky part is now within the inner goroutine. Here, we will need to map the raw AMQP message to one of the actual event structs (as the `EventCreatedEvent` defined before).

Remember how the EventEmitter added an additional `x-event-name` header to the AMQP message when publishing events? This is something that we can use now to map these messages back to their respective struct types. Let's start by extracting the event name from the AMQP message headers:

 All of the following code goes into the inner `range` loop of the `Listen` method.

```
rawEventName, ok := msg.Headers["x-event-name"]
if !ok {
  errors <- fmt.Errorf("msg did not contain x-event-name header")
  msg.Nack(false)
  continue
}

eventName, ok := rawEventName.(string)
if !ok {
  errors <- fmt.Errorf(
    "x-event-name header is not string, but %t",
    rawEventName
  )
  msg.Nack(false)
  continue
}
```

The preceding code tries to read the `x-event-name` header from the AMQP message. Since the `msg.Headers` attribute is basically a `map[string]interface{}`, we will need a few map index and type assertions until we can actually use the event name. In case a message is received that does not contain the required header, an error will be written into the errors channel. Also, the message will be nack'ed (short for negative acknowledgment), indicating to the broker that it could not be successfully processed.

After knowing the event name, we can use a simple switch/case construct to create a new event struct from this name:

```
var event msgqueue.Event

switch eventName {
  case "event.created":
    event = new(contracts.EventCreatedEvent)
  default:
    errors <- fmt.Errorf("event type %s is unknown", eventName)
    continue
}

err := json.Unmarshal(msg.Body, event)
if err != nil {
  errors <- err
  continue
}

events <- event
```

Building the booking service

Now that we have an event listener, we can use it to implement the booking service. Its general architecture will follow that of the event service, so we will not go too much into detail on that matter.

Start by creating a new package todo.com/myevents/bookingservice and create a new main.go file:

```
package main

import "github.com/streadway/amqp"
import "todo.com/myevents/lib/configuration"
import msgqueue_amqp "todo.com/myevents/lib/msgqueue/amqp"
import "flag"

func main() {
  confPath := flag.String("config", "./configuration/config.json", "path to config file")
  flag.Parse()
  config := configuration.ExtractConfiguration(*confPath)

  dblayer, err := dblayer.NewPersistenceLayer(config.Databasetype, config.DBConnection)
```

```
    if err != nil {
      panic(err)
    }

    conn, err := amqp.Dial(config.AMQPMessageBroker)
    if err != nil {
      panic(err)
    }

    eventListener, err := msgqueue_amqp.NewAMQPEventListener(conn)
    if err != nil {
      panic(err)
    }
  }
```

This will set up the booking service with both a database connection and working event listener. We can now use this event listener to listen to the events emitted by the event service. For this, add a new subpackage
todo.com/myevents/bookingservice/listener and create a
new event_listener.go\ file:

```
package listener

import "log"
import "todo.com/myevents/lib/msgqueue"
import "todo.com/myevents/lib/persistence"
import "gopkg.in/mgo.v2/bson"

type EventProcessor struct {
  EventListener msgqueue.EventListener
  Database      persistence.DatabaseHandler
}

func (p *EventProcessor) ProcessEvents() error {
  log.Println("Listening to events...")

  received, errors, err := p.EventListener.Listen("event.created")
  if err != nil {
    return err
  }

  for {
    select {
      case evt := <-received:
        p.handleEvent(evt)
      case err = <-errors:
        log.Printf("received error while processing msg: %s", err)
```

```
        }
      }
    }
```

In the `ProcessEvents()` function, we are calling the event listener's `Listen` function to listen for newly created events. The `Listen` function returns two channels, one for received messages and one for errors that occur during listening. We will then use an infinitely running for loop and a select statement to read from both of these channels at once. Received events will be passed to the `handleEvent` function (which we still need to write), and received errors will be simply printed to the standard output.

Let's continue with the `handleEvent` function:

```
func (p *EventProcessor) handleEvent(event msgqueue.Event) {
  switch e := event.(type) {
    case *contracts.EventCreatedEvent:
      log.Printf("event %s created: %s", e.ID, e)
      p.Database.AddEvent(persistence.Event{ID: bson.ObjectId(e.ID)})
    case *contracts.LocationCreatedEvent:
      log.Printf("location %s created: %s", e.ID, e)
      p.Database.AddLocation(persistence.Location{ID: bson.ObjectId(e.ID)})
    default:
      log.Printf("unknown event: %t", e)
  }
}
```

This function uses a type switch to determine the actual type of the incoming event. Currently, our event listener processes the two events, `EventCreated` and `LocationCreated`, by storing them in their local database.

> In this example, we are using a shared library `todo.com/myevents/lib/persistence` for managing database access. This is for convenience only. In real microservice architectures, individual microservices typically use completely independent persistence layers that might be built on completely different technology stacks.

In our `main.go` file, we can now instantiate the `EventProcessor` and call the `ProcessEvents()` function:

```
func main() {
  // ...

  eventListener, err := msgqueue_amqp.NewAMQPEventListener(conn)
  if err != nil {
    panic(err)
```

```
    }

    processor := &listener.EventProcessor{eventListener, dblayer}
    processor.ProcessEvents()
}
```

Apart from listening to events, the booking service also needs to implement its own REST API that can be used by users to book tickets for a specified event. This will follow the same principles that you have already learned about in Chapter 2, *Building Microservices Using Rest APIs*, and Chapter 3, *Securing Microservices*. For this reason, we will refrain from explaining the Booking Service's REST API in detail and just describe the highlights. You can find a full implementation of the REST service in the code examples for this chapter.

In the main.go file, we will need to move the processor.ProcessEvents() call into its own go-routine. Otherwise, it would block and the program would never reach the ServeAPI method call:

```
func main() {
  // ...

    processor := &listener.EventProcessor{eventListener, dblayer}
    go processor.ProcessEvents()

    rest.ServeAPI(config.RestfulEndpoint, dbhandler, eventEmitter)
}
```

Finally, we will move on to the actual request handler. It is registered for POST requests at /events/{eventID}/bookings; it checks how many bookings are currently placed for this event and whether the event's location still has the capacity for one more booking. In this case, it will create and persist a new booking and emit an EventBooked event. Take a look at the example files to view the full implementation.

Event sourcing

Building your applications using asynchronous messaging opens the door for applying some advanced architectural patterns, one of which you will learn about in this section.

When using messaging, publish/subscribe, and event collaboration, every change in the entire system's state is reflected in the form of an event that is emitted by one of the participating services. Often, each of these services has its own database, keeping its own view on the system's state (at least, as far as required) and staying up to date by continually listening to the events that are published by the other services.

However, the fact that each change in the system state is also represented by a published event presents an interesting opportunity. Imagine that someone recorded and saved each and every event that was published by anyone into an event log. In theory (and also in practice), you can use this event log to reconstruct the entire system state, without having to rely on any other kind of database.

As an example, consider the following (small) event log:

1. 8:00 am—User #1 with name Alice was created
2. 9:00 am—User #2 with name Bob was created
3. 1:00 pm—User #1 was deleted
4. 3:00 pm—User #2 changes name to Cedric

By replaying these events, it is easy to reconstruct the state of your system at the end of the day—there is one user named Cedric. However, there is more. Since each event is timestamped, you can reconstruct the state that your application had at any given point in time (for example, at 10:00 am, your application had two users, Alice and Bob).

Besides point-in-time recovery, event sourcing offers you a complete audit log over everything that happened in your system. Audit logging often is an actual requirement on its own in many cases, but also makes it easier to debug the system in case of errors. Having a complete event log allows you to replicate the system's state at the exact point in time and then replay events step by step to actually reproduce a specific error.

Also, having an event log makes the individual services less dependent on their local databases. In the extreme, you can abandon databases entirely and have each service reconstruct its entire query model from the event log in-memory each time it starts up.

Implementing publish/subscribe and event sourcing with Apache Kafka

In the remainder of this chapter, we will not build our own event sourcing system. Previously, we used RabbitMQ to accomplish messaging between our services. However, RabbitMQ only handles message dispatching, so if you need an event log containing all events, you will need to implement it yourself by listening to all events and persisting them. You will also need to take care of event replaying yourself.

Apache Kafka is a distributed message broker that also ships with an integrated transaction log. It was originally built by LinkedIn and is available as an open source product licensed under the Apache License.

In the preceding section, we already built implementations of the `EventEmitter` and `EventListener` interfaces using an AMQP connection. In this section, we will implement the same interfaces using Kafka.

Kafka quickstart with Docker

Contrary to RabbitMQ, Apache Kafka is a bit more complex to set up. Kafka itself requires a working Zookeeper setup in order to perform leader election, managing cluster state, and persisting cluster-wide configuration data. However, for development purposes, we can use the `spotify/kafka` image. This image comes with a built-in Zookeeper installation, allowing quick and easy setup.

Just as with the RabbitMQ image before, use the `docker run` command to get started quickly:

```
$ docker run -d --name kafka -p 9092:9092 spotify/kafka
```

This will start a single-node Kafka instance and bind it to the localhost TCP port `9092`.

Basic principles of Apache Kafka

Kafka offers a publish/subscribe message broker, but is not based on AMQP and therefore uses a different terminology.

The first basic concept in Kafka is the topic. A topic is something like a category or event name that subscribers can write to. It contains a complete log of all messages that were ever published into this topic. Each topic is divided into a configurable number of partitions. When a new message is published, it needs to contain a partition key. The partition key is used by the broker to decide into which partition of the topic the message should be written.

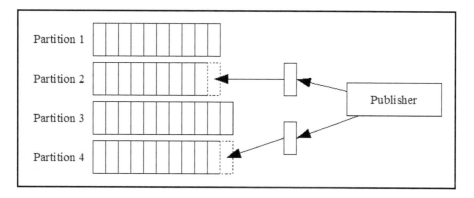

Each Kafka topic consists of a configurable number of partitions; each published message has a partition key, which is used to decide into which partition a message should be saved

The Kafka broker guarantees that within each partition, the order of messages will be the same as in which they were published. For each topic, messages will be kept for a configurable retention period. However, the broker's performance does not degrade significantly when the transaction logs get larger. For this reason, it is entirely possible to operate Kafka with an infinite retention period, and by this way use it as an event log. Of course, you do need to consider that the required disk storage will grow proportionally. Luckily, Kafka supports horizontal scale-out quite well.

From each topic, any number of subscribers (called *consumers* in Kafka jargon) can read messages and any number of publishers (*producers*) can write them. Each consumer defines for itself at which offset in the event log it would like to start consuming. For example, a freshly initialized consumer that only operates in-memory could read the entire event log from the start (offset = 0) to rebuild its entire query model. Another consumer that has a local database and only needs new events that occurred after a certain point in time can start reading the event log at a later point.

Each consumer is a member of a consumer group. A message published in a given topic is published to one consumer of each group. This can be used to implement a publish/subscribe communication, similar to what we have already built with AMQP. The following figure illustrates the different terms and actors in a publish/subscribe architecture using AMQP and Kafka. In both cases, every message that is published in the exchange/topic will be routed to every consumer.

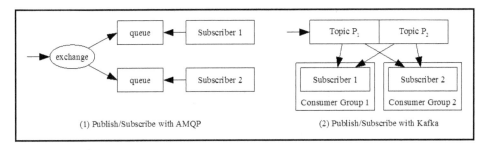

Publish/Subscribe with both AMQP (1) and Apache Kafka (2); each message that is published in the exchange/topic is routed to every subscriber

In AMQP, you can also have multiple subscribers listen on the same queue. In this case, incoming messages will be routed not to all, but to one of the connected subscribers. This can be used to build some kind of load-balancing between different subscriber instances.

The same can be built in Kafka by putting multiple subscriber instances into the same consumer group. In Kafka, however, each subscriber is assigned to a fixed set of (possibly multiple) partitions. For this reason, the number of consumers that can consume a topic in parallel is limited by the number of topic partitions. The following diagram illustrates this example:

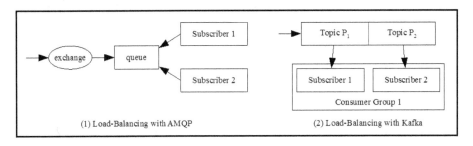

Load-balancing with both AMQP (1) and Apache Kafka (2); each message that is published in the exchange/topic routed to one of the connected subscribers

If you should decide to have multiple consumers within the same consumer group subscribe the same partition of a topic, the broker will simply dispatch all messages in that partition to the consumer that connected last.

Connecting to Kafka with Go

When we connected to an AMQP broker in the previous sections of this chapter, we used the de facto standard library `github.com/streadway/amqp`. For connecting to a Kafka broker, there is a little more diversity among the available Go libraries. At the time of writing this book, the most popular Kafka client libraries for Go are as follows:

1. `github.com/Shopify/sarama` offers full protocol support and is implemented in pure Go. It is licensed under the MIT license. It is actively maintained.
2. `github.com/elodina/go_kafka_client` is also implemented in pure Go. It offers more features than the `Shopify` library, but appears to be less actively maintained. It is licensed under the Apache license.
3. `github.com/confluentinc/confluent-kafka-go` provides a Go wrapper for the `librdkafka` C library (meaning that you will need to have `librdkafka` installed on your system for this library to work). It is reported to be faster than the `Shopify` library since it relies on a highly optimized C library. For the same reason though, it might prove difficult to build. It is actively maintained, although its community seems smaller than the `Shopify` library.

For this chapter, we will use the `github.com/Shopify/sarama` library. Start by installing it via `go get`:

```
$ go get github.com/Shopify/sarama
```

In the previous sections, we have already defined the `EventEmitter` and `EventListener` interfaces in the `todo.com/myevents/lib/msgqueue` package. In this section, we will now add alternative implementations for these two interfaces. Before diving in, let's take a quick look at how to use the `sarama` library to connect to a Kafka broker, in general.

Regardless of whether you intend to publish or consume messages, you will need to start by instantiating a `sarama.Client` struct. For this, you can use the `sarama.NewClient` function. For instantiating a new client, you will need a list of Kafka broker addresses (remember, Kafka is designed for being operated in a cluster, so you can actually connect to many clustered brokers at the same time) and a configuration object. The easiest way to create a configuration object is the `sarama.NewConfig` function:

```
import "github.com/Shopify/sarama"

func main() {
  config := sarama.NewConfig()
  brokers := []string{"localhost:9092"}
  client, err := sarama.NewClient(brokers, config)
```

```
    if err != nil {
      panic(err)
    }
  }
```

Of course, using `localhost` as a single broker works fine in a development setup. For a production setup, the broker list should be read from the environment:

```
func main() {
  brokerList := os.Getenv("KAFKA_BROKERS")
  if brokerList == "" {
    brokerList = "localhost:9092"
  }

  brokers := strings.Split(brokerList, ",")
  config := sarama.NewConfig()

  client, err := sarama.NewClient(brokers, config)
  // ...
}
```

You can use the `config` object to fine-tune various parameters of your Kafka connection. For most purposes, the default settings will do just fine, though.

Publishing messages with Kafka

The Sarama library offers two implementations for publishing messages—the `sarama.SyncProducer` and the `sarama.AsyncProducer`.

The `AsyncProducer` offers an asynchronous interface that uses Go channels both for publishing messages and for checking the success of these operations. It allows high-throughput of messages, but is a bit bulky to use if all you want to do is to emit a single message. For this reason, the `SyncProducer` offers a simpler interface that takes a message for producing and blocks until it receives confirmation from the broker that the message has been successfully published to the event log.

You can instantiate a new Producer using the `sarama.NewSyncProducerFromClient` and `sarama.NewAsyncProducerFromClient` functions. In our example, we will use the `SyncProducer` that you can create as follows:

```
producer, err := sarama.NewSyncProducerFromClient(client)
if err != nil {
  panic(err)
}
```

Let's continue by using the `SyncProducer` to create a Kafka implementation of our `EventEmitter` interface. Start by creating the `todo.com/myevents/lib/msgqueue/kafka` package and the `emitter.go` file within that package:

```
package kafka

type kafkaEventEmitter struct {
  producer sarama.SyncProducer
}
```

Continue by adding a constructor function for instantiating this struct:

```
func NewKafkaEventEmitter(client sarama.Client) (msgqueue.EventEmitter,
error) {
  producer, err := sarama.NewSyncProducerFromClient(client)
  if err != nil {
    return nil, err
  }

  emitter := &kafkaEventEmitter{
    producer: producer,
  }

  return emitter, nil
}
```

In order to emit messages, you will need to construct an instance of the `sarama.ProducerMessage` struct. For this, you will need the topic (which, in our case, is supplied by the `msgqueue.Event`'s `EventName()` method) and the actual message body. The body needs to be supplied as an implementation of the `sarama.Encoder` interface. You can use the `sarama.ByteEncoder` and `sarama.StringEncoder` types to simply typecast a byte array or a string to an `Encoder` implementation:

```
func (e *kafkaEventEmitter) Emit(event msgqueue.Event) error {
  jsonBody, err := json.Marshal(event)
  if err != nil {
    return err
  }

  msg := &sarama.ProducerMessage{
    Topic: event.EventName(),
    Value: sarama.ByteEncoder(jsonBody),
  }

  _, _, err = e.producer.SendMessage(msg)
```

```
    return err
}
```

The key in this code sample is the producer's `SendMessage()` method. Note that we are actually ignoring a few of this method's return values. The first two return values return the number of the partition that the messages were written in and the offset number that the message has in the event log.

The preceding code works, but has one fatal flaw: it creates a new Kafka topic for each event type. While it is entirely possible for a subscriber to consume multiple topics at once, you will have no guaranteed order of processing. This may result in a producer emitting a `location #1 created` and `location #1 updated` sequentially in short order and a subscriber receiving them in the other order.

In order to solve this problem, we will need to do two things:

- All messages must be published on the same topic. This implies that we will need another way to store the actual event name within the message.
- Each message must expose a partition key. We can use the message's partition key to ensure that messages concerning the same entity (that is, the same event, the same user) are stored in a single partition of the event log and are routed to the same consumer in-order.

Let's start with the partitioning key. Remember the `Event` interface in the `todo.com/myevents/lib/msgqueue` package? It looked like this:

```
package msgqueue

type Event interface {
  EventName() string
}
```

Continue by adding a new method `PartitionKey()` to this interface:

```
package msgqueue

type Event interface {
  PartitionKey() string
  EventName() string
}
```

Next, we can modify the existing event structs that we have defined before (for example, `EventCreatedEvent`) to implement this `PartitionKey()` method:

```
func (e *EventCreatedEvent) PartitionKey() string {
  return e.ID
}
```

Now, let's return to the `kafkaEventEmitter`. We can now use each event's `PartitionKey()` method when publishing a message to Kafka. Now, we just need to send the event name alongside the event. To solve this issue, we will use an envelope for the message body: this means that the message body will not just contain the JSON-serialized event object, but rather another object that can contain metadata (like the event name) and the actual event body as payload. Let's define this event in a new file `payload.go` in the package `todo.com/myevents/lib/msgqueue/kafka`:

```
package kafka

type messageEnvelope struct {
  EventName string      `json:"eventName"`
  Payload   interface{} `json:"payload"`
}
```

We can now adjust the `kafkaEventEmitter` to first construct an instance of the `messageEnvelope` struct and then JSON-serialize that:

```
func (e *kafkaEventEmitter) Emit(event msgqueue.Event) error {
  envelope := messageEnvelope{event.EventName(), event}
  jsonBody, err := json.Marshal(&envelope)
  // ...
```

Consuming messages from Kafka

Consuming Messages from a Kafka broker is a little bit more complex than in AMQP. You have already learned that a Kafka topic may consist of many partitions that each consumer can consume one or more (up to all) of these partitions. Kafka architectures allow horizontal scaling by dividing a topic into more partitions and having one consumer subscribe to each partition.

This means that each subscriber needs to know which partitions of a topic exist and which of those it should consume. Some of the libraries that we introduced earlier in this section (especially the Confluent library) actually support automatic subscriber partitioning and automatic group balancing. The `sarama` library does not offer this feature, so our `EventListener` will need to select the partitions it wants to consume manually.

For our example, we will implement the `EventListener` so that it, by default, listens on all available partitions of a topic. We'll add a special property that can be used to explicitly specify the partitions to listen on.

Create a new file `listener.go` in the `todo.com/myevents/lib/msgqueue/kafka` package:

```
package kafka

import "github.com/Shopify/sarama"
import "todo.com/myevents/lib/msgqueue"

type kafkaEventListener struct {
  consumer    sarama.Consumer
  partitions  []int32
}
```

Continue by adding a constructor function for this struct:

```
func NewKafkaEventListener(client sarama.Client, partitions []int32)
(msgqueue.EventListener, error) {
  consumer, err := sarama.NewConsumerFromClient(client)
  if err != nil {
    return nil, err
  }

  listener := &kafkaEventListener{
    consumer: consumer,
    partitions: partitions,
  }

  return listener, nil
}
```

The `Listen()` method of `kafkaEventListener` follows the same interface as the `amqpEventListener` that we implemented in the previous section:

```
func (k *kafkaEventListener) Listen(events ...string) (<-chan
msgqueue.Event, <-chan error, error) {
  var err error

  topic := "events"
  results := make(chan msgqueue.Event)
  errors := make(chan error)
}
```

The first thing to do is to determine which topic partitions should be consumed. We will assume that the listener should listen on all partitions when an empty slice was passed to the NewKafkaEventListener method:

```
func (k *kafkaEventListener) Listen(events ...string) (<-chan
msgqueue.Event, <-chan error, error) {
  var err error

  topic := "events"
  results := make(chan msgqueue.Event)
  errors := make(chan error)

  partitions := k.partitions
  if len(partitions) == 0 {
    partitions, err = k.consumer.partitions(topic)
    if err != nil {
      return nil, nil, err
    }
  }

  log.Printf("topic %s has partitions: %v", topic, partitions)
}
```

A Sarama consumer can only consume one partition. If we want to consume multiple partitions, we will need to start multiple consumers. In order to preserve the EventListener's interface, we will start multiple consumers, each in its own goroutine in the Listen() method and then have them all write to the same results channel:

```
func (k *kafkaEventListener) Listen(events ...string) (<-chan
msgqueue.Event, <-chan error, error) {
  // ...

  log.Printf("topic %s has partitions: %v", topic, partitions)

  for _, partitions := range partitions {
    con, err := k.consumer.ConsumePartition(topic, partition, 0)
    if err != nil {
      return nil, nil, err
    }

    go func() {
      for msg := range con.Messages() {

      }
    }()
  }
}
```

Note the goroutines that are started within the first for loop. Each of these contains an inner for loop that iterates over all messages received in a given partition. We can now JSON-decode the incoming messages and reconstruct the appropriate event types.

 All of the following code examples are placed within the inner for loop of the Listen() method of kafkaEventListener.

```
for msg := range con.Messages() {
  body := messageEnvelope{}
  err := json.Unmarshal(msg.Value, &body)
  if err != nil {
    errors <- fmt.Errorf("could not JSON-decode message: %s", err)
    continue
  }
}
```

We now have a new problem. We have unmarshalled the event body into a messageEnvelope struct. This contains the event name and the actual event body. However, the event body is just typed as interface{}. Ideally, we would need to convert this interface{} type back to the correct event type (for example, contracts.EventCreatedEvent) dependent on the event name. For this, we can use the github.com/mitchellh/mapstructure package that you can install via go get:

$ go get -u github.com/mitchellh/mapstructure

The mapstructure library works similar to the encoding/json library, only that it does not take []byte input variables, but generic interface{} input values. This allows you to take JSON input of unknown structure (by calling json.Unmarshal on an interface{} value) and then later map the already-decoded type of unknown structure to a well-known struct type:

```
for msg := range con.Messages() {
  body := messageEnvelope{}
  err := json.Unmarshal(msg.Value, &body)
  if err != nil {
    errors <- fmt.Errorf("could not JSON-decode message: %s", err)
    continue
  }

  var event msgqueue.Event
  switch body.EventName {
    case "event.created":
      event = contracts.EventCreatedEvent{}
```

```
    case "location.created":
      event = contracts.LocationCreatedEvent{}
    default:
      errors <- fmt.Errorf("unknown event type: %s", body.EventName)
      continue
  }

  cfg := mapstructure.DecoderConfig{
    Result: event,
    TagName: "json",
  }
  err = mapstructure.NewDecoder(&cfg).Decode(body.Payload)
  if err != nil {
    errors <- fmt.Errorf("could not map event %s: %s", body.EventName, err)
  }
}
```

The TagName property in the mapstructure.DecoderConfig struct that is created before doing the actual decoding instructs the mapstructure library to respect the existing `json:"..."` annotations that are already present in the event contracts.

After successfully decoding a message, it can be published into the results channel:

```
for msg := range con.Messages() {
  // ...
  err = mapstructure.NewDecoder(&cfg).Decode(body.Payload)
  if err != nil {
    errors <- fmt.Errorf("could not map event %s: %s", body.EventName, err)
  }

  results <- event
}
```

Our Kafka event listener is now fully functional. Since it implements the msgqueue.EventListener interface, you can use it as a drop-in replacement for the existing AMQP event listener.

There is one caveat, though. When started, our current Kafka event listener always starts consuming from the very start of the event log. Have a closer look at the ConsumePartition call in the preceding code example—its third parameter (in our case, 0) describes the offset in the event log at which the consumer should start consuming.

Using 0 as an offset will instruct the event listener to read the entire event log right from the start. This is the ideal solution if you want to implement event sourcing with Kafka. If you just want to use Kafka as a message broker, your service will need to remember the offset of the last message read from the event log. When your service is restarted, you can then resume consuming from that last known position.

Summary

In this chapter, you learned how to integrate multiple services with asynchronous communication using message queues such as RabbitMQ and Apache Kafka. You also learned about architectural patterns such as event collaboration and event sourcing that help you to build scalable and resilient applications that are well-suited for cloud deployments.

The technologies that we have worked with in this chapter are not tied to any specific cloud provider. You can easily roll your own RabbitMQ or Kafka infrastructure on any cloud infrastructure or your own servers. In Chapter 8, *AWS Part II - S3, SQS, API Gateway, and DynamoDB*, we will take another look at message queues—this time with a special focus on the managed messaging solutions that are offered to you by AWS.

5
Building a Frontend with React

In the previous chapters, you have built multiple microservices with Go and integrated them using both REST web services and asynchronous message queues. However, even the most scalable cloud application is only half as useful without an interface that your users can easily interact with (unless, of course, offering a REST API to your users is your actual product). In order to make the APIs built in the previous chapters more tangible, we will now add a web-based frontend to our application.

For this, we will leave the world of Go programming for a while and take a short side trip to the JavaScript programming world. More precisely, we will take a look at the React framework and will use it to build a frontend application for the (now almost complete) MyEvents backend.

While building the frontend application, we will also get in touch with many components of the incredibly diverse JavaScript ecosystem. For example, we will work with the TypeScript compiler in order to be able to program in a type-safe way. Also, we will use the Webpack module bundler to easily deploy our JavaScript application for easy consumption in all modern web browsers.

In this chapter, we will cover the following topics:

- Setting up a Node.js/TypeScript/React development environment
- Bootstrapping a new project
- React components
- The Webpack module bundler
- Building a React application with a RESTful backend

Getting started with React

For this chapter, we will take a short step outside of the Go ecosystem. For working with React, you will need a development environment offering Node.js, npm, and a TypeScript compiler, which we will set up in the following section.

Setting up Node.js and TypeScript

JavaScript is a dynamically typed language. Although (like Go) it does have a notion of data types, a JavaScript variable can (unlike Go) basically have any type at any time. Since we do not want you to start missing the Go compiler and Go's type safety during our brief excursion into the JavaScript world, we will use TypeScript in this example. TypeScript is a type-safe superset of JavaScript that adds static typing and class-based OOP to JavaScript. You can compile TypeScript to JavaScript using the TypeScript compiler (or short, *tsc*).

First of all, in addition to your Go runtime, you will need a working Node.js runtime set up on your development machine. Take a look at `https://nodejs.org/en/download` to learn how to set up Node.js on your machine. If you are running Linux (or macOS using a package manager such as Homebrew), take a look at `https://nodejs.org/en/download/package-manager`.

After having installed Node.js, continue by installing the TypeScript compiler using the **Node Package Manager (npm)**:

```
$ npm install -g typescript
```

This will download and install the TypeScript compiler into your system's `PATH`. After running the preceding command, you should be able to call tsc on your command line.

In this project, we will also use the Webpack module bundler. A module bundler takes Node.js modules and generates static JavaScript files that can be used in a browser environment. You can install Webpack just as you did for the TypeScript compiler via npm:

```
$ npm install -g webpack
```

Initializing the React project

Start by creating a new directory for your React frontend application. Next, initialize the directory as a new npm package:

```
$ npm init
```

The `npm init` command will prompt you for a few (more or less), important information about your project. In the end, it should generate a `package.json` file, which should look roughly like this:

```
{
    "name": "myevents-ui",
    "version": "1.0.0",
    "description": "",
    "main": "dist/bundle.js",
    "author": "Martin Helmich",
    "license": "MIT"
}
```

In general, our application will have the following directory structure:

- Our TypeScript source files will be placed in the `src/` directory.
- The compiled JavaScript files will be placed in the `dist/` directory. Since we will be using Webpack as a module bundler, our `dist/` directory will most likely contain just one file containing the entire compiled source code.
- The libraries that we will be installing as dependencies via npm will be installed into the `node_modules/` directory.

We can now use npm to add dependencies to our project. Let's start by installing the React and ReactDOM packages:

```
$ npm install --save react@16 react-dom@16 @types/react@16 @types/react-dom@16
```

The `@types` packages are needed for the TypeScript compiler. Since React is a JavaScript (not TypeScript) library, the TypeScript compiler will need additional information about the classes defined by the react library and their method signatures. For example, these **typings** might contain information on which parameter types are needed for certain functions provided by React and their return types.

We will also need a few development dependencies:

```
$ npm install --save-dev typescript awesome-typescript-loader source-map-loader
```

These libraries will be needed by the Webpack module bundler to compile our source files to JavaScript files. However, we will need these dependencies only for *building* the application, not for actually *running* it. For this reason, we declared them as development dependencies using the `--save-dev` flag.

Next, we will need to configure the TypeScript compiler. For this, create a new `tsconfig.json` file in the project directory:

```json
{
  "compilerOptions": {
    "outDir": "./dist/",
    "module": "commonjs",
    "target": "es5",
    "sourceMap": true,
    "noImplicitAny": true,
    "jsx": "react"
  },
  "include": [
    "./src/**/*"
  ]
}
```

Note how we are configuring the TypeScript compiler to load its source files from the `src/` directory using the `include` attribute and to save the compiled output files to `dist/` using the `outDir` attribute.

Lastly, we will also need to configure the Webpack module bundler by creating a `webpack.config.js` file:

```js
module.exports = {
  entry: "./src/index.tsx",
  output: {
    filename: "bundle.js",
    path: __dirname + "/dist"
  },
  resolve: {
    extensions: [".ts", ".tsx"]
  },
  module: {
    rules: [
      {
        test: /\.tsx?$/,
        loader: "awesome-typescript-loader"
      }
    ]
  },
  externals: {
    "react": "React",
    "react-dom": "ReactDOM"
  }
}
```

This file configures Webpack to use the TypeScript loader on all .ts and .tsx files, compile them, and bundle all modules into the dist/bundle.js file. Before you can actually do that, though, you will need to add some source files to compile.

Before doing that, let's take a look at how React actually works.

Basic React principles

A React application is built from **Components**. A component is a JavaScript class that accepts a set of values (called properties, or in short, *props*) and returns a tree of DOM elements that can be rendered by the browser.

Consider the following easy example. We will start with the plain JavaScript implementation and show you how to add static typing using TypeScript later:

```
class HelloWorld extends React.Component {
  render() {
    return <div className="greeting">
      <h1>Hello {this.props.name}!</h1>
    </div>;
  }
}
```

Even if you are used to JavaScript, the syntax will probably seem new to you. Technically, the preceding code example is not plain JavaScript (any browser would refuse to actually run this code), but **JSX**. JSX is a special syntax extension to JavaScript that allows you to directly define DOM elements using their respective HTML representation. This makes defining React components much easier. Without using JSX, the preceding code example will need to be written as follows:

```
class HelloWorld extends React.Component {
  render() {
    return React.createElement("div", {class: "greeting"},
      React.createElement("h1", {}, `Hello ${this.props.name}!`)
    );
  }
}
```

Of course, for actually running the JSX source code in the browser, it needs to be transformed to plain old JavaScript first. This will be done by the Webpack module bundler when actually building the application.

There's also a TypeScript variant of JSX, called **TSX**. It works exactly the same way, but with static typing. When building a React component with TypeScript, you also have the possibility to define an interface for the component props.

Since this is actually a Go book, it is important to note that TypeScript interfaces are a very different thing compared to Go interfaces. While a Go interface describes a set of methods that a struct needs to implement, a TypeScript interface defines properties and/or methods that an object needs to have.

To associate a React component with a props interface, the `React.Component` class has a type parameter that you can specify when extending the class:

```
export interface HelloWorldProps {
  name: string;
}

export class HelloWorld extends React.Component
<HelloWorldProps, any> {
  render() {
    // ...
  }
}
```

Components can be nested into each other. For example, you can now reuse the `HelloWorld` component from earlier in another component:

```
import {HelloWorld} from "./hello_world";

class ExampleComponents extends React.Component<{}, any> {
  render() {
    return <div class="greeting-list">
      <HelloWorld name="Foo"/>
      <HelloWorld name="Bar"/>
    </div>
  }
}
```

One advantage of using TypeScript is that when you are using a component whose props are defined via an interface, the TypeScript compiler checks whether you are actually providing the component with the correct props. For example, omitting the `name` prop in the preceding example (or passing it another value than a string) will trigger a compile error.

The props passed to a React component are treated as immutable. This means that the component will not re-render when one of the prop's values is changed. However, each React component may have an internal state, which can be updated. Every time a component's state is changed, it will be re-rendered. Consider the following example:

```
export interface CounterState {
  counter: number;
}

export class Counter extends React.Component<{}, CounterState> {
  constructor() {
    super();
    this.state = {counter: 0};
  }

  render() {
    return <div>Current count: {this.state.counter}</div>;
  }
}
```

We can now update this state whenever we want using the component's `setState()` method. For example, we can have a timer increment the counter every second:

```
constructor() {
  super();
  this.state = {counter: 0};

  setInterval(() => {
    this.setState({counter: this.state.counter + 1});
  }, 1000);
}
```

Changing the component's state will cause it to be re-rendered. In the preceding example, this would cause the counter to visibly increment by 1 every second.

Of course, we can also combine props and state. One common use case is to use the props that are passed into a component to initialize that component's state:

```
export interface CounterProps {
  start: number;
}

export interface CounterState {
  counter: number
}

export class Counter extends React.Component<CounterProps, CounterState> {
```

```
  constructor(props: CounterProps) {
    super(props);

    this.state = {
      counter: props.start
    };

    setInterval(() => {
      // ...
    }
  }
}
```

Armed with the knowledge about React components, we can now start building the frontend for our MyEvents platform.

Kick-starting the MyEvents frontend

We will start by building a simple React application that gets the list of available events from the server and displays it as a simple list.

Before getting started, we will need to bootstrap our React application. For this, we will need to build an index.html file that can serve as the entry point of our application. Typically, this file will not be long, since most of its logic will be living in the form of React components:

```
<!DOCTYPE html>
<html lang="en">
  <head>
    <meta charset="UTF-8">
    <title>MyEvents</title>
  </head>
  <body>
    <div id="myevents-app"></div>

    <script
src="./node_modules/react/umd/react.production.min.js"></script>
    <script src="./node_modules/react-dom/umd/react-
dom.production.min.js"></script>
    <script src="./dist/bundle.js"></script>
  </body>
</html>
```

Let's take a more detailed look at this HTML file. The `DIV` with the `myevents-app` ID will later be the location at which our React application will be rendered. Most of the file then consists of loading the React libraries from the respective npm packages and loading our actual application bundle (which will be built by Webpack).

To make our application a bit nicer to look at, we will also add the Twitter Bootstrap framework to our frontend. As usual, you can use npm to install Bootstrap:

```
$ npm install --save bootstrap@^3.3.7
```

After installing Bootstrap, you can include the respective CSS file in the header section of your `index.html` file:

```
<!DOCTYPE html>
<html lang="en">
<head>
  <meta charset="UTF-8">
  <title>MyEvents</title>
  <link rel="stylesheet"
href="./node_modules/bootstrap/dist/css/bootstrap.min.css"/>
</head>
<body>
  <!-- ... -->
</body>
</html>
```

To get started, let's now add a new React component. For this, create the `src/components/hello.tsx` file in your project directory:

```
import * as React from "React";

export interface HelloProps {
  name: string;
}

export class Hello extends React.Component<HelloProps, {}> {
  render() {
    return <div>Hello {this.props.name}!</div>;
  }
}
```

The actual entry point of our React application will be placed in the src/index.tsx file. You may remember that this was also the file that we have specified as the entry point for the Webpack module bundler in the webpack.config.js file:

```
import * as React from "react";
import * as ReactDOM from "react-dom";
import {Hello} from "./components/hello";

ReactDOM.render(
  <div className="container">
    <h1>MyEvents</h1>
    <Hello name="World"/>
  </div>,
  document.getElementById("myevents-app")
);
```

Take a look at the className attribute in the preceding code example. When working with plain HTML elements in JSX or TSX, you will need to use className instead of class. This is because class is a reserved keyword in both JavaScript and TypeScript, so using just class would seriously confuse the compiler.

After having created all these files, you can now run the Webpack bundler to create your bundle.js file:

$ webpack

While in development, you can also have the Webpack bundler running continuously, updating your bundle.js file whenever one of the source files changes. Just leave the started process running in a shell window in the background:

$ webpack --watch

You can now open the index.html file in your browser. However, directly opening local files in your browser will cause issues later when making HTTP requests to our backend services. You can use the http-server npm's package to quickly set up an HTTP server that can serve these local files. Simply install it via npm and then run it in your project directory:

$ npm install -g http-server
$ http-server

The Node.js HTTP server will listen at the TCP port `8080` by default, so you can access it by navigating to `http://localhost:8080` in your browser:

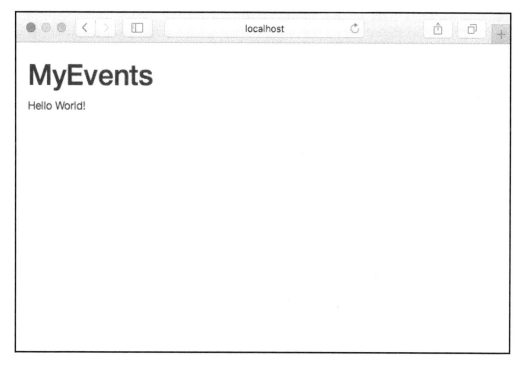

output (http://localhost:8080)

Congratulations! You have just built your first React application. Of course, for the MyEvents platform, we will need a bit more than **Hello World!** One of our first tasks will be loading the available events from the backend service and displaying them in an aesthetically pleasing manner.

Implementing the event list

To display a list of available events, we will need a solution for loading these events from the backend service, more precisely, the event service's REST API that you have built in `Chapter 2`, *Building Microservices Using Rest APIs*, and `Chapter 3`, *Securing Microservices*.

Bringing your own client

React is a modular Framework. Unlike other JavaScript frontend frameworks such as Angular, React does not ship its own library for REST calls, but instead expects you to bring your own. To load data from the server, we will use the fetch API. The fetch API is a newer JavaScript API for doing AJAX calls to backend services that are implemented in many modern browsers (primarily, Firefox and Chrome). For older browsers that do not yet implement the fetch API, there is a `polyfill` library that you can add to your application via `npm`:

```
$ npm install --save whatwg-fetch promise-polyfill
```

You will need to include these two `polyfill` libraries in your `index.html` file alongside the other JavaScript libraries:

```
<script src="./node_modules/react/dist/react.min.js"></script>
<script src="./node_modules/react-dom/dist/react-dom.min.js"></script>
<script src="./node_modules/promise-polyfill/promise.min.js"></script>
<script src="./node_modules/whatwg-fetch/fetch.js"></script>
<script src="./dist/bundle.js"></script>
```

The fetch `polyfill` library will use the browser's fetch API when it is available, and provide its own implementation when it's not available. In a few years, when more browsers support the fetch API, you will be safely able to remove the `polyfill`.

Building the event list components

Let's now think about which React components we will need for our event list. The following diagram shows an overview of the components that we will be building:

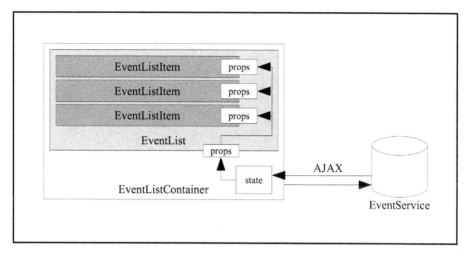

An overview of the components that the event list will be built of

These components will have the following responsibilities:

- The `EventListContainer` component will be responsible for loading the event list from the backend service and managing the event list in its own state. It will then pass the current set of events down to the props of the `EventList` component.
- The `EventList` component will be responsible for rendering the container in which the event list will be presented. For starters, we will choose a simple table view. This table will then be filled with a set of `EventListItem`, one for each event.
- The `EventListItem` component will render a single Event item in the event list.

Technically, we could make the `EventList` component do both—load the events from the backend service and manage the event list presentation. However, this would violate the **single-responsibility principle**; that's why we have two components—one that loads events and passes them to another, and one that presents them to the user.

Let's start by telling the TypeScript compiler how an Event actually looks like. To do this, we will define a TypeScript interface that describes the JSON responses that are delivered by the backend service when GET is used for getting the URL /events. Create a new ./src/models/event.ts file with the following contents:

```
export interface Event {
  ID string;
  Name string;
```

```
    Country string;
    Location {
      ID string;
      Name string;
      Address string;
    };
    StartDate number;
    EndDate number;
    OpenTime: number;
    CloseTime: number;
  }
```

Note how closely this interface definition corresponds with the persistence.Event struct that was defined in the event service's code. In order for frontend and backend to work well together, these two definitions will need to be kept in sync when they change.

You can now continue to build the React components. We will start bottom-up by implementing the EventListItem. For this, create a new src/components/event_list_item.tsx file:

```
import {Event} from "../models/event";
import * as React from "react";

export interface EventListItemProps {
  event: Event;
}

export class EventListItem extends React.Component<EventListItemProps, {}>
{
  render() {
    const start = new Date(this.props.event.StartDate * 1000);
    const end = new Date(this.props.event.EndDate * 1000);

    return <tr>
      <td>{this.props.event.Name}</td>
      <td>{this.props.event.Location.Name}</td>
      <td>{start.toLocaleDateString()}</td>
      <td>{end.toLocaleDateString()}</td>
      <td></td>
    </tr>
  }
}
```

Next, define the `EventList` component in the `src/components/event_list.tsx` file:

```
import {Event} from "../models/event";
import {EventListItem} from "./event_list_item";
import * as React from "react";

export interface EventListProps {
  events: Event[];
}

export class EventList extends React.Component<EventListProps, {}> {
  render() {
    const items = this.props.events.map(e =>
      <EventListItem event={e} />
    );

    return <table className="table">
      <thead>
        <tr>
          <th>Event</th>
          <th>Where</th>
          <th colspan="2">When (start/end)</th>
          <th>Actions</th>
        </tr>
      </thead>
      <tbody>
        {items}
      </tbody>
    </table>
  }
}
```

Note how the `EventList` component uses JavaScript's native `map` function to convert an array of Event objects to a list of `EventListItem` (with that event passed as a prop) very easily. The list of `EventListItem` is then inserted into the body of the table created by the `EventList` component.

Last but not least, we can build the `EventListContainer` component. Within this component, we will use the fetch API to load the events from the server. First, let's implement the definitions for the `EventListContainer` props and state in the `src/components/event_list_container.tsx` file:

```
import * as React from "react";
import {EventList} from "./event_list";
import {Event} from "../models/event";
```

```
export interface EventListContainerProps {
  eventListURL: string;
}

export interface EventListContainerState {
  loading: boolean;
  events: Event[]
}
```

Next, we can implement the actual component:

```
export class EventListContainer extends React.Component
<EventListContainerProps, EventListContainerState> {
  construct(p: EventListContainerProps) {
    super(p);

    this.state = {
      loading: true,
      events: []
    };

    fetch(p.eventListURL)
      .then<Event[]>(response => response.json())
      .then(events => {
        this.setState({
          loading: false,
          events: events
        });
      });
  }
}
```

In the constructor, we will first initialize the component's state. Here, it is important to remember that HTTP operations in JavaScript are usually asynchronous. Although we are calling the `fetch` function in the constructor, the JavaScript runtime will execute this HTTP request asynchronously and the component will be created even when no data has been loaded (yet). For this reason, our component state includes a boolean property named `loading` that indicates whether the data is still loading. Later, the component can adjust its presentation based on this state attribute.

The `fetch` method returns a promise. A promise is a placeholder for a value that is not yet available. You can use the `then(...)` function on a promise instance to run code as soon as the promised value becomes available. You can also chain promise; in this case, the `fetch` function returns a promise for an HTTP response (that is, an instance of the `Response` class). This class in itself has a `json()` function that itself returns another promise for the JSON-decoded value. When a function passed to a `then(...)` call returns another promise, the returned promise will replace the original promise. This means that we can add another `then()` call to the chain that will be called when the HTTP response is available and was successfully JSON-decoded. When that happens, we will update the component's state, indicating that the component is no longer loading, and the `events` property containing the actual event list.

Finally, finish the `EventListContainer` component by adding a `render()` method:

```
render() {
  if (this.state.loading) {
    return <div>Loading...</div>;
  }

  return <EventList events={this.state.events} />;
}
```

In order to actually display the event list on our page, you can now use the `EventListContainer` in the `index.tsx` file:

```
import * as React from "react";
import * as ReactDOM from "react-dom";
import {EventListContainer} from "./components/event_list_container";

ReactDOM.render(
  <div className="container">
    <h1>MyEvents</h1>
    <EventListContainer eventListURL="http://localhost:8181"/>
  </div>,
  document.getElementById("myevents-app")
);
```

In general, it is also considered a good practice to build a root component that can serve as a single point of entry into the application. We can extract the DOM elements from the `ReactDOM.render` call into its own component and then use that in the `ReactDOM.render` call:

```
class App extends React.Component<{}, {}> {
  render() {
    return <div className="container">
      <h1>MyEvents</h1>
      <EventListContainer eventListURL="http://localhost:8181"/>
    </div>
  }
}

ReactDOM.render(
  <App/>
  document.getElementById("myevents-app")
);
```

Enabling CORS in the backend services

Before testing the frontend application, you will need to make sure that the backend services (more precisely, both the event service and the booking service) support **Cross-Origin Resource Sharing (CORS)**. Otherwise, your browser will not execute HTTP requests to any of your backend services, when the frontend is served on `http://localhost:8080` and the backend services run on other TCP ports.

In principle, CORS consists of nothing more than a few additional headers that need to be present in the HTTP response. For example, to allow AJAX requests from another domain, the HTTP response needs to contain an `Access-Control-Allow-Origin` header. An HTTP response with such a header might look like this:

```
HTTP/1.1 200 OK
  Content-Type: application/json; charset=utf-8
  Content-Length: 1524
  Date: Fri, 24 Mar 2017 16:02:55 GMT
  Access-Control-Allow-Origin: http://localhost:8080
```

Since we are using the Gorilla toolkit in both the event and booking service, adding the CORS functionality is easy. First, we will need to go get the `github.com/gorilla/handlers` package:

```
$ go get github.com/gorilla/handlers
```

After that, we can use the `handlers.CORS` function to add the CORS functionality to an existing HTTP server. This allows us to adjust the event service's `rest.go` file as follows:

```
package rest

import (
  // ...
  "github.com/gorilla/mux"
  "github.com/gorilla/handlers"
)

func ServeAPI(endpoint string, dbHandler persistence.DatabaseHandler,
eventEmitter msgqueue.EventEmitter) error {
  handler := newEventHandler(dbHandler, eventEmitter)
  r := mux.NewRouter()

  // ...

  server := handlers.CORS()(r)
  return http.ListenAndServe(endpoint, server)
}
```

Adjust the booking service the same way. After that, you will be able to talk to both services from the frontend application without any issues.

Testing the event list

In order to test your application, make sure that you have an instance of the event service running locally and listening on TCP port `8181`. Also, ensure that you have already created one or two events using the event service's REST API. Then, start the Node.js `http-server` in your frontend application directory and navigate to `http://localhost:8080` in your browser:

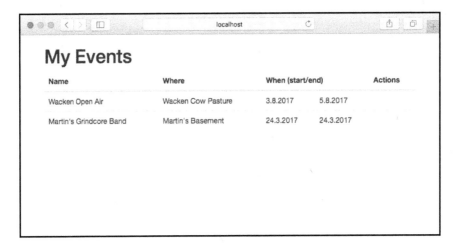

output (http://localhost:8080)

Adding routing and navigation

Before we add more functionalities to our frontend application, let's take the time to add a robust navigation and routing layer. This will allow our application to stay easily maintainable when more features are added.

In order for our application to support multiple application views, we will first add the `react-router-dom` package to our application:

```
$ npm install --save react-router-dom
$ npm install --save-dev @types/react-router-dom
```

The `react-router-dom` package adds a few new components to our application. We can use these in our root component to easily implement routing:

```
import * as React from "react";
import * as ReactDOM from "react-dom";
```

```
import {HashRouter as Router, Route} from "react-router-dom";
// ...

class App extends React.Component<{}, {}> {
  render() {
    const eventList = () => <EventListContainer
eventServiceURL="http://localhost:8181"/>

    return <Router>
      <div className="container">
        <h1>My Events</h1>

        <Route exact path="/" component={eventList}/>
      </div>
    </Router>
  }
}
```

Note how the <Route> component is used within the container; at this point, we can later add multiple Route components and the React router will render these components depending on the current URL. This allows our application to lead the user from one view to another using plain, old links.

Note the eventList constant that is being declared in the preceding render() method. This is because the Route component accepts a component prop, which refers to a component or a function that will be called whenever this Route is matched. However, we cannot specify props that should be passed to the respective component. This is why we are declaring a function that initializes the EventListContainer component with default props, allowing it to be used in the Route component.

Now that we have a working routing layer; let's make sure that our users will always find their way back to the event list. For this, we will add a new navigation bar component that we can use in our root component. Create a new src/components/navigation.tsx file:

```
import * as React from "react";
import {Link} from "react-router-dom";

export interface NavigationProps {
  brandName: string;
}

export class Navigation extends React.Component<NavigationProps, {}> {
}
```

Next, add a `render()` method to the new component:

```
render() {
  return <nav className="navbar navbar-default">
    <div className="container">
      <div className="navbar-header>
        <Link to="/" className="navbar-brand">
          {this.props.brandName}
        </Link>
      </div>

      <ul className="nav navbar-nav">
        <li><Link to="/">Events</Link></li>
      </ul>
    </div>
  </nav>
}
```

Note how our `Navigation` component uses the `Link` component to create links to other React routes, which is admittedly not that complicated yet, given that we only have the `/` route for now.

To actually use our new navigation component, add it to the root component's `render` method:

```
// ...
import {Navigation} from "./components/navigation";

class App extends React.Component<{}, {}> {
  render() {
    const eventList = () => <EventListContainer
eventServiceURL="http://localhost:8181"/>

    return <Router>
      <Navigation brandName="MyEvents"/>
      <div className="container">
        <h1>My Events</h1>

        <Route exact path="/" component={eventList}/>
      </div>
    </Router>
  }
}
```

Implementing the booking process

Now that we have a working routing and navigation in place, we can implement the next piece of functionality—the booking process. For the purpose of this book, we will keep the booking process simple. Each line in the events list that we implemented earlier should get a button that takes the user to the booking form. In this form, they will be prompted for the number of tickets they want to book and can then submit the form. On submitting, the frontend application will perform an HTTP request to the booking service.

Of course, we will implement the booking form as a React component. Just as before, we will keep responsibilities separated and build separate components to handle the backend communication and frontend presentation. The EventBookingFormContainer will be responsible for loading the event record from the event service and saving the actual booking back to the booking service. The EventBookingForm will then be responsible for the actual frontend presentation of the form. In order to make the form presentation easier, we will also introduce a FormRow component. The following diagram gives an overview of these components and how they relate to each other:

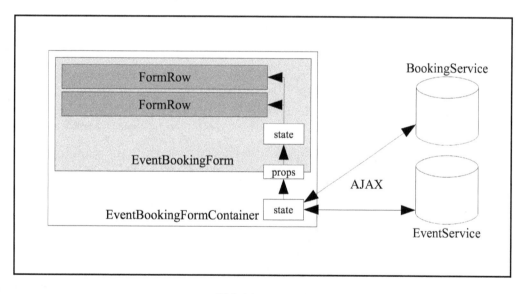

Relation between components

The `FormRow` component will be a purely presentational component to make the Bootstrap framework's form CSS classes easier to use. As before, we will implement these components bottom-up, starting with the innermost component. For this, create the `src/components/form_row.tsx` file:

```
import * as React from "react";

export interface FormRowProps {
  label?: string;
}

export class FormRow extends React.Component<FormRowProps, {}> {
  render() {
    return <div className="form-group">
      <label className="col-sm-2 control-label">
        {this.props.label}
      </label>
      <div className="col-sm-10">
        {this.props.children}
      </div>
    </div>
  }
}
```

In this case, we are using the special prop `children`. Although we did not explicitly define this prop in the `FormRowProps` interface, we can use the `children` prop in any React component. It will contain any DOM elements that were passed as child elements into the current component. This will allow you to use the `FormRow` component as follows:

```
<FormRow label="Some input field">
  <input className="form-control" placeholder="Some value..."/>
</FormRow>
```

Next, we can use the `FormRow` component to build the `EventBookingForm` component. For this, create a new file, called `src/components/event_booking_form.tsx`:

```
import * as React from "react";
import {Event} from "../model/event";
import {FormRow} from "./form_row";

export interface EventBookingFormProps {
  event: Event;
  onSubmit: (seats: number) => any
}

export interface EventBookingFormState {
```

```
    seats: number;
}

export class EventBookingForm
  extends React.Component<EventBookingFormProps, EventBookingFormState> {
    constructor(p:  EventBookingFormProps) {
      super(p);

      this.state = {seats: 1};
    }
}
```

The `EventBookingForm` component has both input props and an internal state. The input properties contain the actual event, for which the booking form should be rendered, and a callback method. We will later configure the booking form to call this callback method whenever the form is submitted. The form's internal state contains a variable for the number of tickets that should be booked.

Now, add a `render()` method to the `EventBookingForm` component:

```
render() {
  return <div>
    <h2>Book tickets for {this.props.event.name}</h2>
    <form className="form-horizontal">
      <FormRow label="Event">
        <p className="form-control-static">
          {this.props.event.name}
        </p>
      </FormRow>
      <FormRow label="Number of tickets">
        <select className="form-control" value={this.state.seats}
onChange={event => this.handleNewAmount(event)}>
          <option value="1">1</option>
          <option value="2">2</option>
          <option value="3">3</option>
          <option value="4">4</option>
        </select>
      </FormRow>
      <FormRow>
        <button className="btn btn-primary"
onClick={() => this.props.onSubmit(this.state.seats)}>
          Submit order
        </button>
      </FormRow>
    </form>
  </div>
}
```

This will generate a small form in which the user will be able to review which event they are booking tickets for, select the desired amount of tickets, and then submit the order. Note how the `onSubmit` prop is called on the button's `onClick` event.

Also, note that the select field's `onChange` event calls a `this.handleNewAmount` method, which we have not defined yet. Let's do this now:

```
import * as React from "react";
import {ChangeEvent} from "react";
// ...

export class EventBookingForm extends
React.Component<EventBookingFormProps, EventBookingFormState> {
  // ...

  private handleNewAmount(event: ChangeEvent<HTMLSelectElement>) {
    const state: EventBookingFormState = {
      seats: parseInt(event.target.value)
    }

    this.setState(state);
  }
}
```

Last but not least, we can now implement the `EventBookingFormContainer` component. This component will be responsible for handling the AJAX communication to the respective backend services (since we are working with event bookings, we will also have to communicate with the booking service that we built in Chapter 4, *Asynchronous Microservice Architectures Using Message Queues*).

Let's start by defining the component's props and state. For this, create a new `src/components/event_booking_form_container.tsx` file:

```
import * as React from "react";
import {EventBookingForm} from "./event_booking_form";
import {Event} from "../model/event";
export class EventBookingFormContainerProps {
  eventID: string;
  eventServiceURL: string;
  bookingServiceURL: string;
}
export class EventBookingFormContainerState {
  state: "loading"|"ready"|"saving"|"done"|"error";
  event?: Event;
}
```

The `EventBookingFormContainer` will need to make AJAX calls to both the event service and the booking service. When a new instance of this component is created, it will be passed an event ID via its properties, and then use that ID to load the respective event's data from the event service into the component's state.

Loading the event data is something that we can do in the component's constructor function that we will define next:

```
export class EventBookingFormContainer
  extends React.Component<EventBookingFormContainerProps,
EventBookingFormContainerState> {
  constructor(p: EventBookingFormContainerProps) {
    super(p);

    this.state = {state: "loading"};

    fetch(p.eventServiceURL + "/events/" + p.eventID)
      .then<Event>(response => response.json())
      .then(event => {
        this.setState({
          state: "ready",
          event: event
        })
      });
  }
}
```

Now, we can add a `render` method to this component that presents the actual booking form as soon as the event has been loaded:

```
render() {
  if (this.state.state === "loading") {
    return <div>Loading...</div>;
  }

  if (this.state.state === "saving") {
    return <div>Saving...</div>;
  }

  if (this.state.state === "done") {
    return <div className="alert alert-success">
      Booking completed! Thank you!
    </div>
  }

  if (this.state.state === "error" || !this.state.event) {
    return <div className="alert alert-danger">
```

```
      Unknown error!
    </div>
  }

  return <EventBookingForm event={this.state.event}
onSubmit={seats => this.handleSubmit(seats)} />
  }
```

This `render()` method basically covers all possible variants of the component's state and then prints the respective status messages. When an event has successfully been loaded, the actual `EventBookingForm` is presented.

Finally, we will need to implement the `handleSubmit` method:

```
private handleSubmit(seats: number) {
   const url = this.props.bookingServiceURL + "/events/" + this.eventID +
"/bookings";
   const payload = {seats: seats};

   this.setState({
     event: this.state.event,
     state: "saving"
   });

   fetch(url, {method: "POST", body: JSON.stringify(payload)})
     .then(response => {
       this.setState({
         event: this.state.event,
         state: response.ok ? "done" : "error"
       });
     })
  }
```

This concludes our work on the booking form. Up until now, we have missed just one little thing—there is no way to access this form yet. Let's now amend this oversight.

Start by adding a new route to the index.tsx file, more precisely, in the App component's render method:

```
render() {
  const eventList = () => <EventListContainer
eventServiceURL="http://localhost:8181" />;
  const eventBooking = ({match}: any) =>
    <EventBookingFormContainer eventID={match.params.id}
      eventServiceURL="http://localhost8181"
      bookingServiceURL="http://localhost:8282" />;

  return <Router>
    <div className="container">
      <h1>My Events</h1>

      <Route exact path="/" component={eventList} />
      <Route path="/events/:id/book" component={eventBooking} />
    </div>
  </Router>
}
```

In this code example, you can see multiple things. First, we are declaring a new local component eventBooking, which basically returns an EventBookingFormContainer component with some default parameters. This component will be passed a prop object with a match attribute (the curly brackets in the parameter declaration are a so-called **destructuring assignment**). This match object contains the route parameters from the /events/:id/book route that was declared in the previous example. This allows us to include an event ID as a route parameter (so, for example, localhost:8080/#/events/58d543209cdd4128c06e59db/book).

Also, for this code to work, we are assuming that you have an instance of the booking service from Chapter 4, *Asynchronous Microservice Architectures Using Message Queues*, running and listening on localhost TCP port 8282.

Lastly, we need to add a button that allows the user to actually reach this route. For this, we will modify the EventListItem component in the src/component/event_list_item.tsx file that you have created in an earlier section of this chapter. We will use the Link component from the react-router-dom package that you have worked with before:

```
import {Link} from "react-router-dom";
// ...

export class EventListItem extends React.Component<EventListItemProps, {}>
{
```

```
render() {
  const start = new Date(this.props.event.StartDate * 1000);
  const end = new Date(this.props.event.EndDate * 1000);

  return <tr>
    <td>{this.props.event.Name}</td>
    <td>{this.props.event.Location.Name}</td>
    <td>{start.toLocaleDateString()}</td>
    <td>{end.toLocaleDateString()}</td>
    <td>
      <Link to={`/events/${this.props.event.ID}/book`}>
        Book now!
      </Link>
    </td>
  </tr>
  }
}
```

In your frontend application, you will now see an additional button labeled **Book now!**:

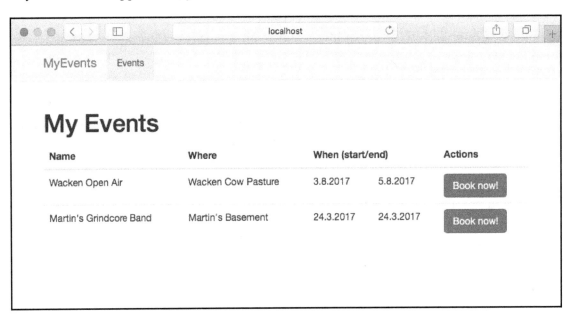

Book now! button

The `EventistItem` components in the event list now contain a link to each event's booking form. Upon clicking one of these buttons, the application will link you to the respective event's actual booking form:

The EventBookingForm in action

Note the URL containing the event ID. Since we have built `EventBookingFormContainer` to load the event data from the event service when it is constructed, we can now even use this URL and open it directly in a browser. The React router will open the booking form immediately and then load the event's data from the event service. This allows you to open subroutes in React applications directly and even share or bookmark these URLs.

Summary

In this chapter, we have given you a glimpse into frontend development with React. Of course, we have only scratched the surface of what is possible with the React framework. In an actual real-world application, we would still need to add quite a lot of features for the frontend application to be actually complete (for example, we would need to add some trivial things, such as a user sign-up and a more sophisticated checkout process).

Up until now, we have spent most of our time doing actual programming, both in the backend with Go and in the frontend with TypeScript. However, there is more to do with software development than just programming. Over the next few chapters, we will concern ourselves with the deployment of our application. This will include both the backend services (such as the Event and booking services built in previous chapters), but also persistence and messaging services (such as databases or message queues). For this, we will take a look at modern container technologies and how to deploy these to the cloud. Stay tuned.

6
Deploying Your Application in Containers

In the past few chapters, we focused on the actual development of our Go application. However, there is more to software engineering than just writing code. Usually, you will also need to concern yourself with the question of how you will deploy your application into its runtime environment. Especially in microservice architectures, where each Service may be built on a completely different technology stack, deployment can quickly become a challenge.

When you are deploying Services that use different technologies (for example, when you have Services written in Go, Node.js, and Java), you will need to provide an environment in which all these Services can actually be run. Using traditional virtual machines or bare-metal servers, this can become quite a hassle. Even though modern cloud providers make quickly spawning and disposing VMs easily, maintaining an infrastructure for all possible kinds of Services becomes an operational challenge.

This is where modern container technologies such asa60;**Docker** or **RKT** shine. Using containers, you can package an application with all its dependencies into a container image and then use that image to quickly spawn a container running your application on any server that can run these containers. The only software that needs to run on your servers themselves (be it virtualized or bare-metal) is the container runtime environment (typically, Docker or RKT).

In this chapter, we will show you how to package the MyEvents application, which we built over the last few chapters, in container images and how to deploy these images. Since we are thinking big, we will also take a look at cluster managers, such as **Kubernetes**, that allows you to deploy containers over many servers at once, allowing you to make your application deployment more resilient and scalable.

In this chapter, we will cover the following topics:

- Using Docker to build and run container images
- Setting up complex multi-container applications with Docker Compose
- Container cloud infrastructures with Kubernetes

What are containers?

Container technologies such as Docker use isolation features offered by modern operating systems, such as **namespaces** and **control groups** (**cgroups**) in Linux. Using these features allows the operating system to isolate multiple running processes from each other to a very large extent. For example, a container runtime might provide two processes with two entirely separate filmount namespaces or two separate networking stacks using network namespaces. In addition to namespaces, cgroups can be used to ensure that each process does not use more than a previously allocated amount of resources (such as CPU time, memory or I/O, and network bandwidth).

In contrast to traditional virtual machines, a container runs completely within the operating system of the host environment; there is no virtualized hardware and OS running on that. Also, in many container runtimes, you do not even have all the typical processes that you will find in a regular operating system. For example, a Docker container will typically not have an init process like regular Linux systems have; instead, the root process (PID 1) in your container will be your application (also, as the container only exists as long as its **PID 1** process exists, it will cease to exist as soon as your application exists).

 Of course, this does not apply to all container runtimes. LXC, for example, will give you a complete Linux system within your container (at least the user-space part of it), including an init process as PID 1.

Most container runtimes also come with a concept of **container images**. These contain prepackaged filesystems from which you can spawn new containers. Many container-based deployments actually use container images as deployment artifacts, in which the actual build artifact (for example, a compiled Go binary, Java application, or Node.js app) are packaged together with their runtime dependencies (which are not that many for compiled Go binaries; however, for other applications, a container image might contain a Java runtime, a Node.js installation, or anything else required for the application to work). Having a container image for your applications can also help make your application scalable and resilient since it is easy to spawn new containers from your application image.

Container runtimes such as Docker also tend to treat containers as **immutable** (meaning that containers are typically not changed in any way after having been started). When deploying your application in containers, the typical way to deploy a new version of your application would be to build a new container image (containing the updated version of your application), then create a new container from that new image and delete the container running the old version of your application.

Introduction to Docker

Currently, the de facto standard for application container runtimes is **Docker**, although there are other runtimes, for example, RKT (pronounced rocket). In this chapter, we will focus on Docker. However, many container runtimes are interoperable and built on common standards. For example, RKT containers can easily be spawned from Docker images. This means that even if you decide to deploy your application using Docker images, you are not running into a vendor lock-in.

Running simple containers

We have worked with Docker before in `Chapter 4`, *Asynchronous Microservice Architectures Using Message Queues*, to quickly set up RabbitMQ and Kafka message brokers; however, we did not go into details on how Docker actually works. We will assume that you already have a working Docker installation on your local machine. If not, take a look at the official installation instructions to learn how you can install Docker on your operating system: `https://docs.docker.com/engine/installation/`.

To test whether your Docker installation is working correctly, try the following command on the command line:

```
$ docker container run --rm hello-world
```

The preceding command uses the new Docker command structure introduced in Docker 1.13. If you are running an older version of Docker, use `docker run` instead of `docker container run`. You can test your current Docker version using the `docker version` command. Also, note that Docker changed its versioning scheme after version 1.13, so the next version after 1.13 will be 17.03.

The Docker run command follows the `docker container run [flags...] [image name] [arguments...]` pattern. In this case, `hello-world` is the name of the image to run, and the `--rm` flag indicates that the container should be removed immediately after it has finished running. When running the preceding command, you should receive an output similar to the one in the following screenshot:

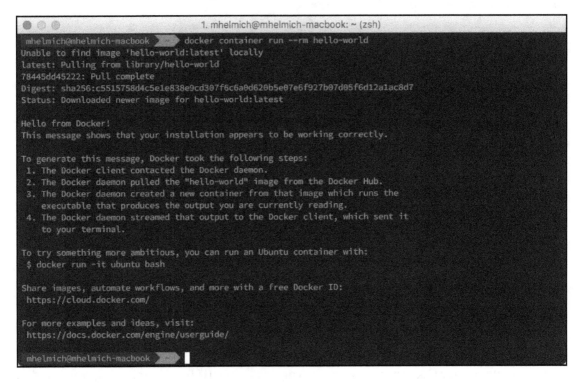

docker container run output

Actually, the `docker run` command did multiple things, here. First of all, it detected that the `hello-world` image was not present on the local machine and downloaded it from the official Docker image registry (if you run the same command again, you will note that the image will not be downloaded since it is already present on the local machine).

It then created a new container from the `hello-world` image that it just downloaded and started that container. The container image consists only of a small program that prints some text to the command line and then immediately exists.

Remember that a Docker container has no init system and typically has one process running in it. As soon as that process terminates, the container will stop running. Since we created the container with the `--rm` flag, the Docker engine will also delete the container automatically after it has stopped running.

Next, let's do something more complex. Execute the following command:

```
$ docker container run -d --name webserver -p 80:80 nginx
```

This command will download the `nginx` image and spawn a new container from it. In contrast to the `hello-world` image, this image will run a web server that runs for an indefinite time. In order to not block your shell indefinitely, the `-d` flag (short for `--detach`) is used to start the new container in the background. The `--name` flag is responsible for giving the new container an actual name (if omitted, a random name will be generated for the container).

The **NGINX** web server running within the container by default listens on TCP port 80. However, each Docker container has its own separate networking stack, so you cannot just access this port by navigating to `http://localhost`. The `-p 80:80` flag tells the Docker Engine to forward the container's TCP port 80 to localhost's port 80. To check whether the container is actually running now, run the following command:

```
$ docker container ls
```

The preceding command lists all currently running containers, the images from which they were created, and their port mappings. You should receive an output similar to the one in the following screenshot:

docker container ls output

When the container is running, you can now access the web server you just started via `http://localhost`.

Building your own images

Up until now, you have worked with publicly available, premade images from the Docker Hub, such as the `nginx` image (or the RabbitMQ and Spotify/Kafka images in Chapter 4, *Asynchronous Microservice Architectures Using Message Queues*). However, with Docker, it is also easy to build your own images. Generally, Docker images are built from a **Dockerfile**. A Dockerfile is a kind of a construction manual for new Docker images and describes how a Docker image should be built, starting from a given base image. Since it rarely makes sense to start with a completely empty filesystem (empty as *in not even a shell or standard libraries*), images are often built on distribution images that contain the user-space tools of popular Linux distributions. Popular base images include *Ubuntu, Debian,* or *CentOS.*

Let's build a short example `Dockerfile`. For demonstration purposes, we will build our own version of the `hello-world` image. For this, create a new empty directory and create a new file named `Dockerfile` with the following contents:

```
FROM debian:jessie
MAINTAINER You <you@example.com>

RUN echo 'Hello World' > /hello.txt
CMD cat /hello.txt
```

The line starting with `FROM` denotes the base image on which you are building your custom image. It always needs to be the first line of a `Dockerfile`. The `MAINTAINER` statement contains only metadata.

The `RUN` statement is executed when the container image is being built (meaning that the final container image will have a `/hello.txt` file with the contents `Hello World` in its filesystem). A `Dockerfile` may contain many such `RUN` statements.

In contrast to that, the `CMD` statement is executed when a container created from the image is being run. The command specified here will be the first and main process (PID 1) of a container created from the image.

You can build the actual Docker image using the `docker image build` command (`docker build` in versions older than 1.13), as follows:

```
$ docker image build -t test-image .
```

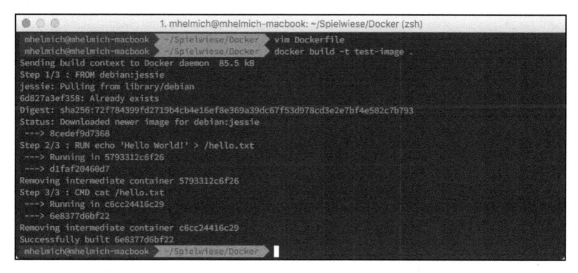

docker image build output

The `-t test-image` flag contains the name that your new image should get. After building the image, you can find it using the `docker image ls` command:

docker image ls output

The name specified with `-t` allows you to create and run a new container from the preceding image using the already known `docker container run` command:

```
$ docker container run --rm test-image
```

As before, this command will create a new container (this time, from our freshly created image), start it (actually, start the command specified by the CMD statement in the Dockerfile), and then remove the container after the command has finished (thanks to the --rm flag).

Networking containers

Often, your application consists of multiple processes that communicate with each other (starting from relatively simple cases such as an application server talking to a database up to complex microservice architectures). When using containers to manage all these processes, you will typically have one container per process. In this section, we will take a look at how you can have multiple Docker containers communicate with each other over their network interfaces.

In order to enable container-to-container communication, Docker offers a network management feature. The command line allows you to create new virtual networks and then add containers to these virtual networks. Containers within one network can communicate with each other and resolve their internal IP addresses via Docker's built-in DNS server.

Let's test this by creating a new network with Docker using the docker network create command:

```
$ docker network create test
```

After this, you will be able to see the new network then running docker network ls:

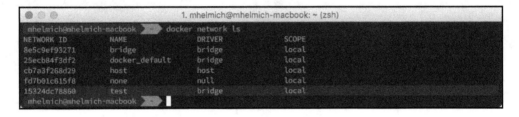

docker network ls output

After having created a new network, you can attach containers to this network. For starters, begin by creating a new container from the nginx image and attaching it to the test network using the --network flag:

```
$ docker container run -d --network=test --name=web nginx
```

Next, create a new container in the same network. Since we have already started a web server, our new container will contain an HTTP client that we will use to connect to our new web server (note that we did not bind the container's HTTP port to the localhost using the –p flag as we did before). For this, we will use the appropriate/curl image. This is an image that basically contains a containerized version of the cURL command-line utility. Since our web server container has the name web, we can now simply use that name for establishing a network connection:

```
$ docker container run --rm --network=test appropriate/curl http://web/
```

This command will simply print the web server's index page to the command line:

```
1. mhelmich@mhelmich-macbook: ~ (zsh)
mhelmich@mhelmich-macbook    docker container run --network=test appropriate/curl http://web
  % Total    % Received % Xferd  Average Speed   Time    Time     Time  Current
                                 Dload  Upload   Total   Spent    Left  Speed
100   612  100   612    0     0   160k      0 --:--:-- --:--:-- --:--:--  597k
<!DOCTYPE html>
<html>
<head>
<title>Welcome to nginx!</title>
<style>
    body {
        width: 35em;
        margin: 0 auto;
        font-family: Tahoma, Verdana, Arial, sans-serif;
    }
</style>
</head>
<body>
<h1>Welcome to nginx!</h1>
<p>If you see this page, the nginx web server is successfully installed and
working. Further configuration is required.</p>

<p>For online documentation and support please refer to
<a href="http://nginx.org/">nginx.org</a>.<br/>
Commercial support is available at
<a href="http://nginx.com/">nginx.com</a>.</p>

<p><em>Thank you for using nginx.</em></p>
</body>
</html>
mhelmich@mhelmich-macbook
```

docker container run output

This demonstrates that the cURL container created from the appropriate/curl image is able to reach the web container via HTTP. When establishing the connection, you can simply use the container's name (in this case, *web*). Docker will automatically resolve this name to the container's IP address.

Armed with the knowledge of Docker images and networking, you can now get to packaging the MyEvents application into container images and running them on Docker.

Working with volumes

An individual Docker container is often very short-lived. Deploying a new version of your application may result in a number of containers being deleted and new ones being spawned. If your application is running in a cloud environment (we will have a look at cloud-based container environments later in this chapter), your container may suffer from a node failure and will be re-scheduled on another cloud instance. This is completely tolerable for stateless applications (in our example, the event service and booking service).

However, this gets difficult for stateful containers (in our example, this would be both the message broker and database containers). After all, if you delete a MongoDB container and create a new one with a similar configuration, the actual data managed by the database will be gone. This is where **volumes** come into play.

Volumes are Docker's way to make data persist beyond the lifecycle of an individual container. They contain files and exist independently of individual containers. Each volume can be *mounted* into an arbitrary number of containers, allowing you to share files between containers.

To test this, create a new volume using the `docker volume create` command:

```
$ docker volume create test
```

This will create a new volume named *test*. You can find this volume again by using the `docker volume ls` command:

```
$ docker volume ls
```

After having created a volume, you can mount it into a container using the `-v` flag of the `docker container run` command:

```
$ docker container run --rm -v test:/my-volume debian:jessie
/bin/bash -c "echo Hello > /my-volume/test.txt"
```

This command creates a new container that has the test volume mounted into the `/my-volume` directory. The container's command will be a bash shell that creates a `test.txt` file within this directory. After this, the container will terminate and be deleted.

To ensure that the files within the volume are still there, you can now mount this volume into a second container:

```
$ docker container run —rm —v test:/my-volume debian:jessie
cat /my-volume/test.txt
```

This container will print the `test.txt` file's contents to the command line. This demonstrates that the test volume still contains all its data, even though the container that initially populated it with data has already been deleted.

Building containers

We will start with building container images for the components of the MyEvents application. As of now, our application consists of three components—two backend services (event and booking service) and the React frontend application. While the frontend application does not contain any kind of backend logic itself, we will at least need a web server to deliver this application to the user. This makes three container images in total that we need to build. Let's start with the backend components.

Building containers for the backend services

Both the event and booking service are Go applications that are compiled into single executable binaries. For this reason, it is not necessary to include any kind of source files or even the Go tool chain in the Docker image.

It is important to note at this point that you will need compiled Linux binaries of your Go applications for the next steps. When on macOS or Windows, you will need to set the GOOS environment variable when invoking `go build`:

```
$ GOOS=linux go build
```

On macOS and Linux, you can check for the correct binary type using the `file` command. For a Linux ELF binary, the `file` command should print a output similar to the following:

```
$ file eventservice
eventservice: ELF 64-bit executable, x86-64, version 1 (SYSV),
statically linked, not stripped
```

Start by compiling Linux binaries for both the event service and the booking service.

When you have compiled both services, continue by defining the Docker image build process for the event service. For this, create a new file named `Dockerfile` in the event service's root directory:

```
FROM debian:jessie

COPY eventservice /eventservice
RUN  useradd eventservice
USER eventservice

ENV LISTEN_URL=0.0.0.0:8181
EXPOSE 8181
CMD ["/eventservice"]
```

This Dockerfile contains some new statements that we did not cover before. The COPY statement copies a file from the host's local filesystem into the container image. This means that we are assuming that you have built your Go application using `go build` before starting the Docker build. The USER command causes all subsequent RUN statements and the CMD statement to run as that user (and not root). The ENV command sets an environment variable that will be available to the application. Finally, the EXPOSE statement declares that containers created from this image will need the TCP port 8181.

Continue by building the container image using the `docker image build` command:

```
$ docker image build -t myevents/eventservice .
```

Next, add a similar Docker file to the `bookingservice`:

```
FROM debian:jessie

COPY bookingservice /bookingservice
RUN  useradd bookingservice
USER bookingservice

ENV LISTEN_URL=0.0.0.0:8181
EXPOSE 8181
CMD ["/bookingservice"]
```

Again, build the image using `docker image build`:

```
$ docker image build -t myevents/bookingservice .
```

To test our new images, we can now spawn the respective containers. However, before starting the actual application containers, we will need to create a virtual network for these container and the required persistence services. Both event and booking service each require a MongoDB instance and a shared AMQP (or Kafka) message broker.

Let's start by creating the container network:

```
$ docker network create myevents
```

Next, add a RabbitMQ container to your network:

```
$ docker container run -d --name rabbitmq --network myevents
rabbitmq:3-management
```

Continue by adding two MongoDB containers:

```
$ docker container run -d --name events-db --network myevents mongo
$ docker container run -d --name bookings-db --network myevents mongo
```

Finally, you can start the actual application containers:

```
$ docker container run \
    --detach \
    --name events \
    --network myevents \
    -e AMQP_BROKER_URL=amqp://guest:guest@rabbitmq:5672/ \
    -e MONGO_URL=mongodb://events-db/events \
    -p 8181:8181 \
    myevents/eventservice

$ docker container run \
    --detach \
    --name bookings \
    --network myevents \
    -e AMQP_BROKER_URL=amqp://guest:guest@rabbitmq:5672/ \
    -e MONGO_URL=mongodb://bookings-db/bookings \
    -p 8282:8181 \
    myevents/bookingservice
```

Note the port mappings. Currently, both services have their REST API listen on TCP port 8181. As long as these two APIs run in different containers, it is completely valid. However, when mapping these ports to host ports (for example, for testing purposes), we would have a port conflict that we resolve here by mapping the booking service's port 8181 to 8282.

Also, note how the -e flags are used to pass environment variables into the running containers. For example, using the MONGO_URL environment variable, it becomes easy to connect the two application containers to different databases.

After having started all these containers, you will be able to reach the event service via http://localhost:8181 and the booking service via http://localhost:8282 from your local machine. The following docker container ls command should now show you five running containers:

docker container ls output

Using static compilation for smaller images

Currently, we are building our application images on top of the debian:jessie image. This image contains the user-space tools and libraries of a typical Debian installation and takes about 123 MB in size (you can find this out using the docker image ls command). Add another 10 MB for the compiled Go application that you are adding to that base image, each of the resulting images will be about 133 MB in size (which does not mean that our two images for the event service and booking service will together take up 266 MB of your disk space. They are both built on the same base image, and Docker is very efficient at optimizing disk space usage for container images).

However, our application does not use most of these tools and libraries, so our container images could be much smaller. By this, we can optimize the local disk space usage (although the Docker Engine is already quite efficient at this), optimize the transfer times when the image is downloaded from an image repository, and reduce the attack surface against malicious users.

Typically, compiled Go binaries have very few dependencies. You do not need any kind of runtime libraries or VMs, and all Go libraries that you use in your project are embedded directly into the resulting executable file. However, if you compile your application in Linux, the Go compiler will link the resulting binary against a few C standard libraries that are typically available on any Linux system. If you are on Linux, you can easily find out against which libraries your program was linked by invoking the `ldd` binary with one of your compiled Go binaries as argument. If your binary is linked against the C standard library, you will receive the following output:

```
$ ldd ./eventservice
    linux-vdso.so.1 (0x00007ffed09b1000)
    libpthread.so.0 => /lib/x86_64-linux-gnu/libpthread.so.0
(0x00007fd523c36000)
    libc.so.6 => /lib/x86_64-linux-gnu/libc.so.6 (0x00007fd52388b000)
    /lib64/ld-linux-x86-64.so.2 (0x0000564d70338000)
```

This means that your Go application actually needs these Linux libraries to run and that you cannot just arbitrarily delete them from your image to make it smaller.

If you cross-compiled your application on Windows or macOS using the `GOOS=linux` environment variable, you will probably not have this issue. As the compiler on those systems do not have access to the Linux standard C libraries, it will, by default, produce a statically linked binary that does not have any dependencies at all. When invoked with such a binary, `ldd` will render the following output:

```
$ ldd ./eventservice
    not a dynamic executable
```

On Linux, you can force the Go compiler to create statically linked binaries by setting the `CGO_ENABLED=0` environment variable for your Go build command:

```
$ CGO_ENABLED=0 go build
$ ldd ./eventservice
    not a dynamic executable
```

Having completely statically linked binary allows you to create a much smaller container image. Instead of building on `debian:jessie` as a base image, you can now use the *scratch* image. The `scratch` image is a special image. It is directly built into the Docker Engine, and you cannot download it from the Docker Hub. What is special about the `scratch` image is that it is completely empty, empty as in does not contain one single file—this means no standard libraries, no system utilities, and not even a shell. Although these properties typically make the scratch image cumbersome to use, it is perfectly suited for building minimal container images for statically linked applications.

Change the event service's `Dockerfile` as follows:

```
FROM scratch

COPY eventservice /eventservice

ENV LISTEN_URL=0.0.0.0:8181
EXPOSE 8181
CMD ["/eventservice"]
```

Next, change the booking service's `Dockerfile` in a similar way. Build both container images again using the `docker image build` command from the preceding code. After that, verify your image size using the `docker image ls` command:

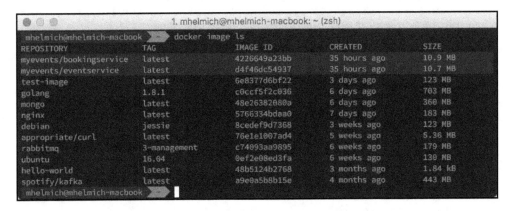

docker image ls output

Building containers for the frontend

Now that we have container images for our backend applications, we can direct our attention to the frontend application. Since this application runs in the user's browser, we do not really need a containerized runtime environment for it. What we do need though is a way to deliver the application to the user. Since the entire application consists of a bit of HTML and JavaScript files, we can build a container image that contains a simple NGINX web server that serves these files to the users.

For this, we will be building on the `nginx:1.11-alpine` image. This image contains a minimal version of the NGINX web server, built on Alpine Linux. Alpine is a Linux distribution optimized for small size. The entire `nginx:1.11-alpine` image is only 50 MB in size.

Add the following `Dockerfile` to your frontend application directory:

```
FROM nginx:1.11-alpine

COPY index.html /usr/share/nginx/html/
COPY dist /usr/share/nginx/html/dist/
COPY node_modules/bootstrap/dist/css/bootstrap.min.css
/usr/share/nginx/html/node_modules/bootstrap/dist/css/bootstrap.min.css
COPY node_modules/react/umd/react.production.min.js
/usr/share/nginx/html/node_modules/react/umd/react.production.min.js
COPY node_modules/react-dom/umd/react-dom.production.min.js
/usr/share/nginx/html/node_modules/react-dom/umd/react-
dom.production.min.js
COPY node_modules/promise-polyfill/promise.min.js
/usr/share/nginx/html/node_modules/promise-polyfill/promise.min.js
COPY node_modules/whatwg-fetch/fetch.js
/usr/share/nginx/html/node_modules/whatwg-fetch/fetch.js
```

Obviously, our web server will need to service both the index.html and the compiled Webpack bundle at dist/bundle.js to the users, so these are copied into the container image with COPY. However, from all the dependencies installed into the node_modules/ directory, our users will need only a very specific subset. For these reasons, we are copying these five files explicitly into the container image, instead of just using COPY for the entire node_modules/ directory.

Before actually building the container image, ensure that you have a recent Webpack build of your application and all dependencies installed. You can also use the -p flag to trigger Webpack to create a production build of your application that will be optimized for size:

```
$ webpack -p
$ npm install
```

After this, build your container:

```
$ docker container build -t myevents/frontend .
```

You can now start this container using the following command:

```
$ docker container run --name frontend -p 80:80 myevents/frontend
```

Note that we are not passing the --network=myevents flag in this case. This is because the frontend container does not actually need to communicate with the backend services directly. All communication is initiated from the user's browser, not from within the actual frontend container.

The `-p 80:80` flag binds the container's TCP port 80 to your local TCP port 80. This allows you to now open `http://localhost` in your browser and view the MyEvents frontend application. If you still have the backend containers from the previous sections running, the application should work out of the box.

Deploying your application with Docker Compose

Up until now, actually deploying the MyEvents application from existing container images involved a number of `docker container run` commands. Although this works reasonably well for testing, it becomes tedious once your application runs in production, especially when you want to deploy updates or scale the application.

One possible solution for this is **Docker Compose**. Compose is a tool that allows you to describe applications composed of multiple containers in a declarative way (in this case, a YAML file that describes which components have built your application).

Docker Compose is part of the regular Docker installation packages, so if you have Docker installed in your local machine, you should also have Docker Compose available. You can easily test this by invoking the following command on your command line:

```
$ docker-compose -v
```

If Compose is not available on your local machine, consult the installation manual at `https://docs.docker.com/compose/install` for a detailed description on how to set up Compose.

Every Compose project is described by a `docker-compose.yml` file. The Compose file will later contain a description of all containers, networks, and volumes that you need for your application. Compose will then try to reconcile the desired state expressed in the Compose file with the actual state of the local Docker engine (for example, by creating, deleting, starting, or stopping containers).

Create such a file at the root of your project directory with the following contents:

```
version: "3"
networks:
  myevents:
```

Note the `version: "3"` declaration in the Compose file. Compose supports multiple declaration formats, the most recent being version 3. In some documentations, examples, or open source projects, you will most likely stumble across Compose files written for older versions. Compose files that do not declare a version at all are interpreted as version 1 files.

Right now, the preceding Compose file does nothing more than declare that your application requires a virtual network named `myevents`. Nevertheless, you can use Compose to reconcile the desired state (one network named `myevents` must exist) by running the following command:

```
$ docker-compose up
```

Right now, the preceding command will print a warning message since we are declaring a container network that is not used by any container.

Containers are declared in the Compose file under the `services`. Each container has a name (used as a key in the YAML structure) and can have various properties (such as the image to be used). Let's continue by adding a new container to the Compose file:

```
version: "3"
networks:
  myevents:
services:
  rabbitmq:
    image: rabbitmq:3-management
    ports:
      - 15672:15672
    networks:
      - myevents
```

This is the RabbitMQ container that you have created manually earlier using the `docker container run -d --network myevents -p 15672:15672 rabbitmq:3-management` command.

You can now create this container by running the following command:

```
$ docker-compose up -d
```

The `-d` flag has the same effect as with the docker container run command; it will cause the container(s) to be started in the background.

As soon as the RabbitMQ container starts running, you can actually invoke `docker-compose up` as many times as you like. Since the already running RabbitMQ container matches the specification from the Compose file, Compose will not take any further action.

Let's continue by adding the two MongoDB containers to the Compose file:

```
version: "3"
networks:
  - myevents
services:
  rabbitmq: #...

  events-db:
    image: mongo
    networks:
      - myevents

  bookings-db:
    image: mongo
    networks:
      - myevents
```

Run `docker-compose up -d` another time. Compose will still not touch the RabbitMQ container, as it is still up to spec. However, it will create two new MongoDB containers.

Next, we can add the two application Services:

```
version: "3"
networks:
  - myevents

services:
  rabbitmq: #...
  events-db: #...
  bookings-db: #...
  events:
    build: path/to/eventservice
    ports:
      - "8181:8181"
    networks:
      - myevents
    environment:
      - AMQP_BROKER_URL=amqp://guest:guest@rabbitmq:15672/
      - MONGO_URL=mongodb://events-db/events
  bookings:
    build: path/to/bookingservice
    ports:
```

```
    - "8282:8181"
networks:
  - myevents
environment:
  - AMQP_BROKER_URL=amqp://guest:guest@rabbitmq:15672/
  - MONGO_URL=mongodb://bookings-db/bookings
```

Note that we are not specifying an `image` attribute for these two containers, but a `build` attribute, instead. This will cause Compose to actually build the images for these containers on-demand from the Dockerfile found in the respective directories.

> It is important to note that the Docker build does not compile your Go binaries. Instead, it will rely on them being already there. In `Chapter 9`, *Continuous Delivery*, you will learn how to use CI pipelines to automate these build steps.

You can also use the `docker-compose` command to trigger individual steps of this pipeline separately. For example, use `docker-compose pull` to download recent versions of all images used in the `Compose` file from the Docker Hub:

```
$ docker-compose pull
```

For containers that do not use a predefined image, use `docker-compose build` to rebuild all images:

```
$ docker-compose build
```

Create the new containers with another `docker-compose up -d`.

> Ensure that you have stopped any previously created containers that might be bound to the TCP ports 8181 or 8282. Use the `docker container ls` and `docker container stop` commands to locate and stop these containers.

You can also use the `docker-compose ps` command to get an overview of the currently running containers associated with the current Compose project:

docker-compose ps output

Finally, add the frontend application to the Compose file:

```
version: "3"
networks:
  - myevents
services:
  rabbitmq: #...
  events-db: #...
  bookings-db: #...
  events: #...
  bookings: #...

  frontend:
    build: path/to/frontend
    ports:
      - "80:80"
```

As you learned in this section, Docker Compose enables you to describe your application's architecture in a declarative way, allowing easy deployment and updates of your application on any server that supports a Docker instance.

Up until now, we have always worked on a single host (most probably, your local machine). This is good for development, but for a production setup, you will need to concern yourself with deploying your application to a remote server. Also, since cloud architectures are all about scale, over the next few sections, we will also take a look at how to manage containerized applications at scale.

Publishing your images

You now have the ability to build container images from your application components and to run containers from these images on your local machine. However, in a production context, the machine on which you have built a container image is rarely the machine that you will run it on. To actually be able to deploy your application to any cloud environment, you will need a way to distribute built container images to any number of hosts.

This is where container registries come into play. In fact, you have already worked with a container registry earlier in this chapter, that is, the Docker Hub. Whenever you use a Docker image that is not present on your local machine (let's say, for example, the `nginx` image), the Docker engine will pull this image from the Docker Hub onto your local machine. However, you can also use a container registry such as the Docker Hub to publish your own container images and then pull them from another instance.

At the Docker Hub (which you can access in your browser via `https://hub.docker.com`), you can register as a user and then upload your own images. For this, click on the **Create Repository** after logging in and choose a new name for your image.

To push a new image into your newly created repository, you will first need to log in with your Docker Hub account on your local machine. Use the following `docker login` command for this:

```
$ docker login
```

Now, you will be able to push images into the new repository. The image names will need to start with your Docker Hub username, followed by a slash:

```
$ docker image build -t martinhelmich/test .
$ docker image push martinhelmich/test
```

By default, images pushed to the Docker Hub will be publicly visible. The Docker Hub also offers the possibility to push private images as a paid feature. Private images can only be pulled after you have successfully authenticated using the `docker login` command.

Of course, you do not have to use the Docker Hub to distribute your own images. There are alternative providers, such as Quay (`https://quay.io`), and all major cloud providers also offer the possibility to host managed container registries for you. However, when using a registry other than the Docker Hub, some of the preceding commands will change slightly. For starters, you will have to tell the `docker login` command the registry that you will be signing in:

```
$ docker login quay.io
```

Also, container images that you want to push will not only need to start with your Docker Hub username, but with the entire registry hostname:

```
$ docker image build -t quay.io/martinhelmich/test .
$ docker image push quay.io/martinhelmich/test
```

If you do not want to entrust your container images to a third-party provider, you can also roll out your own container registry. Fittingly, there is a Docker image that you can use to quickly set up your own registry:

```
$ docker volume create registry-images
$ docker container run \
    --detach \
    -p 5000:5000 \
    -v registry-images:/var/lib/registry \
    --name registry \
    registry:2.6.1
```

This will set up a container registry that is reachable at: `http://localhost:5000`. You can treat it like any other third-party registry:

```
$ docker image build -t localhost:5000/martinhelmich/test .
$ docker image push localhost:5000/martinhelmich/test
```

Having a private container registry listening on `localhost:5000` is fine for development, but for a production setup, you will need additional configuration options. For example, you will need to configure TLS transfer encryption for your registry (by default, the Docker engine will refuse to any non-encrypted Docker registry other than localhost), and you will also need to set up authentication (unless you explicitly intend to run a publicly accessible container registry). Take a look a the registry's official deployment guide to learn how to set up encryption and authentication: `https://docs.docker.com/registry/deploying/`.

Deploying your application to the cloud

To conclude this chapter, we will have a look at how you can deploy your containerized application to a cloud environment.

Container engines, such as, Docker allow you to provision multiple Services in isolated environments, without having to provision separate virtual machines for individual Services. However, as typical for Cloud applications, our container architecture needs to be easily scalable and also resilient to failure.

This is where container orchestration system such as Kubernetes comes into play. These are systems that allow you to deploy containerized applications over entire clusters of hosts. They allow for easy scaling since you can easily add new hosts to an existing cluster (after which new container workloads may automatically be scheduled on them) and also make your system resilient; node failures can be quickly detected, which allows containers on those nodes to be started somewhere else to ensure their availability.

Introduction to Kubernetes

One of the most prominent container orchestrators is Kubernetes (which is Greek for *helmsman*). Kubernetes is an open source product originally developed by Google and now owned by the Cloud Native Computing Foundation.

The following diagram shows the basic architecture of a Kubernetes cluster:

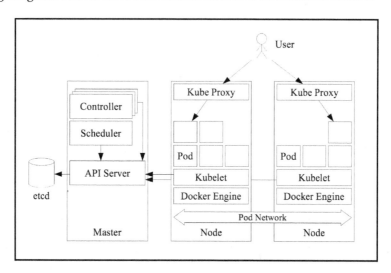

The central component of each Kubernetes cluster is the master server (which, of course, does not have to be an actual single server. In production setups, you will often have multiple master servers that are configured for high availability). The master server stores the entire cluster state in an end data store. The API Server is the component that offers a REST API that can be used by both internal components (such as the scheduler, controllers, or Kubelets) and external users (you!). The scheduler tracks available resources on the individual nodes (such as memory and CPU usage) and decides on which node in the cluster new containers should be scheduled. Controllers are components that manage high-level concepts such as replication controllers or autoscaling groups.

The Kubernetes nodes are the place where the actual application containers managed by the master server are started. Each node runs a Docker Engine and a **Kubelet**. The Kubelet is connected to the master server's REST API and is responsible for actually starting the containers that were scheduled for this node by the scheduler.

In Kubernetes, containers are organized in Pods. A Pod is Kubernetes' smallest possible scheduling unit and consists of one or more Docker containers. All containers in a Pod are guaranteed to be run on the same host. Each Pod will receive an IP address that is unique and routable within the whole cluster (meaning that Pods running on one host will be able to communicate with Pods running on other nodes via their IP addresses).

The Kube Proxy is the component that ensures that users can actually reach your applications. In Kubernetes, you can define Services that group multiple Pods. The Kube Proxy assigns a unique IP address to each Service, and forward network traffic to all Pods matched by a Service. This way, the Kube Proxy also implements a very simple but effective load balancing, when there are multiple instances of an application running in multiple Pods.

You may have noticed that Kubernetes' architecture is quite complex. Setting up a Kubernetes cluster is a challenging task, which we will not cover in detail in this book. For local development and testing, we will use the Minikube tool, which automatically creates a virtualized Kubernetes environment on your local machine. When you are running your application in a public cloud environment, you can also use tools that automatically set up a production-ready Kubernetes environment for you. Some cloud providers even provide managed Kubernetes clusters for you (for example, the **Google Container Engine** and the **Azure Container Service** are both built on Kubernetes).

Setting up a local Kubernetes with Minikube

To get started with Minikube, you will need three tools on your local machine: Minikube itself (which will handle setting up the virtual Kubernetes environment on your machine), VirtualBox (which will be used as a virtualization environment), and kubectl (which is the command-line client for working with Kubernetes). Although we are using Minikube in this example, each and every kubectl command that we are showing in the following sections will work on nearly every Kubernetes cluster, regardless of how it was set up.

Start by setting up VirtualBox. For this, download an installer from the official download page at `https://www.virtualbox.org/wiki/Downloads` and follow the installation instructions for your operating system.

Next, download a recent build of Minikube. You can find all releases
at: `https://github.com/kubernetes/minikube/releases` (at the time of writing, the most
recent release was 0.18.0). Again, follow the installation instructions for your operating
system. Alternatively, use the following command to quickly download and set up
Minikube (replace `linux` with `darwin` or `windows`, respectively):

```
$ curl -Lo minikube
https://storage.googleapis.com/minikube/releases/v0.18.0/minikube-linux-amd
64 && chmod +x minikube && sudo mv minikube /usr/local/bin/
```

Lastly, set up kubectl. You can find the installation instructions
at: `https://kubernetes.io/docs/tasks/kubectl/install`. Alternatively, use the following
command (again, replace `linux` with `darwin` or `windows` as necessary):

```
curl -LO
https://storage.googleapis.com/kubernetes-release/release/1.6.1/bin/linux/a
md64/kubectl && chmod +x kubectl && sudo mv kubectl /usr/local/bin
```

After having set up all the requirements, you can use the `minikube start` command to
start your local Kubernetes environment:

```
$ minikube start
```

This command will download an ISO image, then start a new virtual machine from this
image and install various Kubernetes components. Grab a coffee and do not be surprised if
this takes a few minutes:

minikube start output

The `minikube start` command also creates a configuration file for kubectl that enables
you to use kubectl with your minikube VM without any further configuration. You can find
this file in your home directory at `~/.kube/config`.

To test whether the entire setup works as expected, run the `kubectl get nodes` command. This command will print a list of all nodes that are part of the Kubernetes cluster. In a Minikube setup, you should see exactly one node:

```
$ kubectl get nodes
```

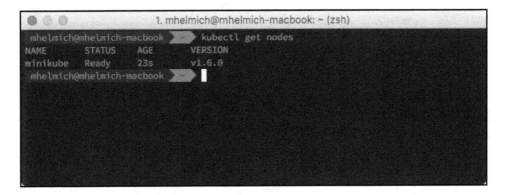

mhelmich@mhelmich-macbook >— > kubectl get nodes
NAME   STATUS   AGE   VERSION
minikube   Ready   23s   v1.6.0
mhelmich@mhelmich-macbook >— >

kubectl get nodes output

Core concepts of Kubernetes

Before diving back into MyEvents, let's take a more thorough look at some of Kubernetes' core concepts. We will start by creating a new Pod that contains a simple NGINX web server.

Kubernetes resources (such as Pods and Services) are usually defined in YAML files that declaratively describe the desired state of your cluster (similar to the Docker Compose configuration files that you have worked with before). For our new NGINX Pod, create a new file named `nginx-pod.yaml` anywhere in your local filesystem:

```yaml
apiVersion: v1
kind: Pod
metadata:
  name: nginx-test
spec:
  containers:
  - name: nginx
    image: nginx
    ports:
      - containerPort: 80
        name: http
        protocol: TCP
```

This so-called manifest file describes what your new Pod should look like. In the `metadata` section, you can set basic metadata, such as the Pod's name or any additional labels (we will need those later). The `spec` section contains the actual specification of what the Pod should look like. As you can see, the `spec.containers` section is formatted as a list; in theory, you could add additional containers here that would then run within the same Pod.

After having created this file, use the `kubectl apply` command to create the Pod:

```
$ kubectl apply -f nginx-pod.yaml
```

After this, you can use the `kubectl get pods` command to verify that your Pod has successfully been created. Note that it may take a few seconds to minutes until the Pod changes its status from `ContainerCreating` to `Running`:

```
$ kubectl get pods
```

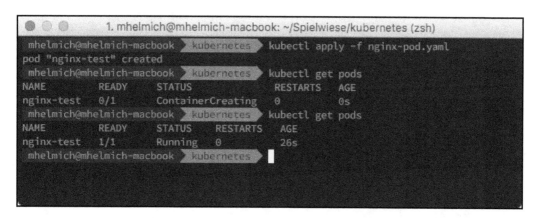

kubectl get pods output

Note that the `kubectl` command communicates directly with the Kubernetes API server (although when using Minikube, that is not a very big distinction, since all components are running on the same virtual machine anyway), not with the cluster nodes. In theory, your Kubernetes cluster could be made of many hosts, and the Kubernetes scheduler would automatically pick the best-suited host on which to run your new Pod on.

There are more things that you can configure for a single Pod. For example, you might want to restrict your application's memory or CPU usage. In this case, you could add the following settings to your newly created Pod manifest:

```
# ...
spec:
  containers:
```

```
     - name: nginx
       image: nginx
       resources:
         limits:
           memory: 128Mi
           cpu: 0.5
       ports: # ...
```

The `resources.limits` section will instruct Kubernetes to create a container with a memory limit of 128 MB and a CPU limit of one half CPU core.

The important thing to note about Kubernetes Pods is that they are not meant to be persistent. Pods may be terminated at a moment's notice and may get lost whenever a node fails. For this reason, it is recommended to use a Kubernetes controller (such as the Deployment controller) to create Pods for you.

Before continuing, delete your Pod using the `kubectl delete` command:

$ kubectl delete pod nginx-test

Next, create a new `nginx-deployment.yaml` file:

```
apiVersion: apps/v1beta1
kind: Deployment
metadata:
  name: nginx-deployment
spec:
  replicas: 2
  template:
    metadata:
      labels:
        app: nginx
    spec:
      containers:
      - name: nginx
        image: nginx
        ports:
        - containerPort: 80
          name: http
          protocol: TCP
```

This manifest will create a so-called Deployment controller for you. A Deployment controller will make sure that a given number of Pods of a given configuration is running at any time—in this case, two Pods (specified in the `spec.replicas` field) that are described by the `spec.template` field (note that the `spec.template` fields matches the Pod definition that we have already written before, minus the name).

As before, create the Deployment using the `kubectl apply` command:

```
$ kubectl apply -f nginx-deployment.yaml
```

Verify the success of your actions using the `kubectl get pods` command. You should note that two Pods will be scheduled (having names like `nginx-deployment-1397492275-qz8k5`):

kubectl get pods output

There's more that you can do with Deployments. For starters, try deleting one of the automatically generated Pods using the `kubectl delete` command (keep in mind that on your machine, you will have a different Pod name):

```
$ kubectl delete pod nginx-deployment-1397492275-qz8k5
```

After deleting the Pod, call `kubectl get pods` again. You will note that the Deployment controller almost immediately created a new Pod.

Also, you might decide that two instances of your application is not sufficient and that you want to scale your application further. For this, you can simply increase the Deployment controller's `spec.scale` property. To increase (or decrease) the scale, you can either edit your existing YAML file and then call `kubectl apply` again. Alternatively, you can directly edit the resource using the `kubectl edit` command:

```
$ kubectl edit deployment nginx-deployment
```

Especially for the `spec.scale` property, there is also a special `kubectl scale` command that you can use:

```
$ kubectl scale --replicas=4 deployment/nginx-deployment
```

kubectl get pods output

Services

Currently, we have four NGINX containers running, but no way to actually access them. This is where Services come into play. Create a new YAML file named `nginx-service.yaml`:

```
apiVersion: v1
kind: Service
metadata:
  name: nginx
spec:
  type: NodePort
  selector:
    app: nginx
  ports:
  - name: http
    port: 80
```

Note that the `spec.selector` property matches the `metadata.labels` property that you have specified in the Deployment manifest. All Pods created by a Deployment controller will have a given set of labels (which are really just arbitrary key/value mappings). The `spec.selector` property of a Service now specifies which labels a Pod should have to be recognized by this Service. Also, note the `type: NodePort` property, which is going to be important later.

After creating the file, use `kubectl apply` as usual to create the service definition:

```
● ◐ ◌                1. mhelmich@mhelmich-macbook: ~/Spielwiese/kubernetes (zsh)
mhelmich@mhelmich-macbook ▶ kubernetes ▶ kubectl apply -f nginx-service.yaml
service "nginx" created
mhelmich@mhelmich-macbook ▶ kubernetes ▶ kubectl get services
NAME          CLUSTER-IP    EXTERNAL-IP   PORT(S)       AGE
kubernetes    10.0.0.1      <none>        443/TCP       2h
nginx         10.0.0.223    <nodes>       80:31455/TCP  2s
mhelmich@mhelmich-macbook ▶ kubernetes ▶ ▊
```

kubectl apply output

<pre>$ kubectl apply -f nginx-service.yaml

Next, call `kubectl get services` to inspect the newly created Service definition.

In the `kubectl get services` output, you will find your newly created `nginx` Service (along with the Kubernetes Service, which is always there).

Remember the `type: NodePort` property that you specified when creating the Service? The effect of this property is that the Kube proxy on each node now opened up a TCP port. The port number of this port is chosen randomly. In the preceding example, this is the TCP port 31455. You can use this Port to connect to your Service from outside the Kubernetes cluster (for example, from your local machine). Any and all traffic received on this port is forwarded to one of the Pods matched by the `selector` specified in the Service's specification.

The special thing about services is that typically they will have a (much) longer lifespan than your average Pod. When new Pods are added (maybe because you have increased the replica count of the Deployment controller), these will automatically be added. Also, when Pods are removed (again, maybe because of a changed replica count, but also because of a node failure or just because a Pod was manually deleted), they will stop receiving traffic.

If you are using Minikube, you can now use the `minikube service` command to quickly find a node's public IP address to open this service in your browser:

```
$ minikube service nginx
```

In addition to the node port, also note the cluster IP property in the preceding output; this is an IP address that you can use within the cluster to reach any Pod matched by this Service. So, in this example, you could start a new Pod running your own application, and use the IP address `10.0.0.223` to access the `nginx` Service within this application. Also, since IP addresses are cumbersome to work with, you will also be able to use the Service name (`nginx`, in this case) as a DNS name.

Persistent volumes

Often, you will need a place to store files and data in a persistent way. Since individual Pods are fairly short-lived in a Kubernetes environment, it is usually not a good solution to store files directly in a container's filesystem. In Kubernetes, this issue is solved using persistent volumes, which are basically a more flexible abstraction of the Docker volumes that you have already worked with before.

To create a new persistent volume, create a new `example-volume.yaml` file with the following contents:

```
apiVersion: v1
kind: PersistentVolume
metadata:
  name: volume01
spec:
  capacity:
    storage: 1Gi
  accessModes:
  - ReadWriteOnce
  - ReadWriteMany
  hostPath:
    path: /data/volume01
```

Create the volume using `kubectl apply -f example-volume.yaml`. After this, you can find it again by running `kubectl get pv`.

The preceding manifest file creates a new volume that stores its files in the `/data/volume01` directory on the host that the volume is used on.

Other than in a local development environment, using a hostPath volume for persistent data is a terrible idea. If a Pod using this Persistent Volume is rescheduled on another node, it does not have access to the same data that it had before. Kubernetes support a large variety of volume types that you can use to make volumes accessible across multiple hosts.

For example, in AWS, you could use the following volume definition:

```
apiVersion: v1
kind: PersistentVolume
metadata:
  name: volume01
spec:
  capacity:
    storage: 1Gi
  accessModes:
  - ReadWriteOnce
  awsElasticBlockStore:
    volumeID: <volume-id>
    fsType: ext4
```

Before using a persistent volume in a Pod, you will need to claim it. Kubernetes makes an important distinction between creating persistent volumes and using them in containers. This is because the person creating a persistent volume and the one using (claiming) it are often different. Also, by decoupling the creation of volumes and their usage, Kubernetes also decouples the usage of volumes in Pods from the actual underlying storage technology.

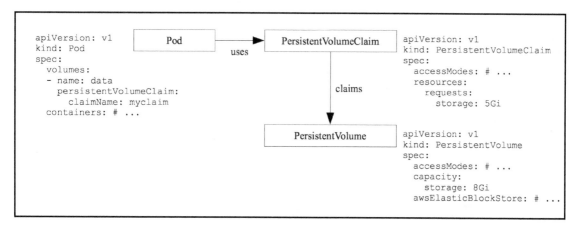

Next, create a `PersistentVolumeClaim` by creating a `example-volume-claim.yaml` file and then calling `kubectl apply -f example-volume-claim.yaml`:

```
apiVersion: v1
kind: PersistentVolumeClaim
metadata:
  name: my-data
spec:
  accessModes:
    - ReadWriteOnce
```

```
resources:
  requests:
    storage: 1Gi
```

When calling `kubectl get pv` again, you will find that the status field of the `volume01` volume has changed to `Bound`. You can now use the newly created persistent volume claim when creating a Pod or Deployment:

```
apiVersion: v1
kind: Pod
spec:
  volumes:
  - name: data
    persistentVolumeClaim:
      claimName: my-data
  containers:
  - name: nginx
    image: nginx
    volumeMounts:
    - mountPath: "/usr/share/nginx/html"
      name: data
```

When you operate your Kubernetes cluster in a cloud environment, Kubernetes is also able to create new persistent volumes automatically by talking to the cloud provider's API, for example, to create new EBS devices.

Deploying MyEvents to Kubernetes

Now that you took your first steps with Kubernetes, we can work on deploying the MyEvents application into a Kubernetes cluster.

Creating the RabbitMQ broker

Let's start by creating the RabbitMQ broker. Since RabbitMQ is not a stateless component, we will use a special controller offered by Kubernetes—the `StatefulSet` Controller. This works similar to a Deployment controller, but will create Pods with a persistent identity.

To create a new `StatefulSet`, create a new file named `rabbitmq-statefulset.yaml`:

```
apiVersion: apps/v1beta1
kind: StatefulSet
metadata:
  name: rmq
spec:
  serviceName: amqp-broker
  replicas: 1
  template:
    metadata:
      labels:
        myevents/app: amqp-broker
    spec:
      containers:
      - name: rmq
        image: rabbitmq:3-management
        ports:
        - containerPort: 5672
          name: amqp
        - containerPort: 15672
          name: http
```

This definition is missing one important thing, though, that is, persistence. Currently, if the RabbitMQ Pod should fail for any reason, a new one will be scheduled without any of the state (in this case, exchanges, queues, and not-yet-dispatched messages) that the broker previously had. For this reason, we should also declare a persistent volume that can be used by this `StatefulSet`. Instead of manually creating a new `PersistentVolume` and a new `PersistentVolumeClaim`, we can simply declare a `volumeClaimTemplate` for the `StatefulSet` and let Kubernetes provision the new volume automatically. In a Minikube environment this is possible, because Minikube ships with an automatic provisioner for such volumes. In cloud environments, you will find similar volume provisioners.

Add the following section to the `StatefulSet`:

```
apiVersion: apps/v1beta1
kind: StatefulSet
metadata:
  name: rmq
spec:
  serviceName: amqp-broker
  replicas: 1
  template: # ...
  volumeClaimTemplates:
  - metadata:
      name: data
```

```
      annotations:
        volume.alpha.kubernetes.io/storage-class: standard
    spec:
      accessModes: ["ReadWriteOnce"]
      resources:
        requests:
          storage: 1Gi
```

The `volumeClaimTemplate` will instruct the `StatefulSet` controller to automatically provision a new `PersistentVolume` and a new `PersistentVolumeClaim` for each instance of the `StatefulSet`. If you increase the replica count, the controller will automatically create more volumes.

The last thing left to do is actually use the volume claim within the `rabbitmq` container. For this, modify the container spec as follows:

```
    containers:
    - name: rmq
      image: rabbitmq:3-management
      ports: # ...
      volumeMounts:
      - name: data
        mountPath: /var/lib/rabbitmq
```

Create the `StatefulSet` using `kubectl apply -f rabbitmq-statefulset.yaml`. After this, you should see a new Pod named `rmq-0` starting up when you run `kubectl get pods`. You should also see the automatically generated persistent volumes and the respective claims when running `kubectl get pv` and `kubectl get pvc`, respectively.

Next, create a `Service` to allow other Pods to access your RabbitMQ broker:

```
    apiVersion: v1
    kind: Service
    metadata:
      name: amqp-broker
    spec:
      selector:
        myevents/app: amqp-broker
      ports:
      - port: 5672
        name: amqp
```

As usual, create the Service using `kubectl apply -f rabbitmq-service.yaml`. After creating the Service, you will be able to resolve it via DNS using the hostname `amqp-broker` (or in its long form, `amqp-broker.default.svc.cluster.local`).

Creating the MongoDB containers

Next, let's create the MongoDB containers. Conceptually, they are not much different than the RabbitMQ container that you created in the preceding section. Just as before, we will use a `StatefulSet` with automatically provisioned volumes. Place the following contents in a new file called `events-db-statefulset.yaml` and then call `kubectl apply` on this file:

```yaml
apiVersion: apps/v1beta1
kind: StatefulSet
metadata:
  name: events-db
spec:
  serviceName: events-db
  replicas: 1
  template:
    metadata:
      labels:
        myevents/app: events
        myevents/tier: database
    spec:
      containers:
      - name: mongo
        image: mongo:3.4.3
        ports:
        - containerPort: 27017
          name: mongo
        volumeMounts:
        - name: database
          mountPath: /data/db
  volumeClaimTemplates:
  - metadata:
      name: data
      annotations:
        volume.alpha.kubernetes.io/storage-class: standard
    spec:
      accessModes: ["ReadWriteOnce"]
      resources:
        requests:
          storage: 1Gi
```

Next, define a Service that matches this `StatefulSet` by creating a new file, `events-db-service.yaml`, and calling `kubectl apply`:

```
apiVersion: v1
kind: Service
metadata:
  name: events-db
spec:
  clusterIP: None
  selector:
    myevents/app: events
    myevents/tier: database
  ports:
  - port: 27017
    name: mongo
```

Now, we need to repeat this for the booking service's MongoDB containers. You can reuse almost the same definitions from above; simply replace `events` with `bookings` and create the `StatefulSet` and Service `bookings-db`.

Making images available to Kubernetes

Before you can now deploy your actual microservices, you need to make sure that the Kubernetes cluster has access to your images. Typically, you will need to have your self-built images available in a container registry for this. If you are using Minikube and want to save yourself the hassle of setting up your own image registry, you can do the following instead:

```
$ eval $(minikube docker-env)
$ docker image build -t myevents/eventservice .
```

The first command will instruct your local shell to connect not to your local Docker Engine, but the Docker Engine within the Minikube VM, instead. Then, using a regular `docker container build` command, you can build the container image you are going to use directly on the Minikube VM.

If your images are available in a private registry (like, for example, the Docker Hub, Quay.io or a self-hosted registry), you will need to configure your Kubernetes cluster so that it is authorized to actually access these images. For this, you will add your registry credentials as a `Secret` object. For this, use the `kubectl create secret` command:

```
$ kubectl create secret docker-registry my-private-registry \
    --docker-server https://index.docker.io/v1/ \
    --docker-username <your-username> \
    --docker-password <your-password> \
    --docker-email <your-email>
```

In the code example above, `my-private-registry` is an arbitrarily chosen name for your set of Docker credentials. The `--docker-server` flag `https://index.docker.io/v1/` specifies the URL of the official Docker Hub. If you are using a third-party registry, remember to change this value accordingly.

You can now use this newly created `Secret` object when creating a new Pod, by adding an `imagePullSecrets` attribute to the Pod specification:

```
apiVersion: v1
kind: Pod
metadata:
  name: example-from-private-registry
spec:
  containers:
  - name: secret
    image: quay.io/martins-private-registry/secret-application:v1.2.3
  imagePullSecrets:
  - name: my-private-registry
```

Using the `imagePullSecrets` attribute also works when you are creating Pods using a `StatefulSet` or a Deploymet controller.

Deploying the MyEvents components

Now that you have your container images available on your Kubernetes cluster (either by building them locally on your Minikube VM or by pushing them to a registry and authorizing your cluster to access that registry), we can begin deploying the actual event service. Since the event service itself is stateless, we will deploy it using a regular Deployment object, not as `StatefulSet`.

Continue by creating a new file—events-deployment.yaml—with the following contents:

```
apiVersion: apps/v1beta1
kind: Deployment
metadata:
  name: eventservice
spec:
  replicas: 2
  template:
    metadata:
      labels:
        myevents/app: events
        myevents/tier: api
    spec:
      containers:
      - name: api
        image: myevents/eventservice
        imagePullPolicy: Never
        ports:
        - containerPort: 8181
          name: http
        environment:
        - name: MONGO_URL
          value: mongodb://events-db/events
        - name: AMQP_BROKER_URL
          value: amqp://guest:guest@amqp-broker:5672/
```

Note the imagePullPolicy: Never property. This is necessary if you have built the myevents/eventservice image directly on the Minikube VM. If you have an actual container registry available to which you can push your image, you should omit this property (and add a imagePullSecrets attribute, instead).

Next, create the respective Service by creating a new file, events-service.yaml:

```
apiVersion: v1
kind: Service
metadata:
  name: events
spec:
  selector:
    myevents/app: events
    myevents/tier: api
  ports:
  - port: 80
    targetPort: 8181
    name: http
```

Create both Deployment and Service with the respective `kubectl apply` calls. Shortly thereafter, you should see the respective containers showing up in the `kubectl get pods` output.

Proceed similarly for the booking service. You can find the full manifest files for the booking service in the code examples of this book.

Finally, let's deploy the frontend application. Create another Deployment with the following manifest:

```
apiVersion: apps/v1beta1
kind: Deployment
metadata:
  name: frontend
spec:
  replicas: 2
  template:
    metadata:
      labels:
        myevents/app: frontend
    spec:
      containers:
      - name: frontend
        image: myevents/frontend
        imagePullPolicy: Never
        ports:
        - containerPort: 80
          name: http
```

Create the corresponding `Service` with the following manifest:

```
apiVersion: v1
kind: Service
metadata:
  name: frontend
spec:
  selector:
    myevents/app: frontend
  ports:
  - port: 80
    targetPort: 80
    name: http
```

Configuring HTTP Ingress

At this point, you have all required services for the MyEvents application running in your Kubernetes cluster. However, there is no convenient way (yet) to access these services from outside the cluster. One possible solution to make them accessible would be to use **NodePort** services (which we have done before in one of the previous sections). However, this would result in your services being exposed at some randomly chosen high TCP ports, which is not desirable for a production setup (HTTP(S) services should be available at TCP ports 80 and 443).

If your Kubernetes cluster is running in a public cloud environment (more precisely, AWS, GCE, or Azure), you can create a `LoadBalancer Service` as follows:

```yaml
apiVersion: v1
kind: Service
metadata:
  name: frontend
spec:
  type: LoadBalancer
  selector:
    myevents/app: frontend
  # ...
```

This will provision the appropriate cloud provider resources (for example, an **Elastic Load Balancer** in AWS) to make your service publicly accessible at a standard port.

However, Kubernetes also offers another feature that allows you to handle incoming HTTP traffic called **Ingress**. Ingress resources offer you a more fine-grained control of how your HTTP services should be accessible from the outside world. For example, our application consists of two backend services and one frontend application, all three of which need to be publicly accessible via HTTP. While it is possible to create separate `LoadBalancer` services for each of these components, this would result in each of these three services receiving its own IP address and requiring its own hostname (for example, serving the frontend app on `https://myevents.example`, and the two backend services on `https://events.myevents.example` and `https://bookings.myevents.example`). This may get cumbersome to use, and in many microservice architecture, there is often a requirement to present a single entry point for external API access. Using Ingress, we can declare a path-to-service mapping that, for example, makes all backend services accessible at `https://api.myevents.example`.

`https://github.com/kubernetes/ingress/blob/master/controllers/`
`nginx/README.md.`

Before using Ingress resources, you will need to enable an Ingress controller for your Kubernetes clusters. This is highly specific to your individual environment; some cloud-providers offer special solutions for handling Kubernetes Ingress traffic, while in other environments, you will need to run your own. Using Minikube, however, enabling Ingress is a simple command:

```
$ minikube addons enable ingress
```

If instead, you intend to run your own Ingress controller on Kubernetes, take a look at the official documentation of the NGINX Ingress controller. It may seem complicated at first, but just as many internal Kubernetes services, an Ingress controller also just consists of Deployment and Service recources.

After enabling the Ingress controller in Minikube, your Minikube VM will start responding to HTTP requests on ports 80 and 443. To determine which IP address you need to connect to, run the minikube ip command.

To make our services accessible to the open world, create a new Kubernetes resource in a new file—ingress.yaml—with the following contents:

```
apiVersions: extensions/v1beta1
kind: Ingress
metadata:
  name: myevents
spec:
  rules:
  - host: api.myevents.example
    http:
      paths:
      - path: /events
        backend:
          serviceName: events
          servicePort: 80
      - path: /bookings
        backend:
          serviceName: bookings
          servicePort: 80
  - host: www.myevents.example
    http:
      paths:
```

```
        - backend:
            serviceName: frontend
            servicePort: 80
```

Create the Ingress resource using `kubectl apply -f ingress.yaml`. Of course, the `myevents.example` domain will not be publicly accessible (that's the entire point of the `.example` top-level domain); so, to actually test this setup, you can add a few entries to your host file (`/etc/hosts` on macOS and Linux; `C:\Windows\System32\drivers\etc\hosts` on Windows):

```
192.168.99.100 api.myevents.example
192.168.99.100 www.myevents.example
```

Typically, `192.168.99.100` should be the (only locally routable) IP address of the Minikube VM. Cross-check with the output of the `minikube ip` command to be sure.

Summary

In this chapter, you learned how to use container technologies such as Docker to package your application, including all its dependencies into container images. You learned how to build container images from your application and deploy them in a production container environment built on Kubernetes.

We will get back to building container images in Chapter 9, where you will learn how to further automate your container build tool chain, allowing you to completely automate your application deployment, starting with a git push command and ending with an updated container image running in your Kubernetes cloud.

Up until now, we have been fairly cloud-agnostic. Each and every example that we have looked at so far will work in any major public or private cloud, be it AWS, Azure, GCE, or OpenStack. If fact, container technologies are often considered an excellent way to abstract from the individual quirks of the cloud providers and avoid a (potentially costly) vendor lock-in.

All this will change in the next two chapters, where we will take a look at one of the major cloud providers—**Amazon Web Services** (**AWS**). You will learn about the intricacies of each of these providers, how to deploy the MyEvents application onto these platforms, and how to use the unique features offered by them.

7
AWS I – Fundamentals, AWS SDK for Go, and EC2

Welcome to a new step in our journey to learn cloud programming in the Go language. In this chapter, we'll start discussing cloud technologies by covering the popular **Amazon Web Services** (**AWS**) platform. AWS was among the first cloud platforms to be offered for customers to use in their start-ups, their enterprises, and even for their personal side projects. AWS was launched by Amazon in 2006 and has been growing continuously ever since. Due to the large size of the topic, we will divide the material into two chapters.

In this chapter, we will cover the following topics:

- The fundamentals of AWS
- The AWS SDK for Go
- How to set up and secure EC2 instances

AWS fundamentals

The simplest definition of AWS is that it's a service provided by Amazon, where you can buy virtual machines, databases, message queues, RESTful API endpoints, and all kinds of software products hosted on their cloud platform. To fully appreciate AWS, we will need to cover some of the major services that are offered on the platform. We will then dig deeper to learn how to reap the power of Go to build applications capable of utilizing the services AWS provides via its cloud APIs.

- **Elastic Compute Cloud (EC2)**: The **Elastic Compute Cloud (EC2)** is one of the most popular services provided by AWS. It can simply be described as a service to be used when needing to spin new server instances on AWS. EC2 is special in that it makes the process of starting servers and allocating resources practically easy for users and developers. EC2 allows auto-scaling, which means that applications can automatically scale up and down based on the user's needs. The service supports multiple setups and operating systems.
- **Simple Storage Service (S3)**: S3 allows developers to store different types of data for later retrieval and data analysis. S3 is another popular AWS service that is used by numerous developers all over the world. Typically, developers store images, photos, videos, and similar types of data on S3. The service is reliable, scales well, and easy to use. The use cases for S3 are plentiful; it can be used for web sites, mobile applications, IOT sensors, and more.
- **Simple Queue Service (SQS)**: SQS is a hosted message queue service provided by AWS. In a nutshell, we can describe a message queue as a piece of software that can reliably receive messages, queue them, and deliver them between other applications. SQS is a scalable, reliable, and distributed hosted message queue.
- **Amazon API Gateway**: Amazon API gateway is a hosted service that enables developers to create secure web APIs at scale. It not only allows you to create and publish APIs, but also exposes sophisticated features such as access control, authorization, API versioning, and status monitoring.

- **DynamoDB**: DynamoDB is a NoSQL database that is hosted in AWS and provided as a service. The database is flexible, reliable, and scalable with a latency of only few milliseconds. NoSQL is a term used to describe databases that are nonrelational and enjoy high performance. A nonrelational database is a type of database that doesn't use tables with relations to store data. DynamoDB makes use of two data models: a document store and a key-value store. A document store database stores data in a collection of document files, whereas a key-value store puts data in simple key value pairs. In the next chapter, you will learn how to build Go applications in AWS that are capable of utilizing the power of DynamoDB.
- **AWS SDK for Go**: The AWS SDK for Go is a collection of Go libraries that empower developers to write applications that can interact with the AWS ecosystem. Those libraries are the tools we'll utilize to make use of the different AWS services that we have mentioned so far, such as EC2, S3, DynamoDB, and SQS.

Throughout this chapter and the next one, we will be covering those technologies in deeper detail. Every single topic we will discuss in this chapter is massive and can be covered in entire books. So, instead of covering every single aspect of each AWS service, we will provide practical insights into each service and how to utilize them as a whole to build powerful production grade applications. Before diving deep into each AWS service, let's cover some general concepts in the AWS world.

The AWS console

The AWS console is the web portal that provides us access to the multitude of services and features that AWS offers. To access the portal, you first need to navigate to `aws.amazon.com`, and then choose the **Sign In to the Console** option, as follows:

Once you sign in to the console, you will be greeted with a web page that showcases the services provided by AWS:

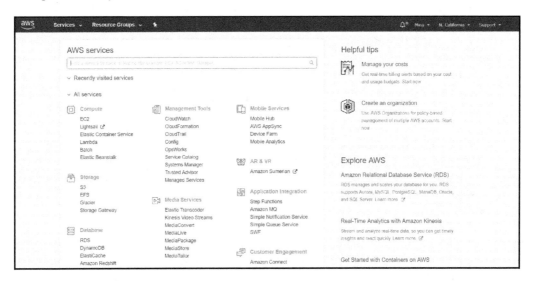

AWS command-line interface (CLI)

AWS CLI is an open source tool that provides commands to interact with AWS services. AWS CLI is cross-platform; it can run on Linux, macOS, and Windows. In this chapter, we will use the tool for certain tasks, such as copying files from an `S3` folder to an EC2 instance. AWS CLI can perform tasks that are similar to those performed by the AWS console; this includes configuration, deployment, and monitoring of AWS services. The tool can be found at `https://aws.amazon.com/cli/`.

AWS regions and zones

AWS services are hosted on multiple geographical locations around the world. In the world of AWS, locations consist of regions and availability zones. Each region is an independent geographical location. Each region contains multiple isolated internal locations known as availability zones. Some services — such as Amazon EC2, for example—give you full power as to which regions to use for your service deployment. You can also replicate resources across regions. You can find a list of available AWS regions at `http://docs.aws.amazon.com/AWSEC2/latest/UserGuide/using-regions-availability-zones.html#concepts-available-regions`.

For complex application deployments in AWS, developers typically deploy their microservices into multiple regions. This ensures that the application will enjoy high availability, even if any Amazon data center in a certain region suffers from a failure.

AWS tags

AWS tags is another important concept in the AWS universe. It allows you to categorize your different AWS resources properly. This is very useful, especially when you use numerous AWS services for different things. For example, you can set one or more tags to identify the S3 storage bucket that you use for your mobile application. The same tags can then be used to identify the EC2 instance you use for that mobile application backend. A tag is a key value pair; the value is optional.

A good resource for better understanding AWS tags can be found at: `https://aws.amazon.com/answers/account-management/aws-tagging-strategies/`.

AWS Elastic Beanstalk

Before we start to practically dive into AWS services, it is important to mention a useful service in the AWS ecosystem called *Elastic Beanstalk*. The purpose of this service is to provide an easy-to-use configuration wizard via the AWS console, which allows you to quickly deploy and scale your applications on AWS.

This service is useful in multiple scenarios, and we encourage the reader to explore it after reading this chapter and the next chapter of the book. However, we will not be focusing on Elastic Beanstalk in this book. That is because the purpose of this book when it comes to AWS is to provide you a practical foundational knowledge on the inner workings of the main AWS services. This knowledge will make it easy for you to not only deploy and run applications on AWS, but also to have a good grasp of how things work, and make tweaks when necessary. The foundational knowledge is also what you would need to then move your skills to the next level beyond this book.

Covering AWS Beanstalk without diving into the key AWS services that make AWS a great choice for developers will not be enough for you to obtain enough knowledge to be effective in the long run. However, if you take a look at AWS Beanstalk after going through this chapter and the next chapter of the book, you will be able to understand what happens behind the scenes.

The service can be found at `https://aws.amazon.com/elasticbeanstalk/`.

AWS services

Now, it's time to learn how to utilize the power of Go to interact with AWS and build cloud native applications. In this section, we'll start a practical dive into some AWS services needed to build modern production grade cloud applications.

AWS SDK for Go

As mentioned earlier, the AWS SDK for Go is a collection of libraries that enables Go to expose the power of AWS. In order to utilize the SDK, there are some key concepts we need to cover first.

The first step we will need to do is to install the AWS SDK for Go; this is done by running the following command:

```
go get -u github.com/aws/aws-sdk-go/...
```

Like any other Go package, this command will deploy the AWS SDK libraries to our development machine.

Configuring the AWS region

The second step is to specify the AWS region; this helps identify where to send the SDK requests when making calls. There is no default region for the SDK, which is why we must specify one. There are two ways to do that:

- Assigning the region value to an environmental variable called `AWS_REGION`. An example of a region value is `us-west-2` or `us-east-2`.
- Specifying it in the code—more to that later.

Configuring AWS SDK authentication

The third step is to achieve proper AWS authentication; this step is more involved, but very important to ensure the security of our code that is interacting with different AWS services. To do this, we will need to provide security credentials to our applications in order to make secure calls to AWS.

There are two main ways to generate the credentials you need to make your code works when talking to AWS via the SDK:

- Creating a user, which is simply an identity that represents a person or a service. You can assign individual permissions to users directly or assemble multiple users into a group that allow users to share permissions. The AWS SDK for Go requires users to be secured using AWS access keys to authenticate requests you send to AWS. An AWS access key is composed of two pieces: an access key ID and a secret access key. This is what we use when running applications from our local servers.
- The next way is to create a role. A role is very similar to a user in that it's an identity with specific permissions assigned to it. However, a role is not meant to be assigned to people; it instead is assigned to whoever needs it based on specific conditions. For example, a role can be attached to an EC2 instance, which would allow applications running on this EC2 instance to make secure calls to AWS without specifying a distinct user. This is the recommended approach when running applications on EC2 instances, where the applications are expected to make AWS API calls.

Creating IAM Users

If you are running your application from your own local machine, the recommended way to create access keys is to create a user that has specific permissions to access the AWS services that you would like your code to utilize. This is done by creating a user in the **AWS identity and access management (IAM)**.

To create a user in IAM, we will first need to log in to the AWS main web console, then click on **IAM**, which should be under the **Security, Identity & Compliance** category:

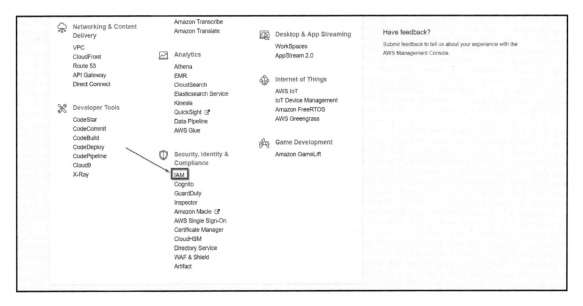

Next, we will need to click on the **User** option on the right-hand side, then click on **Add user** to create a new IAM user:

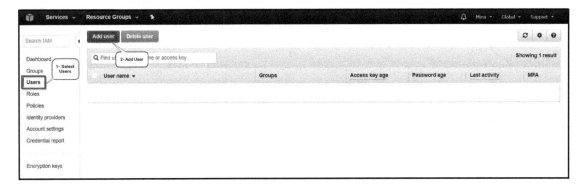

From there, you will be treated with a user creation wizard to help you create a user and generate access keys. In the first step of this wizard, you will get to choose a username and select the AWS access type for the user. The AWS access type consists of two main types: programmatic access or AWS management console access. Obviously, to create users capable of being used by the AWS SDK, we will need to select programmatic access, as follows:

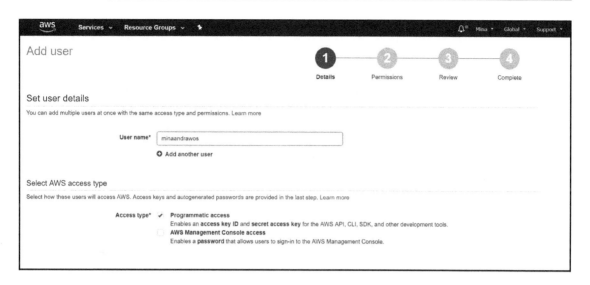

The next step will involve attaching permissions to the user being created. There are three approaches for assigning permissions to users. However, before we discuss the three approaches, we will need first to understand the concept of policies. A policy is simply a flexible approach to define permissions. For example, a new policy can be created to define a read-only access to a specific S3 folder. Any user or group who then get this policy attached to them will only be permitted a read-only access to this specific S3 folder. AWS provides a number of precreated policies that we can use in our configuration. For example, there is a policy called **AmazonS3FullAccess**, which allows full access to S3 to its holders. Now, let's return to the three approaches for assigning permissions to users:

- **Adding the user to a group**: A group is an entity that can have its own policies. Multiple users can be added to one or more groups. You can think of a group simply as a folder of users. Users under a specific group will enjoy access to all permissions allowed by the policies of the said group. The configuration wizard in this step will allow you to create a new group and assign policies to it, if need be. This is typically the recommended way to assign permissions to users.

- **Copying permissions from existing users**: This allows the new user to enjoy all groups and policies already configured for a different user. This is good to use, for example, to add a user to a new team.

- **Attaching existing policies directly**: This allows assigning policies directly to the new users without going through groups or copying from other users. The disadvantage of this approach is that if each user get assigned individual policies without the sense of order provided by groups, it becomes tedious to manage the users as they grow in numbers.

The following is a screenshot of the three options being presented:

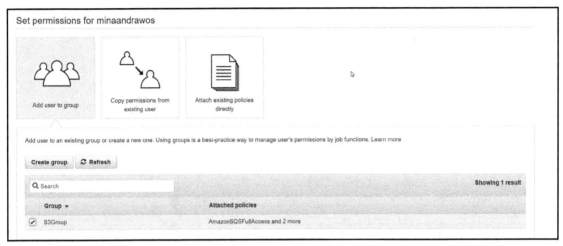

Once this setting of permissions is done, we get to review our choices and proceed to create a new user. Once a new user gets created, we will get an option to download the user's access keys as a CSV file. We must do that in order to be able to utilize those access keys later in our applications. An access key is composed of the access key ID and the secret access key value.

Once you have your access keys, there are multiple approaches to allow your code to use them; we will discuss three of them:

Utilizing a environmental variables directly: There are two main environmental variables that our AWS SDK code will look for, and a third environmental variable, which is optional. We will only discuss the two main environmental variables:

- `AWS_ACCESS_KEY_ID`: Where we set the key ID of our access key
- `AWS_SECRET_ACCESS_KEY`: Where we set the secret key value of our access key

Environmental variables are typically checked, by default, by the SDK before moving on to the next approach.

Utilizing a credentials file: The credentials file is a plain text file that will host your access keys. The file must be named `credentials` and needs to be located in the `.aws/` folder of the home directory of your computer. The home directory will obviously vary depending on your operating system. In Windows, you can point out your home directory using the environmental variable `%UserProfile%`. In Unix platforms, you use an environmental variable called `$HOME` or just `~`. The credentials file is of the `.ini` format and can look like this:

```
[default]
aws_access_key_id = <YOUR_DEFAULT_ACCESS_KEY_ID>
aws_secret_access_key = <YOUR_DEFAULT_SECRET_ACCESS_KEY>

[test-account]
aws_access_key_id = <YOUR_TEST_ACCESS_KEY_ID>
aws_secret_access_key = <YOUR_TEST_SECRET_ACCESS_KEY>

[prod-account]
; work profile
aws_access_key_id = <YOUR_PROD_ACCESS_KEY_ID>
aws_secret_access_key = <YOUR_PROD_SECRET_ACCESS_KEY>
```

The names between the square brackets are called **profiles**. As shown from the preceding snippet, your credentials file can specify different access keys mapped to different profiles. However, then comes an important question, what would be the profile to use for our application? For this, we would need to create an environmental variable called `AWS_PROFILE`, which will specify the profile name and the name of the application that it is assigned to. For example, let's say our application is called `testAWSapp`, and that we want it to utilize the `test-account` profile, we will then set the `AWS_PROFILE` environmental variable as follows:

```
$ AWS_PROFILE=test-account testAWSapp
```

If the `AWS_PROFILE` environmental variable is not set, the *default* profile gets picked up by default.

Hardcoding the access keys in your application: This is typically not recommended for security reasons. So although it is technically possible, do not try this in any production systems since anyone who would have access to your application code (maybe in GitHub) will be able to retrieve and use your access keys.

Creating IAM Roles

As mentioned earlier, IAM roles are recommended if your application is running on an Amazon EC2 instance. Creating an IAM role via the AWS console starts similar to creating an IAM user:

1. We first log in to the AWS console (`aws.amazon.com`)
2. We then select IAM from under the **Security, Identity & Compliance** category

From there, we will take a different path. This time, we click on **Roles** on the right-hand side, then select **Create new role**:

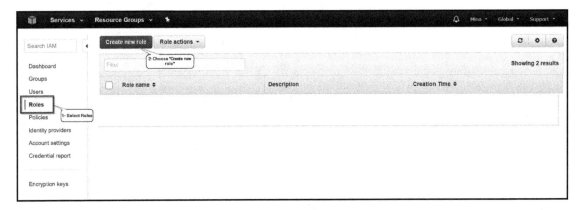

After selecting to create a new role, we will get treated with the role creation wizard.

We first get asked to select a role type. For our case, we will need to select the **EC2 Service role**, then **Amazon EC2**:

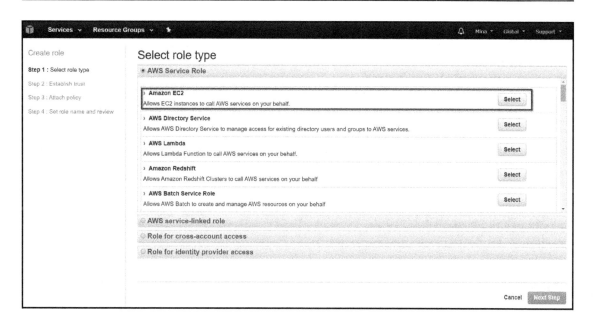

From there, we will click on **Next Step**. We will then need to select the policies that our new role will use:

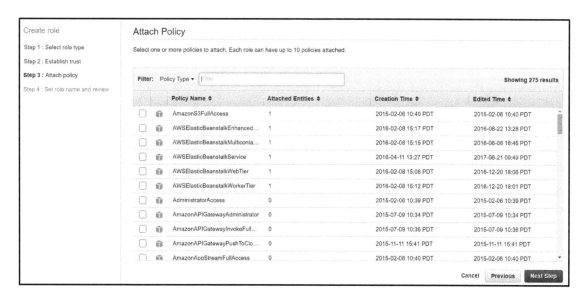

For the purpose of our application, let's select the following four policies:

- **AmazonS3FullAccess**
- **AmazonSQSFullAccess**
- **AmazonDynamoDBFullAccess**
- **AmazonAPIGatewayAdministrator**

We will click on **Next step** again, then, we move to the final step where we get to set the role name, review our configuration, and then click on **Create role** to create a new role. For our purposes, I created a new role called EC2_S3_API_SQS_Dynamo:

Once we click on **Create role**, a new role with our selected policies gets created.

This role can then be attached on an EC2 instance, where our application code will run. We will explore how to do that in the EC2 section.

The fundamentals of the AWS SDK for Go

In order to harness the power of the AWS SDK for Go, there are two key concepts we will need to cover.

Sessions

The first concept is the idea of sessions. A session is an object from the SDK that contains configuration information that we can then use with other objects to communicate with AWS services.

The `session` objects can be shared and used by different pieces of code. The object should be cached and reused. Creating a new `session` object involves loading the configuration data, so reusing it saves resources. `session` objects are safe to use concurrently as long as they don't get modified.

To create a new `session` object, we can simply write the following code:

```
session, err := session.NewSession()
```

This will create a new `session` and store it in a variable called session. If we create a new `session` via the preceding code, default configurations would be utilized. If we need to override a configuration, we can pass a pointer to an object of the `aws.Config` type struct as an argument to the `NewSession()` struct. Let's say we want to set `Region`:

```
session, err := session.NewSession(&aws.Config{
    Region: aws.String("us-east-2"),
})
```

Another constructor we can use to create a new session is called `NewSessionWithOptions()`; this helps override some of the environmental variables we used to provide information needed to create a session. For example, we discussed earlier how we can define a profile to host the credentials to be utilized by our application. Here is how this would look like:

```
session,err := session.NewSessionWithOptions(session.Options{
    Profile: "test-account",
})
```

Service clients

The second concept is the idea of service clients. A service client is an object that provides API access to a specific AWS service such as S3 or SQS.

Service client objects are created from session objects. Here is an example of a piece of code that makes use of an S3 service client to obtain a list of buckets (an S3 bucket is simply a container of files and folders), then prints out the name of each bucket individually:

```go
//Don't forget to import github.com/aws/aws-sdk-go/service/s3

sess, err := session.NewSession(&aws.Config{
    Region: aws.String("us-west-1"),
})
if err != nil {
    log.Fatal(err)
}
s3Svc := s3.New(sess)
results, err := s3Svc.ListBuckets(nil)
if err != nil {
    log.Fatal("Unable to get bucket list")
}

fmt.Println("Buckets:")
for _, b := range results.Buckets {
    log.Printf("Bucket: %s \n", aws.StringValue(b.Name))
}
```

Service client objects are typically safe to use concurrently as long as you ensure that you don't change the configuration in your concurrent code.

Under the hood, service clients make use of Restful API calls to interact with AWS. However, they take care of all the tedious code involved with building and securing HTTP requests for you.

As we go through this chapter and the next chapter, we will create session and service client objects to access the different AWS services. Sessions and service clients are the building coding blocks that we need to build proper AWS cloud native applications. The SDK allows you to dive deep into the underlying requests; this is typically helpful if we want to perform some operations on multiple requests before they get sent out.

Most of the API method calls of the AWS SDK adhere to the following pattern:

1. The API method name would typically describe a certain operation. For example, let's say that we have an **Simple Queue Service (SQS)** service client object, and that we need to get the URL address of a certain queue. The method name will be `GetQueueUrl`.

2. The input argument to the API method typically looks like <method name>Input; so, in case of the `GetQueueUrl` method, it's input type is `GetQueueUrlInput`.

3. The output type from the API method is typically similar to <method name>Output; so, in case of the `GetQueueURL` method, it's output type is `GetQueueUrlOutput`.

Native datatypes

Another important remark regarding the SDK methods is that almost all of the datatypes used as arguments or in struct fields are pointers, even if the data type is native. For example, instead of using a string datatype for a string value, the SDK tends to use *string instead, same with ints and other types. In order to make life easier for the developer, the AWS SDK for Go provides helper methods to convert between native datatypes and their pointers while ensuring nil checks are performed to avoid runtime panics.

The helper method to convert a native data type into a pointer to the same data type follows this pattern: `aws.<datatype>`. For example, if we call `aws.String("hello")`, the method will return a pointer to a string where the `Hello` value is stored. If we call `aws.Int(1)`, the method returns a pointer to an int of value 1.

On the other hand, the method to convert a pointer back to its data type while doing nil checks follows this pattern: `aws.<datatype>Value`. So, for example, if we call `aws.IntValue(p)`, where p is a pointer to an int of value 1, the result returned is simply an int with value 1. To clarify further, here is the implementation of `aws.IntValue` inside the SDK code:

```
func IntValue(v *int) int {
  if v != nil {
    return *v
  }
  return 0
}
```

Shared configuration

Since it is likely that different microservices would need to use the same configuration settings when interacting with AWS, the AWS provides an option to make use of what is called shared configuration. Shared configuration is basically a configuration file that is stored locally. The filename and path is .aws/config. Remember that the .aws folder would exist in the home folder of our operating system; the folder was covered before when discussing the credentials file.

The configuration file should follow an ini-like format similar to the credentials file. It also supports profiles in a similar way to what we covered earlier in the credentials file. Here is an example of what .aws/config should look like:

```
[default]
region=us-west-2
```

To allow microservices in a particular server to make use of the AWS configuration file of said server, there are two methods:

1. Set the AWS_SDK_LOAD_CONFIG environmental variable to true; this will cause the SDK code to use the configuration file.
2. When creating the session object, utilize the NewSessionWithOptions constructor to enable using shared configuration. Here is what the code would look like:

```
sess, err := session.NewSessionWithOptions(session.Options{
    SharedConfigState: SharedConfigEnable,
})
```

For the full AWS Go SDK documentation, you can visit https://docs.aws.amazon.com/sdk-for-go/api/.

Pagination methods

Some API operations can return a huge number of results. For example, let's say that we need to issue an API call to retrieve a list of items from an S3 bucket. Now, let's assume the S3 bucket contains tons of items, and returning all of them in one API call is not efficient. The AWS Go SDK provides a feature called **Pagination** to help in that scenario. With pagination, you get your results in multiple pages.

You can read each page at a time, and then move to the next page of items when ready to process new items. API calls that support pagination is similar to <method name>Pages. For example, the pagination API method call that corresponds to the `ListObjects` S3 method is `ListObjectsPages`. The `ListObjectPages` method will iterate over the pages resulted from the `ListObject` operation. It takes two arguments—the first argument is of the `ListObjectInput` type, which will tell `ListObjectPages` about the name of the S3 bucket we are trying to read as well as the maximum number of keys we want per page. The second argument is a function that gets called with the response data for each page. Here is what the function signature looks like:

```
func(*ListObjectsOutput, bool) bool
```

This argument function has two arguments of its own. The first argument carries the results of our operation; in our case, the results will be hosted in an object of type `ListObjectsOutput`. The second argument is of the `bool` type, which is basically a flag that is true if we are at the last page. The function return type is `bool`; we can use the return value to stop iterating over pages if we wish so. This means that whenever we return false, the pagination will stop.

Here is an example from the SDK documentation that showcases Pagination perfectly, utilizing the methods we discussed. The following code will use pagination to go through a list of items contained in an S3 bucket. We will request a maximum of 10 keys per page. We will print object keys per page, then we will exit once we go through three pages at most. Here is what the code will look like:

```
svc, err := s3.NewSession(sess)
if err != nil {
    fmt.Println("Error creating session ", err)
}
inputparams := &s3.ListObjectsInput{
    Bucket: aws.String("mybucket"),
    MaxKeys: aws.Int64(10),
}
pageNum := 0
svc.ListObjectsPages(inputparams, func(page *s3.ListObjectsOutput, lastPage
bool) bool {
    pageNum++
    for _, value := range page.Contents {
        fmt.Println(*value.Key)
    }
    return pageNum < 3
})
```

Waiters

Waiters are API calls that allow us to wait until a certain operation is completed. Most waiter methods typically adhere to the WaitUntil<action> format. For example, when working with the DynamoDB database, there is an API method call named `WaitUntilTableExists`, which will simply wait till a condition is met.

Handling Errors

The AWS Go SDK returns errors of the `awserr.Error` type, which is a special interface type in the AWS SDK that satisfies the generic Go error interface type. The `awserr.Error` supports three main methods:

- `Code()` : Returns the error code related to the problem
- `Message()`: Returns a string description of the error
- `OrigErr()`: Returns the original error that is wrapped with the `awserr.Error` type; for example, if the problem is related to networking, `OrigErr()` returns the original error that probably belonged to the Go net package

In order to expose and make use of the `awserr.Error` type, we will need to make use of the type assertion feature in Go.

Let's showcase how to make use of the `awserr.Error` type with a practical example. Let's assume that in our application, we use a Dynamodb service client object to retrieve an item from a Dynamodb table via the item ID. However, we made a mistake in the table name and now it doesn't exist, which will cause the call to fail. Code will look like:

```
result, err := dynamodbsvc.GetItem(&dynamodb.GetItemInput{
  Key: map[string]*dynamodb.AttributeValue{
    "ID": {
      N: aws.String("9485"),
    },
  },
  TableName: aws.String("bla"),
})
if err != nil {
  if v, ok := err.(awserr.Error); ok {
    log.Println("AWS ERROR...")
    if v.Code() == dynamodb.ErrCodeResourceNotFoundException {
      log.Println("Requested resource was not found...")
      return
    }
  }
}
```

From the preceding code, if the `dynamodbsvc.GetItem()` method fails and we can't get the item, we capture whether an error occurred, then we use Go's type assertion to obtain the underlying `awserr.Error` type from our error object. We then proceed to check the error code and compare it to the error code in our SDK that indicates a resource not found problem. If it's indeed a resource not found problem, we print a message indicating as such then return. The following is the specific piece of code from the preceding code where we did the error detection and handling as described in the current paragraph:

```
if err != nil {
  if v, ok := err.(awserr.Error); ok {
    log.Println("AWS ERROR...")
    if v.Code() == dynamodb.ErrCodeResourceNotFoundException {
      log.Println("Requested resource was not found...")
      return
    }
  }
}
```

Elastic Compute Cloud (EC2)

Similarly to any other AWS service, we will start from the AWS console in order to be able to initiate and deploy EC2 instances. As mentioned earlier, EC2 can simply be described as a service to be used when needing to spin new server instances on AWS. Let's explore the steps we will need to take to create, then access EC2 instances.

Creating EC2 instances

In the AWS console main screen, we will need to choose EC2 in order to start a new EC2 instance:

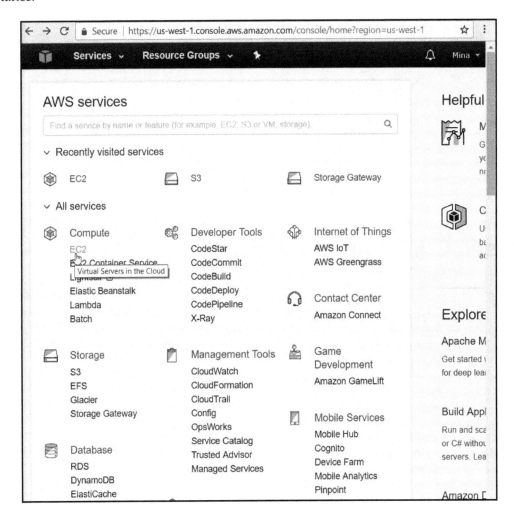

The next screen will expose lots of different options to manage EC2 instances. For now, what we need to do is to click on the **Launch Instance** button. You will note that the AWS region is shown here:

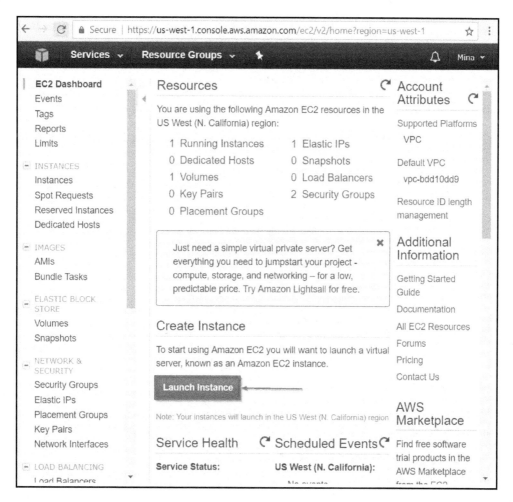

Afterward, we will get to select the image to use as our virtual server on the cloud. An **Amazon Machine Image** (**AMI**) is an acronym to describe an Amazon virtual server image combined with all the information it needs to be launched. An AMI includes a template that describes the operating system, the applications in the virtual server, the launch permissions that specify which AWS account can use the AMI to launch instances of the virtual server image, and a device mapping to specify the volumes to be attached to the instance once it launches. Amazon provides a number of premade AMIs that we can use right away. However, you can also create your own.

The following is what the AMI selection screen in the AWS console looks like:

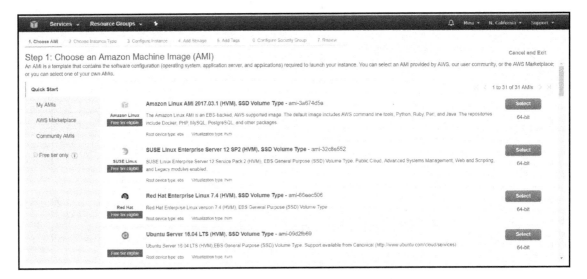

As you can tell from the AMI descriptions, an AMI defines operating systems, command-line tools, programming language environments such as Python, Ruby, and Pert.

For now, let's select the **Amazon Linux AMI** option to proceed to the next step. In this step, we get to select our desired server image. Here is where you get to select the number of CPU cores, the memory, and network performance among other things. You would note the term EBS being under Instance Storage. **Elastic Block Store** (**EBS**), which provides cloud hosted storage volumes and offers high availability, scalability, and durability. Each EBS gets replicated within its availability zone.

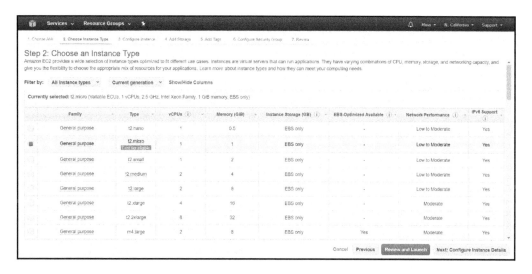

Next, we can click on either the **Review and Launch** button to launch the AMI or the **Next: Configure Instance Details** button to look deeper into the configuration options for the instance. Deeper configuration options include the number of instances, the subnet, the network address, among others.

Configuring the instance details is also where we assign an IAM role (which we discussed earlier) to the EC2. The IAM role we created earlier in the chapter was called EC2_S3_API_SQS_Dynamo, which will allow applications running on this EC2 instance to access S3 service, the API gateway service, the SQS service, and the Dynamo database. Here is what the configuration page will look like:

For the purpose of this chapter, we will click on **Review and Launch** to review then launch the instance. Let's take a look at the review page:

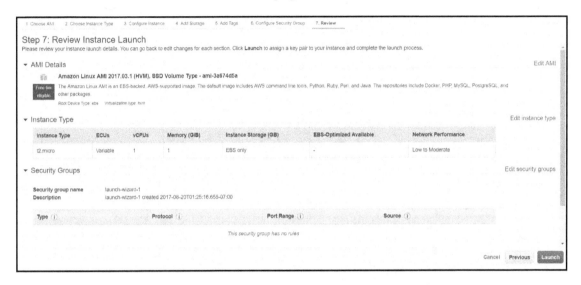

Once we are satisfied with all the settings, we can go ahead and click on Launch. This will show a dialog requesting a public-private key pair. The concept of public key encryption was discussed in Chapter 3 in more detail. In a nutshell, we can describe public-private key encryption as a method of encryption, where you can share a public key with other people so that they encrypt messages before they send them to you. The encrypted message can then only be decrypted via the private key that only you possess.

For AWS, in order to allow developers to connect to their services securely, AWS requests developers to select a public-private key pair to secure access. The public key is stored in AWS, whereas the private key is stored by the developer.

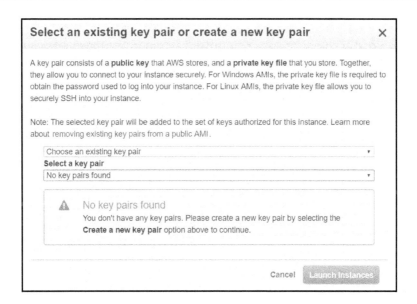

If you don't already have a public-private key pair with AWS, this is the step where we can create one. AWS also allows you to proceed without creating a key, which will obviously be less secure and not recommended in production applications. So let's take a look at the three options we get when click on the first list box:

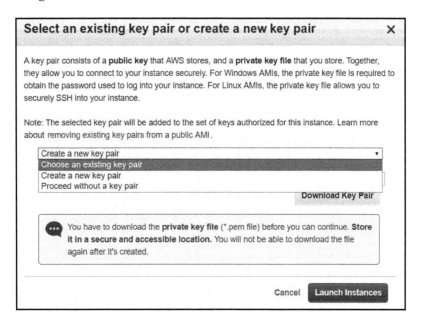

If you select the option to create a new key pair, you will get the option to name your key pair and to download the private key. You must download the private key and store it in a secure location so that you can make use of it later:

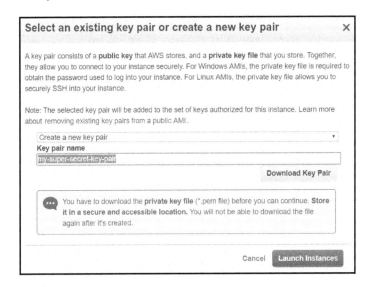

Finally, after we download the private key and are ready to launch the instance(s), we can click on the **Launch Instances** button. This will initiate the process of starting the instance(s) and show us a status indicating as such. Here is what the next screen typically looks like:

Perfect; with this step done, we have our own Linux virtual machine running in the Amazon Cloud. Let's find out how to connect to it and explore it.

Accessing EC2 instances

In order to get access to an EC2 instance that we have already created, we need to first log in to the AWS console, then select EC2 as before. This will provide you access to the EC2 dashboard. From there, we will need to click on instances in order to access the currently created EC2 instances under our account.

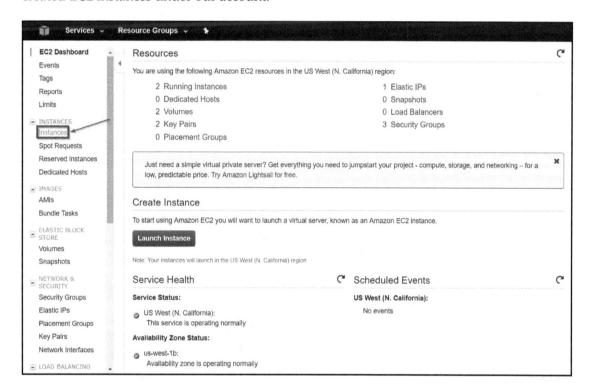

This will open up a list of EC2 instances that were already created. The instance we just created is the first one; you will note that its instance ID matches with the instance ID that was shown when we created the instance earlier.

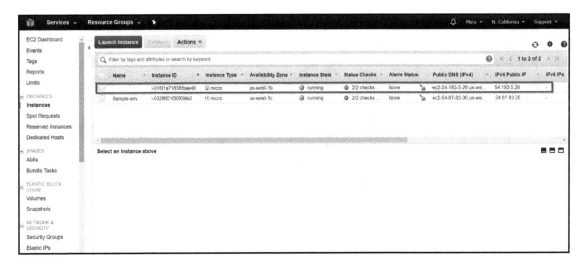

The preceding screenshot shows us that the instance is currently running on AWS. We can connect to it like any remote server if we so desire. Let's explore how to do that.

The first step is to select the instance in question, then click on the **Connect** button. This will not connect directly to your instance; however, it will provide a list of useful instructions of how to establish the connection to your EC2 instance. In order to establish the connection, you will need to utilize the SSH protocol combined with the private encryption key that was downloaded earlier to remotely log in to the EC2 virtual server. **Secure Shell** (**SSH**) is a protocol mostly used to securely login to remote computers by users.

The approach to invoke SSH can be different from one operating system to another. For example, if you are using the Windows operating system, then you should use the popular PuTTY tool (found at `https://www.chiark.greenend.org.uk/~sgtatham/putty/latest.html`) to establish the SSH connection to the EC2 instance. If you are using macOS or Linux, you can use the SSH command directly.

Accessing EC2 instances from a Linux or macOS machine

In order to access EC2 instances created on AWS from a Linux or a macOS machine, we will need to use the SSH command.

The first step is to ensure that the connection private key—which we downloaded earlier when we created the EC2 instance—is secure and cannot be accessed by external parties. This is typically done by executing the following command on the terminal:

```
chmod 400 my-super-secret-key-pair.pem
```

`my-super-secret-key-pair.pem` is the name of the file that contains the private key. Obviously, if the filename is different, then you will need to ensure that the command will target the correct filename. For the preceding command to work, we will need to run it from the same folder as where the key is located. Otherwise, we will need to specify the path to the key.

After we ensure that the key is protected against public access, we will need to make use of the SSH command to connect to our EC2 instance. For this, we will need three pieces of information: the private key filename, the EC2 image username, and the DNS name of the connection. We already know the key filename, which means we now need to figure out the username and the DNS name of the connection. The username will depend on the EC2 instance operating system. The following table shows the operating system to username mapping:

Operating System	User Name
Amazon Linux	`ec2-user`
RHEL (Red Hat Enterprise Linux)	`ec2-user` or root
Ubuntu	ubuntu or root
Centos	centos
Fedora	`ec2-user`
SUSE	`ec2-user` or root

For other operating systems, if `ec2-user` or root don't work, check with the **Amazon Machine Image (AMI)** provider.

Now, the remaining piece of information we need is the DNS name of the connection to the EC2 instance. We can find it by simply looking at the EC2 instance details on the status page:

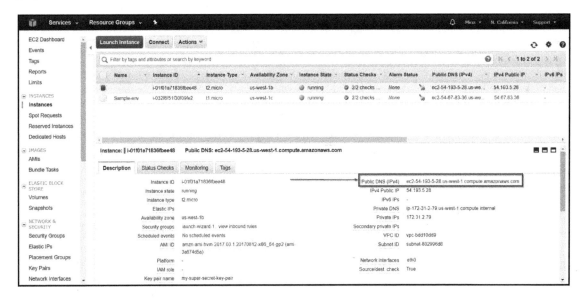

With this, we have all what we need to execute an SSH command to access our EC2 instance; the command will look as follows:

```
ssh -i "my-super-secret-key-pair.pem" ec2-user@ec2-54-193-5-28.us-
west-1.compute.amazonaws.com
```

The private key name in the preceding command is `my-super-secret-key-pair.pem`, the username is `ec2-user`, whereas the DNS is `ec2-54-193-5-28.us-west-1.compute.amazonaws.com`.

This command will allow us access to the EC2 instance that we just created; here is what the screen will look like:

```
       __|  __|_  )
       _|  (     /   Amazon Linux AMI
      ___|\___|___|

https://aws.amazon.com/amazon-linux-ami/2017.03-release-notes/
[ec2-user@ip-172-31-2-79 ~]$
[ec2-user@ip-172-31-2-79 ~]$
```

Accessing EC2 from Windows

To access EC2 from Windows, we can either use a Windows version of the SSH tool we covered in the preceding section or we can use PuTTY. PuTTY is a very popular SSH and telnet client that can run on Windows or Unix. To download PuTTY, we need to visit `https://www.chiark.greenend.org.uk/~sgtatham/PuTTY/latest.html`. Once we download PuTTY, install and run it, the main screen will look similar to this:

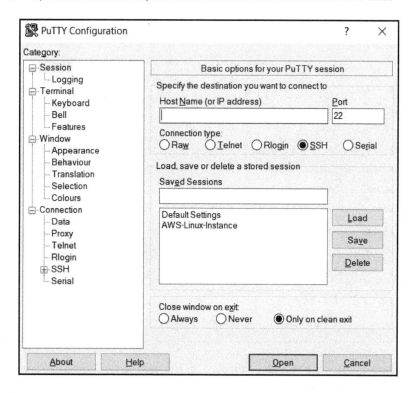

Before we can use PuTTY to connect to our EC2 instance, we will need to convert the private key file that we obtained earlier into a different file type that can be easily consumed by the PuTTY software.

To perform the private key conversion, we will need the help of a tool called **PuTTYgen**, which gets installed with PuTTY. PuTTYgen can be found under **All Programs>PuTTY>PuTTYgen**. Here is what PuTTYgen looks like after it starts:

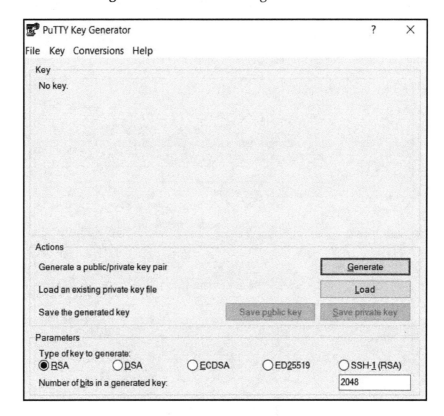

Under **Parameters**, ensure that **RSA** is selected as the encryption algorithm, with **2048** as the number of bits in the generated key.

To proceed, let's click on the **Load** button in order to be able to load our AWS private key into the tool. The **Load** button will open a dialog to allow us to select the private key file. We will need to select the option to show all files in order to make the private key file viewable:

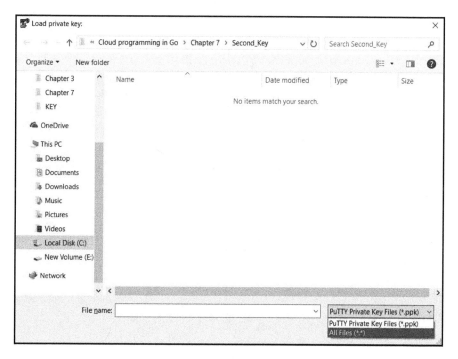

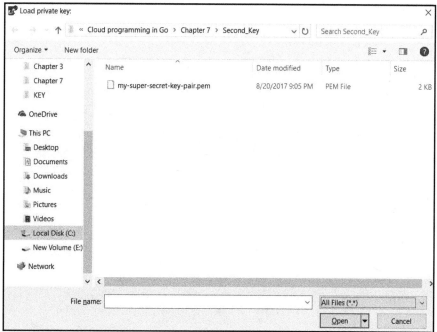

We can then select the key, then click on **Open** in order for the key to get loaded into the PuTTYgen tool. The next step is to click on **Save Private Key** to finish the key conversion. A warning will show up inquiring whether you are sure you want to save this key without a passphrase to protect it; click on **Yes**. The passphrase is supposed to be an extra layer of protection; however, it requires user input to work. So, if we want to automate the SSH connection to the EC2 instance, we shouldn't have the passphrase enabled. After we click on **Yes**, we can select the filename for the converted file; then, we click on **Save** to create and save the file. The PuTTY private key is of the ∗.ppk type.

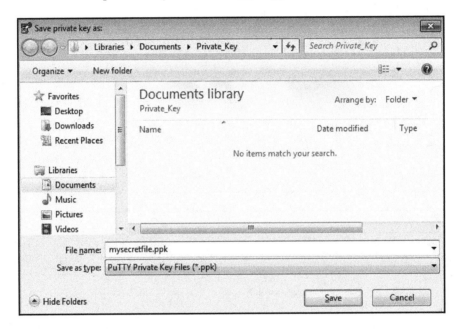

Perfect; we now have a PuTTY private key ready for our use case. The next step is to open the PuTTY tool in order to use this key to connect to the EC2 instance via SSH.

After we open PuTTY, we need to go to the **SSH** option under the **Connection** category, then from there, navigate to the **Auth** option. At the **Auth** window, we will search for the option to load the PuTTY private key file we created earlier.

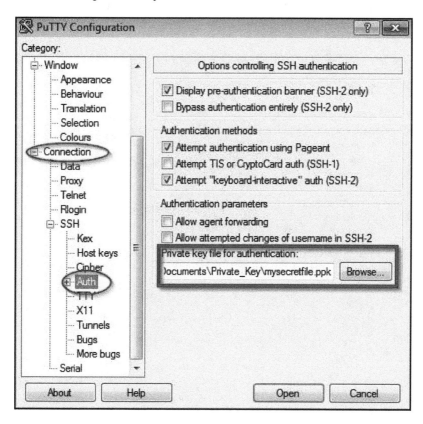

Next, we will need to click on the **Session category** on the right-hand side. Then, under the **Host Name (or IP address)** field on the right-hand side, we will need to enter the username and the public DNS address in the following format: `username@DNS public` name. In our case, it looks like this: `ec2-user@ec2-54-193-5-28.us-west-1.compute.amazonaws.com`:

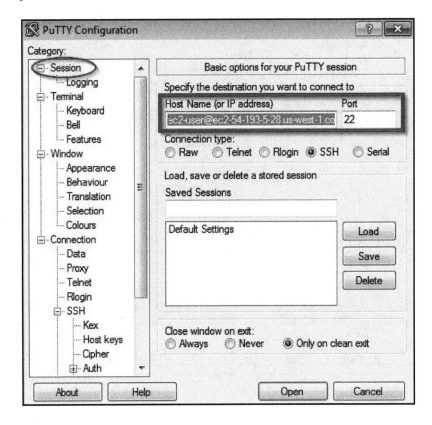

From there, we can click on **Open** to open a session to the EC2 instance. The first time we try to open the session, we will get a message asking whether we trust the server we are trying to connect to. If we trust it, we need to click on **Yes**, which will cache the server's host key into the registry.

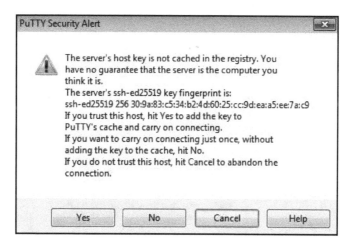

This will open up a secure session to our EC2 instance; we can then use it however we like:

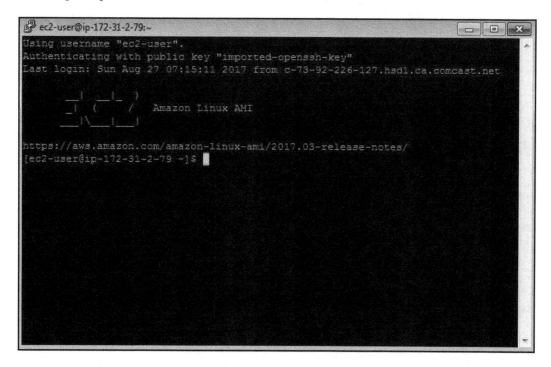

PuTTY has the ability to save existing session information. After we finish our configuration, we can choose a name then click on **Save** as shown in the following figure in order to save the session information:

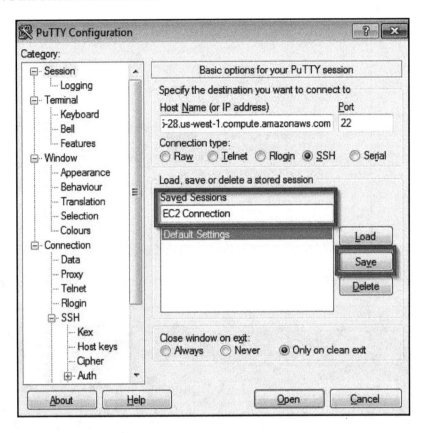

Security groups

Great! This covers enough practical knowledge about how to configure and set up an EC2 instance in different operating systems. Now, there is an additional topic we need to cover, that is, **Security Groups**. You can think of a security group as a collection of firewall rules around your EC2 instance. For example, by adding a security rule, you can allow applications running on your EC2 to accept HTTP traffic. You can create rules to allow access to specific TCP or UDP ports, and much more.

Since we are expected to deploy web services to our EC2 instances, such as the *events microservice*. We need to create a security group that allows HTTP traffic, then assign the group to our EC2 instance.

The first step we will need to do is to open up the EC2 dashboard by going to the AWS console main screen, then selecting EC2 as we did before. Once we are inside the EC2 dashboard, we can click on **Security Groups** on the left-hand side, which will be under the **Network & Security** category:

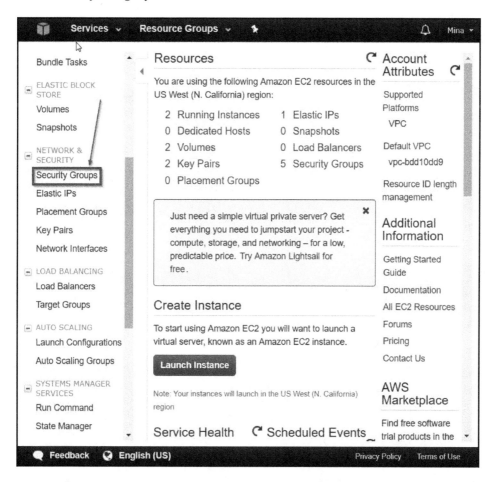

The security groups dashboard will show a list of all the **Security Groups** that have been already created. The dashboard allows us to create new groups or edit existing groups. Since, in our case, we are creating a new group, we will need to click on **Create Security Group** on the upper left-hand side of the dashboard.

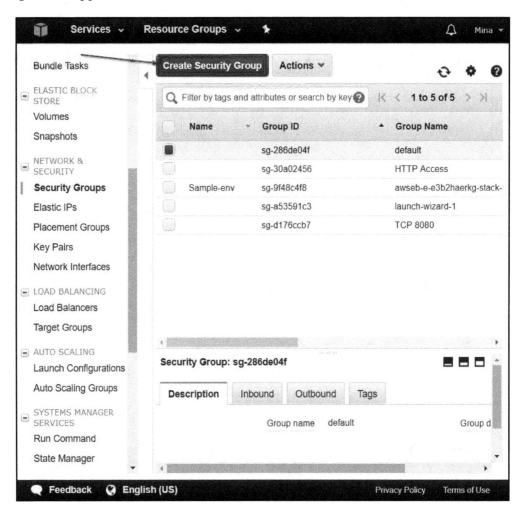

A form window will come up with fields that we need to fill in order to create our security group. First, we will need to provide a name for the security group, an optional description, the name of the virtual private cloud where our security group will apply. A virtual private cloud is simply defined as a logically isolated section in the AWS cloud; we can define our own.

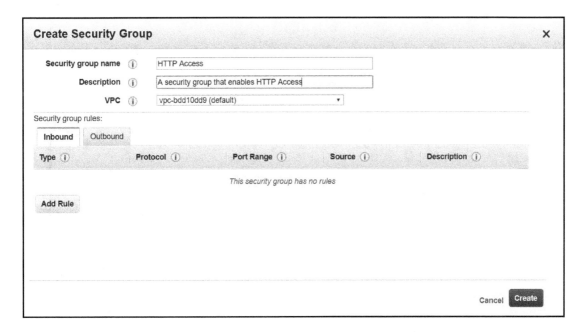

In the preceding screenshot, we named our security group **HTTP Access**; we described it as the security group to enable HTTP access, and then we choose the default VPC.

The next step is to click on the **Add Rule** button to start defining the rules that will compose our security group. After we click on it, a new row will appear inside the **Security group rules** section. We need to click on the listbox under the **Type** column, then select **HTTP**. Here is what the result will look like:

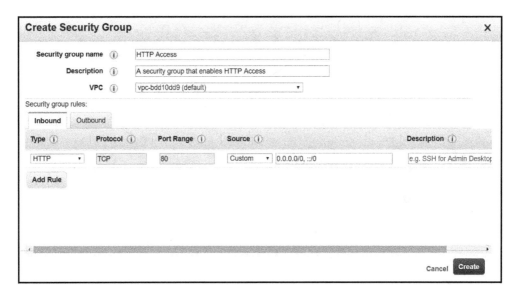

You will note that the protocol, port range, and source fields will be filled up for you. TCP is the underlying protocol for HTTP, whereas port 80 is the HTTP port.

We can also add an HTTPS rule if we would like; we will follow the same steps, except when we choose the **Type**, where **HTTPS** will be chosen instead of **HTTP**. You can also explore the rest of the options to discover what other exceptions can be created under a security rule.

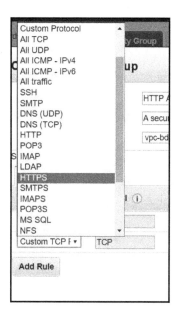

Once a security group is created, we will find it in the list of our security groups:

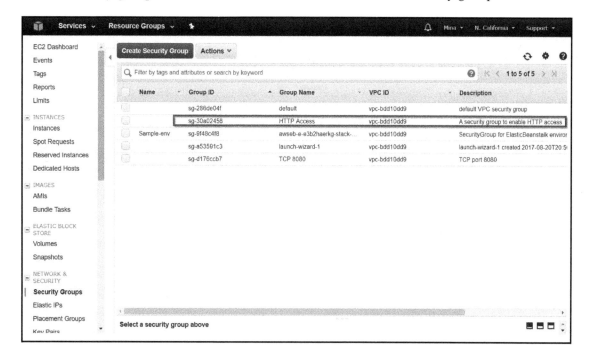

Once we have a security group created, we can attach it to an existing EC2 instance. This is done by going back to the EC2 Dashboard, then selecting **Running instances**, and then selecting the instance of interest from the list of EC2 instances. From there, we click on **Actions**, then **Networking**, and then **Change Security Groups**:

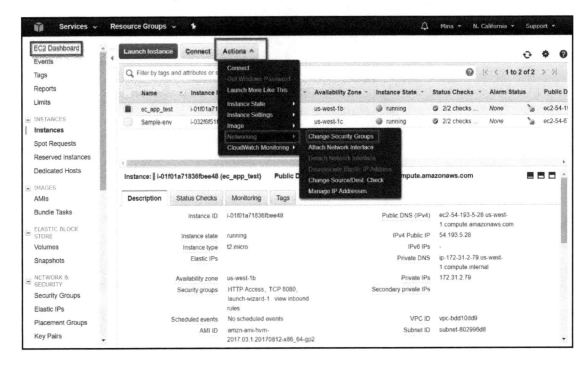

From there, we can choose the **Security Groups** that we would like to attach to our instance:

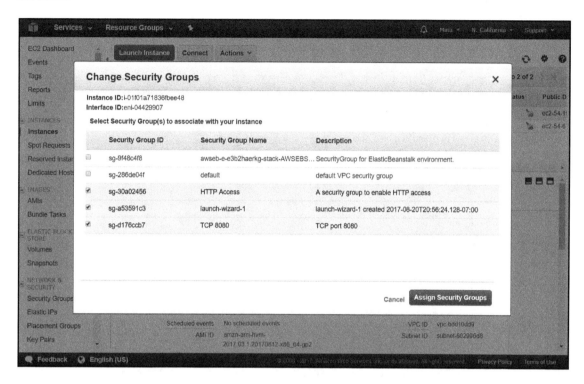

Perfect; with this, our EC2 instance now allows HTTP access to applications running inside it.

Another important remark is that we can assign security groups to EC2 instances at the time of the EC2 instance creation. We access this option by clicking on **Configure Instance Details** while creating a new instance, then following the configuration wizard to the **Configure Security Group** option.

Summary

In this chapter, we started covering AWS, by learning how to configure EC2 and how to work with the AWS SDK for Go. In the next chapter, we'll continue to dive deeper into AWS, by learning about some of the key AWS services and how to write Go code that can make proper use of them.

8

AWS II – S3, SQS, API Gateway, and DynamoDB

In this chapter, we'll continue covering the massive topic of Amazon Web Services. In this chapter, we'll cover the S3 service, SQS service, AWS API Gateway service, and DynamoDB service. Every single one of these services is a powerful tool in your arsenal to build production applications deployed on the cloud.

We will cover the following topics in this chapter:

- The AWS S3 storage service
- The SQS message queue service
- The AWS API gateway service
- The DynamoDB database service

Simple Storage Service (S3)

Amazon S3 is an AWS service responsible for storing and analyzing data. The data typically includes files of all sorts and shapes (including music files, photos, text files, and video files). S3, for example, can be utilized to store code files for static data. Let's take a tour of how to use the S3 service in AWS.

Configuring S3

The S3 service stores files in buckets. Each bucket can hold files directly or can include a number of folders, and, in turn, each folder can hold a number of files.

We will use the AWS web console to configure S3, similar to what we did with EC2. The first step will be to navigate to the AWS web console and then select S3:

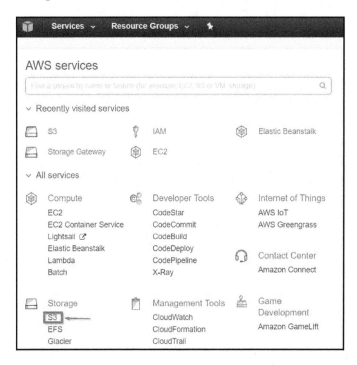

This will open the Amazon S3 console; from there, we can click on **Create bucket** to create a new bucket to store data folders:

This will start a wizard that will walk you through the different steps needed to properly create a bucket. This will give you the power to set the bucket name, enable versioning or logging, set tags, and set permissions. Once done, a new bucket will get created for you. The bucket name has to be unique so that it won't get conflicted with buckets used by other AWS users.

I created a bucket called `mnandbucket`; it will show up in the list of buckets in my S3 main web page. If you have more buckets than what the page can show, you can search for buckets in the search bar:

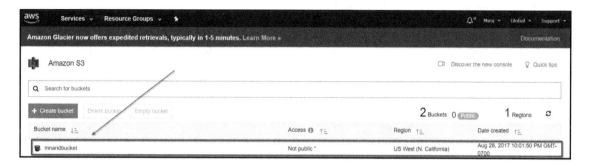

Once we enter a bucket, we can then create folders and upload files:

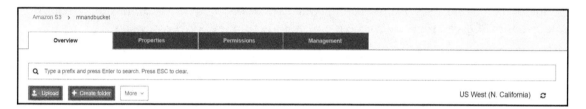

Perfect! With that, we have a practical idea of what S3 is about.

You can download this file from `https://www.packtpub.com/sites/default/files/downloads/CloudNativeprogrammingwithGolang_ColorImages.pdf`.
The code bundle for the book is also hosted on GitHub at `https://github.com/PacktPublishing/Cloud-Native-Programming-with-Golang`.

S3 storage can be utilized to store our application files for later use. So, for example, say we built our `events` microservice to run in a Linux environment, and the filename for the application is simply `events`. We can then simply store the file in an S3 folder; then, whenever we need an EC2 instance to obtain the file, we can use the AWS command-line tools in the Ec2 instance to achieve that.

We first need to ensure that the AWS roles are properly defined to allow our EC2 instance to access the S3 storage as was covered earlier. Then, from there, to copy the file from S3 to our EC2 instance, we will need to issue the following command from our EC2 instance:

```
aws s3 cp s3://<my_bucket>/<my_folder>/events my_local_events_copy
```

The preceding command will retrieve the `events` file from the S3 storage, then copy it to a new file called `my_local_events_copy`, which will live in the current folder. `<my_bucket>` and `<my_folder>` represent the bucket and the folder where the events file exists on the S3 storage, respectively.

After we copy an executable file to EC2, we will need to give it access to execute via the Linux `chmod` command. This is achieved utilizing the following command:

```
chmod u+x <my_executable_file>
```

In the preceding command, `<my_executable_file>` is the file that we would like to obtain enough access in our EC2 instance to execute.

Simple Queue Service (SQS)

As mentioned earlier, SQS is the message queue provided by AWS. Applications that can interact with SQS can send and receive messages within the AWS ecosystem.

Let's start by discussing how to configure an SQS from the Amazon console. As usual, the first step is to log in to the Amazon console and then select our service from the main dashboard. The service name in this case will be called **Simple Queue Service**:

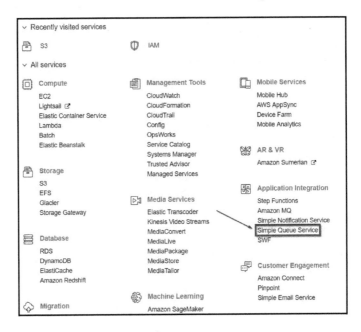

From there, we will need to either click on **Getting started** or on **Create New Queue**. The queue creation page will offer us the ability to configure the behavior of the new queue. For example, we can set the maximum message size allowed, the number of days we can retain a message, or even the wait time to receive a message:

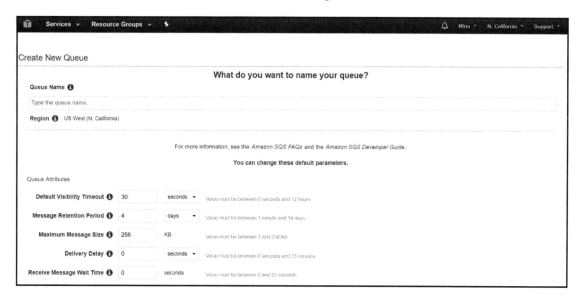

Once you are satisfied with your settings, click on **Create Queue**—I picked the name eventqueue.

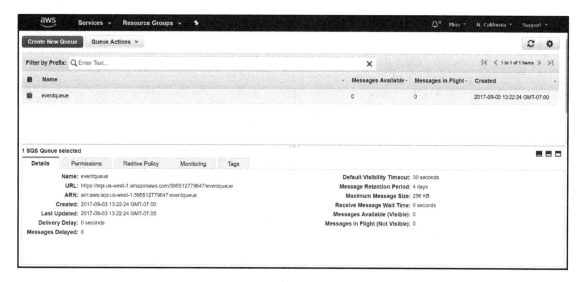

This will create a new AWS SQS queue that we can utilize in our code. Now, it's time to discuss how we can write code to interact with our new queue.

Perfect! With our queue created, we are ready to write some code to send and receive messages via the newly created AWS SQS queue. Let's start with exploring the code we need to write in order to send some data.

The docs for the AWS SDK Go SQS package can be found at `https://godoc.org/github.com/aws/aws-sdk-go/service/sqs`.

As any other AWS service, there are two first key steps we will need to get out of the way:

- Obtaining or creating a session object
- Creating a service client for our desired AWS service

The preceding steps are covered via the following code:

```
sess, err := session.NewSession(&aws.Config{
  Region: aws.String("us-west-1"),
})
if err != nil {
  log.Fatal(err)
}
sqsSvc := sqs.New(sess)
```

The preceding code sets the region via the code when calling the `NewSession()` constructor; however, we have the choice to use a shared configuration instead, as mentioned in the preceding chapter. I made use of `log.Fatal()` in this code since it's only testing code, so if anything fails, I would want to exit with the error message reported.

Next, we will need to obtain the message queue URL. The URL is important because it serves as a unique identifier for the message queue in the SDK method calls. We can obtain the URL either from the AWS console SQS page, where the URL of our queue will show in the **Details** tab when the queue is selected or via code by utilizing the queue name we chose when creating our queue. In my case, I called my queue `eventqueue`; so, let's take a look at how we can obtain the URL from that name through our code:

```
QUResult, err := sqsSvc.GetQueueUrl(&sqs.GetQueueUrlInput{
  QueueName: aws.String("eventqueue"),
})
if err != nil {
  log.Fatal(err)
}
```

The `QUResult` object is of the `*GetQueueUrlOutput` type, which is a pointer to a struct that contains a field called `QueueUrl` of the `*string` type. This field should have our queue URL if the `GetQueueUrl()` method is executed successfully.

Perfect! Now that we have the URL of our queue, we are ready to send some data over the message queue. However, before we do that, we will need to cover some important definitions to understand the code that is yet to come.

- **Message body**: A message body is simply the core message we are trying to send. For example, if I want to send a hello message via SQS, then the message body would be hello.
- **Message attributes**: Message attributes are a collection of structured metadata items. You can think of them simply as a list of key value pairs that you can define and send with your message. Message attributes are optional; however, they can be powerful because they allow sending messages that are more structured and sophisticated than just text. Message attributes allow us to understand what the message might contain before we start processing the message body. We can include up to 10 message attributes per message. Message attributes support three main data types: string, number, and binary. A Binary type represents binary data such as compressed files and images.

Now, let's return to our sample code; let's say that we want to send a message via SQS for our events app to represent a customer reservation for some concerts; our message will have the following properties:

- **Message attributes**: We would like two message attributes:
    - `message_type`: The type of the message we are trying to send—in our case, the value of this attribute will be "RESERVATION"
    - `Count`: The number of reservations included in this message
- **Message body**: This entails the reservation data in JSON format. The data includes the customer names reserving the concert and the event name (the concert, in this case)

Here is what the code will look like:

```
sendResult, err := sqsSvc.SendMessage(&sqs.SendMessageInput{
    MessageAttributes: map[string]*sqs.MessageAttributeValue{
        "message_type": &sqs.MessageAttributeValue{
            DataType: aws.String("String"),
            StringValue: aws.String("RESERVATION"),
        },
        "Count": &sqs.MessageAttributeValue{
```

```
        DataType: aws.String("Number"),
        StringValue: aws.String("2"),
    },
},
MessageBody: aws.String("[{customer:'Kevin S',event:'Pink Floyd
Concert'},{customer:'Angela     T',event:'Cold Play Concert'}]"),
    QueueUrl: QUResult.QueueUrl,
})
```

The preceding code makes use of the `SendMessage()` method to send the message. `SendMessage()` takes an argument of the `*SendMessageInput{}` type, which is where we define the message attributes, message body, and where we identify the queue URL.

Afterward, we can then check whether any error occurred. We can obtain the ID for the message we created via the following code:

```
if err != nil {
    log.Fatal(err)
}
log.Println("Message sent successfully", *sendResult.MessageId)
```

Perfect! With this piece of sample code, we now know how to send message over SQS. Now, let's learn how to receive them.

There are some concepts that we will need to cover and questions we will need answered before we start looking into the message receiving code. Let's assume that we have a microservice architecture where more than one microservices are reading messages from an SQS message queue. An important question to answer is, what do we do after one of our services receives a message? Should that message be allowed to be received by the other services afterward? The answer for those two questions depends on the purpose of the said message. If the message is supposed to be consumed and processed once, then we will need to ensure that the first service to properly receive this message should then delete it from the queue.

In the world of AWS SQS, a message does not get deleted from the queue when it gets received in a standard queue. We will instead need to explicitly delete the message from the queue after we receive it in order to ensure that it disappears, if that's our intention. However, there is another complication. Let's assume that microservice A received a message and started processing it. However, before microservice A got to deleting the message from the queue, microservice B received the message and started processing it, which we don't want.

To avoid that scenario, SQS introduces a concept called **visibility timeout**. A visibility timeout simply makes a message invisible for a certain period of time after it gets received by one consumer. This timeout gives us some time to decide what to do with the message before other consumers get to see it and process it.

One important remark is that there is not always a guarantee against receiving a message twice. The reason for that is because SQS queues are typically distributed among multiple servers. There are rare cases where a delete request doesn't reach the server because it is offline, which means the message might survive despite a delete request.

Another important concept in the world of SQS is long polling or wait time. Since SQS is distributed and might have some delays every now and then, some messages might be slow to be received. If we care about receiving messages even if they are slow, then we will need to wait longer when listening to incoming messages.

The following is a sample piece of code that shows receiving a message from a queue:

```
QUResult, err := sqsSvc.GetQueueUrl(&sqs.GetQueueUrlInput{
  QueueName: aws.String("eventqueue"),
})
if err != nil {
  log.Fatal(err)
}
recvMsgResult, err := sqsSvc.ReceiveMessage(&sqs.ReceiveMessageInput{
  AttributeNames: []*string{
    aws.String(sqs.MessageSystemAttributeNameSentTimestamp),
  },
  MessageAttributeNames: []*string{
    aws.String(sqs.QueueAttributeNameAll),
  },
  QueueUrl: QUResult.QueueUrl,
  MaxNumberOfMessages: aws.Int64(10),
  WaitTimeSeconds: aws.Int64(20),
})
```

In the preceding code, we attempt to listen to incoming message from the SQS queue, which we created. We use the `GetQueueURL()` method as before to retrieve the queue URL to utilize in the `ReceiveMessage()` method.

The `ReceiveMessage()` method allows us to specify the message attributes (which we discussed earlier) that we would like to capture, as well as the general system attributes. System attributes are general properties of the message, such as the time stamp that came with it. In the preceding code, we ask for all the message attributes, but only for the message time stamp system attribute.

We set the maximum number of messages we would like to receive in a single call to be 10. It is important to point out that this is only the maximum number of message requested, so it is common to receive less. Finally, we will set the polling time to be a maximum of 20 seconds. If we receive messages faster than 20 seconds, the call returns with the captured messages without having to wait.

Now, what should we do with the captured messages? For the sake of showcasing code, let's say that we would like to print the message body and message attributes to the standard output. Afterward, we delete the messages. Here is what this would look like:

```
for i, msg := range recvMsgResult.Messages {
    log.Println("Message:", i, *msg.Body)
    for key, value := range msg.MessageAttributes {
       log.Println("Message attribute:", key,
aws.StringValue(value.StringValue))
    }

    for key, value := range msg.Attributes {
       log.Println("Attribute: ", key, *value)
    }

    log.Println("Deleting message...")
    resultDelete, err := sqsSvc.DeleteMessage(&sqs.DeleteMessageInput{
       QueueUrl: QUResult.QueueUrl,
       ReceiptHandle: msg.ReceiptHandle,
    })
    if err != nil {
       log.Fatal("Delete Error", err)
    }
    log.Println("Message deleted... ")
}
```

Note that in the preceding code, we used an object called `msg.ReceiptHandle` in the `DeleteMessage()` method in order to identify the message we would like to delete. ReceiptHandle is an object that we obtain whenever we receive a message from the queue; the purpose of this object is to allow us to delete the message that we received afterward. Whenever a message is received, a ReceiptHandle is created.

Also, we received the message in the preceding code and then dissect it:

- We call `msg.Body` to retrieve the body of our message
- We call `msg.MessageAttributes` to obtain the message attributes of our message
- We call `msg.Attributes` to obtain the system attributes that came with our message

With that, we have enough knowledge to implement an SQS message queue emitter and listener for our `events` application. In a previous chapter, we created two key interface that need to be implemented for message queues in our application. One of them was the emitter interface, which was responsible for sending a message over a message queue. The other was the listener interface, which was responsible for receiving a message from a message queue.

As a quick refresher, how is what the emitter interface looked like:

```
package msgqueue

// EventEmitter describes an interface for a class that emits events
type EventEmitter interface {
  Emit(e Event) error
}
```

Also, here is what the listener interface looked like:

```
package msgqueue

// EventListener describes an interface for a class that can listen to
events.
type EventListener interface {
 Listen(events ...string) (<-chan Event, <-chan error, error)
 Mapper() EventMapper
 }
```

The `Listen` method takes a list of event names, then return those events in a channel, as well as any errors occurred while trying to receive the events via the message queue. This is called the channel generator pattern.

So, for our application to support the SQS message queue, we will need to implement those two interfaces. Let's start with the `Emitter` interface. We'll create a new folder inside `./src/lib/msgqueue`; the new folder name will be `sqs`. Inside the `sqs` folder, we create two files—`emitter.go` and `listener.go`. `emitter.go` is where we will implement the emitter interface.

We start by creating a new object to implement the emitter interface—the object is called `SQSEmitter`. It will contain the SQS service client object, as well as the URL of our queue:

```
type SQSEmitter struct {
  sqsSvc *sqs.SQS
  QueueURL *string
}
```

We will then need to create a constructor for our emitter. In the constructor, we'll create the SQS service client from either an existing session or from a newly created session. We will also utilize the `GetQueueUrl` method in order to obtain the URL of our queue. Here is what this will look like:

```
func NewSQSEventEmitter(s *session.Session, queueName string) (emitter
msgqueue.EventEmitter, err error) {
  if s == nil {
    s, err = session.NewSession()
    if err != nil {
      return
    }
  }
  svc := sqs.New(s)
  QUResult, err := svc.GetQueueUrl(&sqs.GetQueueUrlInput{
    QueueName: aws.String(queueName),
  })
  if err != nil {
    return
  }
  emitter = &SQSEmitter{
    sqsSvc: svc,
    QueueURL: QUResult.QueueUrl,
  }
  return
}
```

The next step is to implement the `Emit()` method of the emitter interface. The message we will emit should have the following properties:

- It will contain a single message attribute called `event_name`, which will hold the name of the event we are trying to send. As covered before, in this book, an event name describes the type of the event our application is trying to process. We had three event names—`eventCreated`, `locationCreated`, and `eventBooked`. Remember here that `eventCreated` and `eventBooked`, refer to application events (and not message queue events) being created or booked, like concerts or circus acts for example.
- It will contain a message body, which will hold the event data. The message body will be in JSON format.

Here is what the code will look like:

```
func (sqsEmit *SQSEmitter) Emit(event msgqueue.Event) error {
    data, err := json.Marshal(event)
    if err != nil {
        return err
    }
    _, err = sqsEmit.sqsSvc.SendMessage(&sqs.SendMessageInput{
        MessageAttributes: map[string]*sqs.MessageAttributeValue{
            "event_name": &sqs.MessageAttributeValue{
                DataType: aws.String("string"),
                StringValue: aws.String(event.EventName()),
            },
        },
        MessageBody: aws.String(string(data)),
        QueueUrl: sqsEmit.QueueURL,
    })
    return err
}
```

With this, we have an SQS message queue implementation for the emitter interface. Now, let's discuss the listener interface.

The listener interface will be implemented in the `./src/lib/msgqueue/listener.go` file. We start with the object that will implement the interface. The object name is `SQSListener`. It will contain the message queue event type mapper, the SQS client service object, the URL of the queue, the maximum number of messages to be received from one API call, the wait time for messages to be received, and the visibility timeout. Here is what this will look like:

```
type SQSListener struct {
    mapper msgqueue.EventMapper
    sqsSvc *sqs.SQS
```

```
    queueURL *string
    maxNumberOfMessages int64
    waitTime int64
    visibilityTimeOut int64
}
```

We will first start with the constructor; the code will be similar to the constructor we built for the emitter. We will ensure that we have an AWS session object, a service client object, and obtain the URL of our queue based on the queue name:

```
func NewSQSListener(s *session.Session, queueName string, maxMsgs, wtTime,
visTO int64) (listener msgqueue.EventListener, err error) {
  if s == nil {
    s, err = session.NewSession()
    if err != nil {
      return
    }
  }
  svc := sqs.New(s)
  QUResult, err := svc.GetQueueUrl(&sqs.GetQueueUrlInput{
    QueueName: aws.String(queueName),
  })
  if err != nil {
    return
  }
  listener = &SQSListener{
    sqsSvc: svc,
    queueURL: QUResult.QueueUrl,
    mapper: msgqueue.NewEventMapper(),
    maxNumberOfMessages: maxMsgs,
    waitTime: wtTime,
    visibilityTimeOut: visTO,
  }
  return
}
```

Afterward, we will need to implement the `Listen()` method of the `listener` interface. The method does the following:

- It takes a list of event names as arguments
- It listens to incoming messages
- When it receives a message, it checks the message event name and compares it with the list of event names that were passed as arguments

- If a message is received that does not belong to a requested event, it gets ignored
- If a message is received that belongs to a known event, it gets passed through the a Go channel of the 'Event' type to the outside world
- Messages that are accepted get deleted after they pass through the Go channel
- Any errors that occur get passed through another Go channel for error objects

Let's focus on the code that will listen and receive messages for the time being. We will create a new method called `receiveMessage()` for that. Here is how it is broken down:

1. First, we receive messages and pass any errors to a Go error channel:

```
func (sqsListener *SQSListener) receiveMessage(eventCh chan
msgqueue.Event, errorCh chan error, events ...string) {
   recvMsgResult, err :=
sqsListener.sqsSvc.ReceiveMessage(&sqs.ReceiveMessageInput{
      MessageAttributeNames: []*string{
        aws.String(sqs.QueueAttributeNameAll),
      },
      QueueUrl: sqsListener.queueURL,
      MaxNumberOfMessages:
aws.Int64(sqsListener.maxNumberOfMessages),
      WaitTimeSeconds: aws.Int64(sqsListener.waitTime),
      VisibilityTimeout:
aws.Int64(sqsListener.visibilityTimeOut),
   })
   if err != nil {
     errorCh <- err
   }
```

2. We then go through the received messages one by one and check their message attributes—if the event name does not belong to the list of requested event names, we ignore it by moving to the next message:

```
bContinue := false
for _, msg := range recvMsgResult.Messages {
  value, ok := msg.MessageAttributes["event_name"]
  if !ok {
    continue
  }
  eventName := aws.StringValue(value.StringValue)
  for _, event := range events {
    if strings.EqualFold(eventName, event) {
      bContinue = true
      break
    }
  }
```

```
    }

    if !bContinue {
      continue
    }
```

3. If we continue, we retrieve the message body, then use our event mapper object to translate it to an Event type that we can use in our external code. The event mapper object was created in Chapter 4, *Asynchronous Microservice Architectures Using Message Queues*; it simply takes an event name and the binary form of the event, then it returns an Event object to us. After that, we obtain the event object and pass it to the events channel. If we detect errors, we pass the error to the errors channel, then move to the next message:

```
message := aws.StringValue(msg.Body)
event, err := sqsListener.mapper.MapEvent(eventName,
[]byte(message))
if err != nil {
  errorCh <- err
  continue
}
eventCh <- event
```

4. Finally, if we reach to this point without errors, then we know we succeeded in processing the message. So, the next step will be to delete the message so that it won't be processed by someone else:

```
    _, err =
sqsListener.sqsSvc.DeleteMessage(&sqs.DeleteMessageInput{
        QueueUrl: sqsListener.queueURL,
        ReceiptHandle: msg.ReceiptHandle,
    })

    if err != nil {
      errorCh <- err
    }
  }
}
```

This is great. You might wonder, however, how come we didn't put this code directly in the Listen() method? The answer is simple: we did that to clean up our code and avoid one massive method. This is because the piece of code we just covered needs to be called in a loop so that we keep receiving messages from the message queue continuously.

Now, let's look at the `Listen()` method. The method will need to call `receiveMessage()` in a loop inside a goroutine. The reason why a goroutine is needed is because otherwise the `Listen()` method would block its calling thread. Here is what this will look like:

```
func (sqsListener *SQSListener) Listen(events ...string) (<-chan
msgqueue.Event, <-chan error, error) {
  if sqsListener == nil {
    return nil, nil, errors.New("SQSListener: the Listen() method was
called on a nil pointer")
  }
  eventCh := make(chan msgqueue.Event)
  errorCh := make(chan error)
  go func() {
    for {
      sqsListener.receiveMessage(eventCh, errorCh)
    }
  }()

  return eventCh, errorCh, nil
}
```

The preceding code first ensures that the `*SQSListener` object is not nil, then it creates the events and the errors Go channels to be utilized for communicating the results of the `receiveMessage()` method to the outside world.

AWS API gateway

The next step in our quest to dive into cloud native applications is to take a tour into the AWS API gateway. As mentioned earlier, the AWS API gateway is a hosted service that allows developers to build flexible APIs for their applications. In this section, we will go through a practical introduction about the service and how it can be used.

Similar to the other services that we have covered so far, we will create an API gateway via the AWS console. The first step, as usual, would be to visit and log in to the AWS console at `aws.amazon.com`.

The second step would be to go to the home page, and then select **API Gateway** from under **Application Services**:

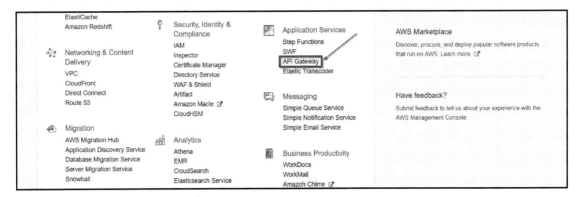

Next, we will need to select **API** from the left-hand side, then click on **Create API**. This will start the process of creating a new API to use for our application:

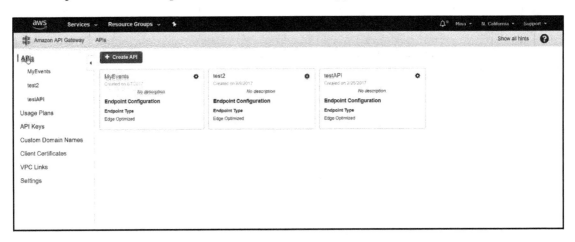

From there, we get to pick a name of our new API, as follows:

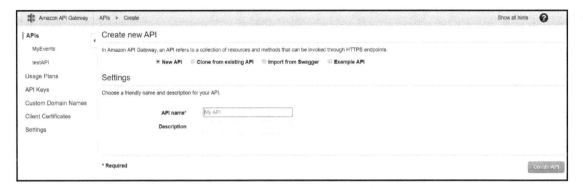

Now, after creating the API, we will need to create mappings between the AWS API gateway, and the addresses of the RESTful APIs embedded in our MyEvents application. The MyEvents application included more than one microservice. One of those microservices was the events services; it supported several tasks that could be activated via its RESTful API. As a refresher, here is a quick summary of the API tasks and examples of their relative URL addresses:

1. **Searching for events**:
   - **ID**: The relative URL is `/events/id/3434`, method is `GET`, and no data expected in the HTTP body
   - **Name**: The relative URL is `/events/name/jazz_concert`, method is `GET`, and no data expected in the HTTP body
2. **Retrieving all events at once**: The relative URL is `/events`, method is `GET`, and no data expected in the HTTP body
3. **Creating a new event**: The relative URL is `/events`, method is `POST`, and the expected data in the HTTP body needs to be the JSON representation of the new event we would like to add. Let's say we would like to add the event of `opera aida` that would play in the U.S. Then, the HTTP body would look like this:

```
{
    name: "opera aida",
    startdate: 768346784368,
    enddate: 43988943,
    duration: 120, //in minutes
    location:{
        id : 3 , //=>assign as an index
        name: "West Street Opera House",
        address: "11 west street, AZ 73646",
```

```
            country: "U.S.A",
            opentime: 7,
            clostime: 20
            Hall: {
                name : "Cesar hall",
                location : "second floor, room 2210",
                capacity: 10
            }
        }
    }
}
```

Let's explore the events microservice API task by task and learn how to get the AWS API gateway to act as a front door to the application.

From the preceding description, we have three relative URLs:

- /events/id/{id}, where {id} is a number. We support GET HTTP requests with that URL.
- /events/name/{name}, where {name} is a string. We support GET HTTP requests with that URL
- /events, where we support GET and POST requests with this URL.

To represent those relative URLs with their methods in our AWS API gateway, we will need to perform the following:

1. Create a new resource and call it events. We will first visit our newly created API page. Then, from there, we will create a new resource by clicking on **Actions** and selecting **Create Resource**:

2. Ensure that you set both the name and the path to `events` on the new resource:

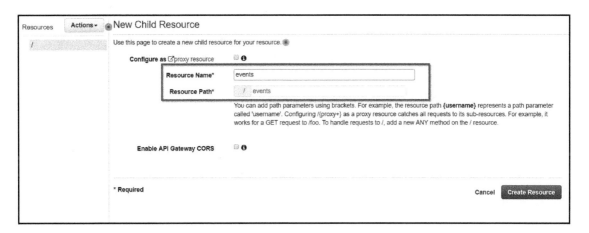

3. Afterwards, select the newly created `events` resource and create a new resource called `id`. Select the `events` resource again, but this time, create a new resource called `name`. Here is what this will look like:

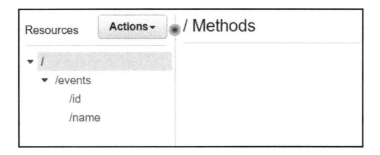

4. Select the `id` resource, then create a new resource. This time, call the resource name `id` again; however, the resource path needs to be `{id}`. This is important because it indicates that `id` is a parameter that can accept other values. Meaning that this resource can represent a relative URL that looks like this `/events/id/3232`:

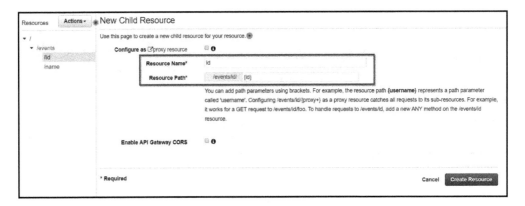

5. Similar to step 4, we will select the `name` resource, then create another resource underneath, which will have the resource name as `name` and the resource path as `{name}`. Here is what this will end up looking like:

6. Now, this should cover all our relative URLs. We need to attach the supported HTTP methods to their corresponding resources. First, we will go the `events` resource and then attach a `GET` method as well as a `POST` method to it. To do that, we need to click on s, then select **Create Method**:

7. We can then select **GET** as the method type:

8. We then select the integration type of **HTTP**. From there, we will need to set the endpoint URL. The endpoint URL needs to be the absolute path of the API endpoint that corresponds to this resource. In our case, since we are under the 'events' resource, the absolute address for the resource on the 'events' microservice would be `<EC2 DNS Address>/events`. Let's assume that the DNS is `http://ec2.myevents.com`; this will make the absolute path `http://ec2.myevents.com/events`. Here is what this configuration will look like:

9. We will repeat the preceding step; however, this time we will create a POST method.

10. We select the {id} resource, then create a new GET method. The EndPoint URL needs to include the {id}; here is what this will look like:

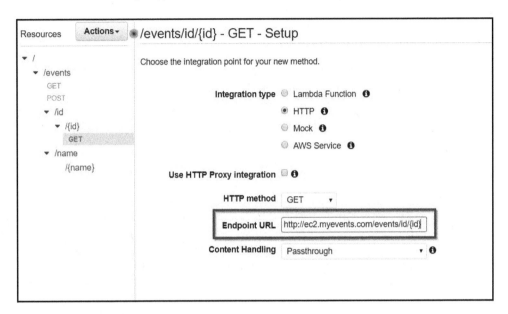

11. We will repeat the same step with the {name} resource; here is what the Endpoint URL will look like:
    `http://ec2.myevents.com/events/name/{name}`.

Perfect! With this, we created AWS API gateway mappings to our events microservice API. We can use the same technique to add more resources in our MyEvents API that would point to other microservices that belong to the MyEvents application. The next step is to deploy the API. The first thing we need to do is to create a new stage. A stage is a way to identify a deployed RESTful API that is callable by users. We will need to create a stage before we can deploy a RESTful API. To deploy an API, we will need to click on **Actions** and then on **Deploy API**:

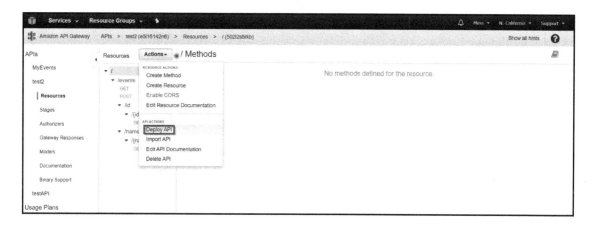

If we don't already have a stage, we will need to select **[New Stage]** as our **Deployment stage**, then pick a stage name, and finally click on **Deploy**. I will call my stage `beta`:

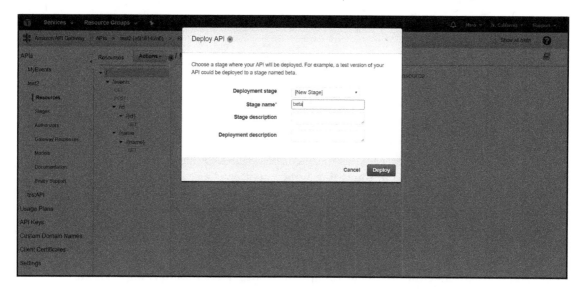

Once we deploy our RESTful API resources to a stage, we can start using it. We can find out the API URLs for our AWS API gateway door to our events microservice by navigating to **Stages**, then clicking on the desired resource to explore, the selected resource API URL is defined here as `Invoke URL`. In the below figure, we selected the **events** resource, the API URL can be found on the right hand side:

DynamoDB

DynamoDB is a very important part of the AWS ecosystem; it typically serves as the backend database for numerous cloud native applications. DynamoDB is a distributed high-performance database hosted in the cloud, which is offered as a service by AWS.

DynamoDB components

Before we discuss how to write code that can interact with DynamoDB, we will need to first cover some important concepts regarding the database. DynamoDB consists of the following components:

- **Tables**: Like a typical database engine, DynamoDB stores data in a collection of tables. For example, in our MyEvents application, we can have an `events` table that would store events information such as concert names and start dates. Similarly, we can also have a `bookings` table to host booking information for our users. We can also have a `users` table to store our users information.

- **Items**: Items are nothing more than the rows of the DynamoDB tables. Information inside an item is known as attributes. If we take the `events` table as an example, an item would be a single event in that table. Similarly, if we take the `users` table as an example, each item is a user. Each item in the table needs a unique identifier, also known as primary key, that will distinguish the item from all the other items in the table.
- **Attributes**: As mentioned in the previous point, attributes represent the information inside an item. Each item consists of one or more attributes. You can think of an attribute as the holders of your data. Each attribute consists of an attribute name and attribute value. If we take the `events` table as an example, each `event` item will have an `ID` attribute to represent the event ID, a `name` attribute to represent an event name, a `startdate` attribute, an `enddate` attribute, and so on.

The item primary key is the only attribute in an item that must be defined beforehand. However, any other attribute inside an item doesn't need to be predefined. This makes DynamoDB a schemaless database, which means that the structure of the database table does not need to be defined before filling the table with data.

Most of the attributes in DynamoDB are scalar. This means that they can have only one value. An example of a scalar attribute is a string attribute or number attribute. Some attributes can be nested, where an attribute can host another attribute and so on. Attributes are allowed to get nested up to 32 levels deep.

Attribute value data types

As mentioned earlier, each DynamoDB attribute consists of an attribute name and an attribute value. The attribute value in turn consists of two pieces: the value's data type name, and the value data. In this section, we'll focus on the data types.

There are three main data types categories:

- **Scalar Types**: This is the simplest data type; it represents a single value. The scalar type category encompasses the following data type names:
    - `S`: This is simply a string type; it utilizes the UTF-8 encoding; the length of the string must be between zero and 400 KB.
    - `N`: This is a number type. They can be positive, negative, or simply zero. They can go up to 38 digits precision.

- B: An attribute of type binary. Binary data includes compressed texts, encrypted data, or images. The length needs to be between 0 and 400 KB. Our applications must encode binary data values in base64-encoded format before sending them to DynamoDB.
- *BOOL*: An attribute of Boolean. It can be either true or false.

- **Document Types**: The document types is a complex structure with nested attributes. There are two data types name that fall under this category:
    - L: An attribute of type list. This type can store an ordered collection of values. There are no restrictions on the data types that can be stored in a list.
    - *Map*: A map type stores data in an unordered collection of name-value pairs.

- **Set Types**: A set type can represent multiple scalar values. All items in a set type must be of the same type. There are three data type names that fall under this category:
    - *NS*: A set of numbers
    - SS: A set of strings
    - BS: A set of binary values

Primary keys

As mentioned earlier, the only part of a DynamoDB table item that needs to be defined beforehand is the primary key. In this section, we'll take a deeper look into the primary keys of the DynamoDB database engine. The main task of the primary key is to uniquely identify each item in a table so that no two items can have the same key.

DynamoDB supports two different kinds of primary keys:

- **Partition key**: This is a simple type of primary key. It is composed of one attribute known as the partition key. DynamoDB stores its data in multiple partitions. A partition is the storage layer for a DynamoDB table, backed by solid state hard drives. The partition key's value is used as an input to an internal hash function, which generates an output that determines the partition in which the item will be stored.

- **Composite key**: This type of key is composed of two attributes. The first attribute is the partition key which we discussed earlier, whereas the second attribute is what is known as the 'sort key'. If you utilize a composite key as your primary key, then more than one item can share the same partition key. Items with the same partition key are stored together. The sort key is then utilized to sort items with the same partition key. The sort key must be unique for each item.

Each primary key attribute must be a scalar, which means it can only hold a single value. There are three datatypes allowed for primary key attributes—a string, number, or binary.

Secondary indexes

Primary keys in DynamoDB provide efficient and fast access to items in tables, when we query the items via their primary keys. However, there are a lot of scenarios where we may want to query items in tables via attributes other than the primary keys. DynamoDB allows us to create secondary indexes that target attributes different than primary key attributes. These indexes enable us to run efficient queries on nonprimary key items.

A secondary index is nothing more than a data structure that contains a subset of attributes from a table. A table is allowed to have multiple secondary indexes, which provides flexibility when querying data from tables.

In order to further understand secondary queries, we will need to cover some basic definitions:

- **Base Table**: Each and every secondary index belongs to exactly one table. The table from which the index is based and from where the index obtains its data is called the base table.
- **Projected attributes**: Project attributes are the attributes that get copied from the base table into the index. DynamoDB copies these attributes into the data structure of the index, along with the primary keys of the base table.
- **Global secondary index**: An index with a partition key and a sort key that are different from those on the base table. This type of index is considered `global` because queries performed on that index can span all the data in the base table. You can create a global secondary index either at the same time you create a table or at a later time.

- **Local secondary index**: An index with the same partition key as the base table, but a different sort key. This type of index is `local` because every partition of a local secondary index is associated with the base table partition that has the same partition key value. You can only create a local secondary index at the same time when you create a table.

Creating tables

Let's make use of the AWS web console to create DynamoDB tables that we can then access later in our code. The first step is to visit the AWS management console main dashboard, then click on **DynamoDB**:

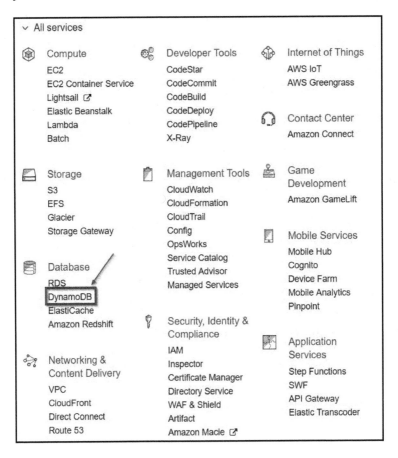

After clicking on **DynamoDB**, we will move to the **DynamoDB** main dashboard, where we can create a new table:

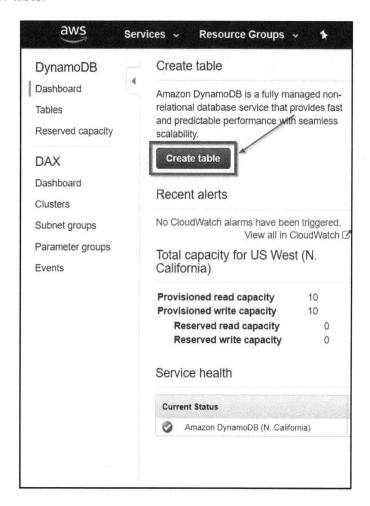

The next step is to pick the table name and the primary keys. As we mentioned earlier, the primary key in DynamoDB can consist of up to two attributes—the partition key and the sort key. Let's say we are creating a table called `events`. Let's use a simple primary key that consists only of a partition key called `ID` that is of the `Binary` type:

We will also leave the default settings. We will revisit some of those settings such as secondary indexes later. After we are done with the configuration, we will need to click on **Create** to create the table. We will then repeat the process with all other tables that we would like to create:

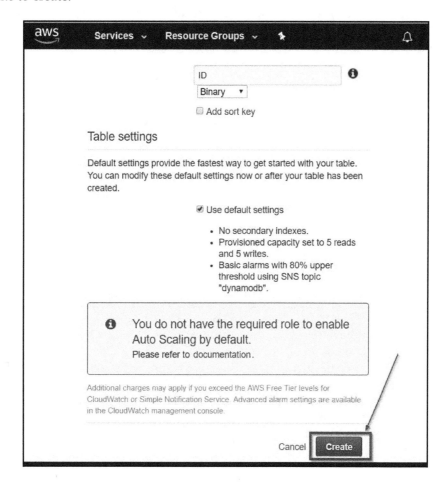

Once a table is created, we can now connect to it, edit it, and read from it through our code. However, before we start discussing code, we will need to create a secondary index. To do that, we will need to first visit our newly created table by selecting the **Tables** option on the left-hand side. We will then select the `events` table from tables list. Afterward, we will need to pick the **Indexes** tab, then click on **Create Index** to create a new secondary index:

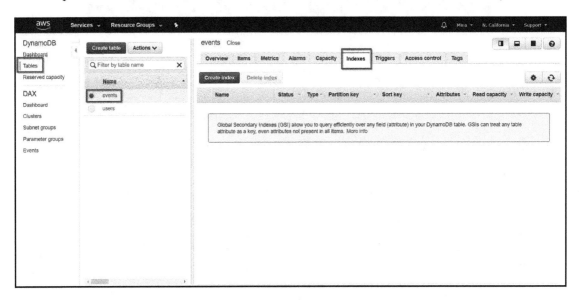

The secondary index name needs to be the attribute name from our table that we would like to use as our secondary index. In our case, the attribute that we would like to use for queries is the event name. This attribute represents the index that we need in order to run an efficient query when querying for events by their names instead of their IDs. Here is what the **Create index** dialog looks like; let's fill the different fields, then click on **Create Index**:

Perfect! With this step, we now have our table ready for our code. Note that in the screenshot above how the index name is `EventName-index`. We will utilize that name later in our Go code.

The Go language and DynamoDB

Amazon has provided the Go language with powerful packages that we can utilize to build applications that can efficiently interact with DynamoDB. The main package can be found at `https://docs.aws.amazon.com/sdk-for-go/api/service/dynamodb/`.

Before we start diving into the code, let's take a refresher on the `DatabaseHandler` interface we discussed in `Chapter 2`, *Building Microservices Using Rest APIs*. This interface represents the database handler layer of our microservices, which is where the database access code lives. In case of the `events` service, this interface supported four methods. Here is what it looked like:

```
type DatabaseHandler interface {
  AddEvent(Event) ([]byte, error)
  FindEvent([]byte) (Event, error)
  FindEventByName(string) (Event, error)
  FindAllAvailableEvents() ([]Event, error)
}
```

In our quest to gain a practical understanding on how to write applications that can work with DynamoDB, we will implement the preceding four methods to utilize DynamoDB as the backend database.

Similar to other AWS services, the AWS Go SDK provides a service client object that we can use to interact with DynamoDB. Also, similar to other AWS services, we will need to obtain a session object first, then use it to create a DynamoDB service client object. Here is what that code should look like:

```
sess, err := session.NewSession(&aws.Config{
  Region: aws.String("us-west-1"),
})
if err != nil {
  //handler error, let's assume we log it then exit.
  log.Fatal(err)
}
dynamodbsvc := dynamodb.New(sess)
```

`dynamodbsvc` ends up being our service client object, which we can then use to interact with DynamoDB.

Now, we will need to create a new file called dynamolayer.go, which will exist under the relative folder `./lib/persistence/dynamolayer`, which is under our application:

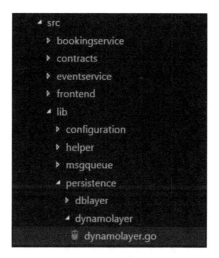

The `dynamolayer.go` file is where our code will live. The first step we will need to follow in order to implement the `databasehandler` interface is to create a `struct` type, which will implement the interface methods. Let's call the new type `DynamoDBLayer`; here is what the code will look like:

```
type DynamoDBLayer struct {
  service *dynamodb.DynamoDB
}
```

The `DynamoDBLayer` struct contains one field of type `*dynamodb.DynamoDB`; this struct field represents the AWS service client for DynamoDB, which is the key object type we'll use in our code to interact with DynamoDB.

The next step is to write some constructors to initialize the `DynamoDBLayer` struct. We will create two constructors—the first constructor assumes that we don't have an existing AWS session object to use in our code. It will take a single string argument, which represents our AWS region (for example, `us-west-1`). It will then utilize the region string to create a session object targeting that region. Afterward, the session object will be used to create a DynamoDB service client object, which can be assigned to a new `DynamoDBLayer` object. Here is what the first constructor will look like:

```
func NewDynamoDBLayerByRegion(region string) (persistence.DatabaseHandler,
error) {
  sess, err := session.NewSession(&aws.Config{
    Region: aws.String(region),
  })
  if err != nil {
    return nil, err
```

```
    }
    return &DynamoDBLayer{
        service: dynamodb.New(sess),
    }, nil
}
```

The second constructor is the one we would use if we already had an existing AWS session object. It takes the session object as an argument, then use it to create a new DynamoDB service client, which we can assign to a new `DynamoDBLayer` object. Here is what the code will look like:

```
func NewDynamoDBLayerBySession(sess *session.Session)
persistence.DatabaseHandler {
    return &DynamoDBLayer{
        service: dynamodb.New(sess),
    }
}
```

Perfect! Now, with the constructors out of the way, let's implement the `DatabaseHandler` interface methods.

Before we continue writing our code, we will need to first cover two important concepts:

- `*dynamoDB.AttributeValue`: This is a struct type that lives inside the dynamodb Go package. It represents a DynamoDB item attribute value.
- `dynamodbattribute`: This is a subpackage that falls underneath the dynamodb package. The docs for this package can be found at: `https://docs.aws.amazon.com/sdk-for-go/api/service/dynamodb/dynamodbattribute/`. The package is responsible for converting between Go types and `dynamoDB.AttributeValues`. This provides a very convenient way to convert Go types inside our application into types that can be understood by the dynamoDB package methods, and vice versa. `dynamodbattribute` can convert slices, maps, structs, and even scalar values to and from `dynamoDB.AttributeValues` by utilizing marshal and unmarshal methods.

We will be utilizing the power of the dynamoDB.AttributeValue type as well as the dynamodbattribute package from now on to write code capable of working with DynamoDB.

The first DatabaseHandler interface method that we will cover is the AddEvent() method. This method takes an argument of the Event type, and then adds it as an item into the events table in the database. Before we start covering the method's code, we will need to first understand the AWS SDK components that we'll need to utilize:

- AddEvent() will need to make use of an AWS SDK method called PutItem()
- The PutItem() method takes an argument of the PutItemInput type
- PutItemInput needs two pieces of information to serve our purposes—the table name, and the item that we would like to add
- The table name field of the PutItemInput type is of the *string type, whereas the item is of the map[string]*AttributeValue type
- In order to convert our Go type Event into map[string]*AttributeValue, which as per the preceding point is the item field type we will need for PutItemInput, we can utilize a method called dynamodbattribute.MarshalMap()

There is one more important remark we will need to cover; the following is what our Event type looks like:

```
type Event struct {
  ID bson.ObjectId `bson:"_id"`
  Name string
  Duration int
  StartDate int64
  EndDate int64
  Location Location
}
```

It contains all the key information we typically need to describe an event such as a concert. However, when working with DynamoDB, there is one issue with the `Event` type—the keyword `Name` is a reserved keyword in the DynamoDB world. This means that if we leave the struct like this, we won't be able to use the `Name` field of the Event struct in our queries. Fortunately, the `dynamodbattribute` package supports a struct tag called `dynamodbav`, which allows us to mask the struct field name with another name. This will allow us to use the struct field Name in our Go code, but have it exposed as a different name to DynamoDB. The following is what the code will look like after adding the struct field:

```go
type Event struct {
  ID bson.ObjectId `bson:"_id"`
  Name string `dynamodbav:"EventName"`
  Duration int
  StartDate int64
  EndDate int64
  Location Location
}
```

In the preceding code, we utilized the `dynamodbav` struct tag to define the `Name` struct field as `EventName` when interfacing with DynamoDB.

Perfect! Now, let's look at the `AddEvent()` method code:

```go
func (dynamoLayer *DynamoDBLayer) AddEvent(event persistence.Event)
([]byte, error) {
  av, err := dynamodbattribute.MarshalMap(event)
  if err != nil {
    return nil, err
  }
  _, err = dynamoLayer.service.PutItem(&dynamodb.PutItemInput{
    TableName: aws.String("events"),
    Item: av,
  })
  if err != nil {
    return nil, err
  }
  return []byte(event.ID), nil
}
```

The first step in the preceding code was to marshal the event object to `map[string]*AttributeValue`. The next step was to call the `PutItem()` method, which belongs to the DynamoDB service client. `PutItem` took an argument of the `PutItemInput` type as discussed earlier, which contained the table name and the marshaled item data that we would like to add. At the end, if no errors occur, we will return a byte representation of the event ID.

The next `DatabaseHandler` interface method that we will need to discuss is `FindEvent()`. This method retrieves an event via its ID. Remember here that when we created the `events` table, we set the ID attribute as its key. Here are some points we will need to cover to understand the incoming piece of code:

- `FindEvent()` utilizes an AWS SDK method called `GetItem()`.
- `FindEvent()` takes an argument of the `GetItemInput` type.
- The `GetItemInput` type needs two pieces of information: the table name and the value of the item key.
- The `GetItem()` method returns a struct type called `GetItemOutput`, which has a field called `Item`. The `Item` field is where our retrieved database table item will be hosted.
- The item obtained from the database will be represented with the `map[string]*AttributeValue` type. We can then make use of the `dynamodbattribute.UnmarshalMap()` function to convert it to an `Event` type.

Here is what the code will look like at the end:

```
func (dynamoLayer *DynamoDBLayer) FindEvent(id []byte) (persistence.Event,
error) {
  //create a GetItemInput object with the information we need to search for
our event via it's ID attribute
  input := &dynamodb.GetItemInput{
    Key: map[string]*dynamodb.AttributeValue{
      "ID": {
        B: id,
      },
    },
    TableName: aws.String("events"),
  }
  //Get the item via the GetItem method
  result, err := dynamoLayer.service.GetItem(input)
  if err != nil {
    return persistence.Event{}, err
  }
  //Utilize dynamodbattribute.UnmarshalMap to unmarshal the data retrieved
into an Event object
  event := persistence.Event{}
  err = dynamodbattribute.UnmarshalMap(result.Item, &event)
  return event, err
}
```

Note in the preceding code that the `Key` field of the `GetItemInput` struct was of the `map[string]*AttributeValue` type. The key to this map is the attribute name, which is `ID` in our case, whereas the value of this map is of the `*AttributeValue` type and is as follows:

```
{
    B: id,
}
```

The `B` in the preceding code is a struct field in `AttributeValue`, which represents a binary type, whereas `id` is simply the byte slice argument that got passed to our `FindEvent()` method. The reason why we used the binary type field is because our ID key attribute of the events table was of type binary.

Let's now move to the third `DatabaseHandler` interface method for the events microservice, which is the `FindEventByName()` method. This method retrieves an event via its name. Remember that when we created the `events` table earlier, we set the `EventName` attribute as the secondary index. The reason why we did that is because we wanted the ability to query items from the `events` table via the event names. Again, before we start covering the code, here is what we need to know about the method:

- `FindEventByName()` utilizes an AWS SDK method called `Query()` in order to query the database.
- The `Query()` method takes an argument of the `QueryInput` type, which needs four pieces of information:
    - The query that we would like to execute, in our case, the query is simply `EventName = :n`.
    - The value of `:n` in the above expression. This is a parameter that we will need to fill with the name of the event we are trying to find.
    - The index name that we would like to utilize for our query. In our case, the secondary index we created for the EventName attribute was called `EventName-index`
    - The table name where we would like to run the query.
- If the `Query()` method succeeds, we get our result items as slice of maps; the result items will be of the `[]map[string]*AttributeValue` type. Since we only seek a single item, we can just retrieve the first item of that map slice.

- The `Query()` method returns an object of the type `QueryOutput` struct, which contains a field called `Items`. The `Items` field is where our query result set will be hosted.
- We then will need to utilize the `dynamodbattribute.UnmarshalMap()` function in order to convert the item of the `map[string]*AttributeValue` type into an `Event` type.

Here is what the code will look like:

```
func (dynamoLayer *DynamoDBLayer) FindEventByName(name string)
(persistence.Event, error) {
  //Create the QueryInput type with the information we need to execute the
query
  input := &dynamodb.QueryInput{
    KeyConditionExpression: aws.String("EventName = :n"),
    ExpressionAttributeValues: map[string]*dynamodb.AttributeValue{
      ":n": {
        S: aws.String(name),
      },
    },
    IndexName: aws.String("EventName-index"),
    TableName: aws.String("events"),
  }
  // Execute the query
  result, err := dynamoLayer.service.Query(input)
  if err != nil {
    return persistence.Event{}, err
  }
  //Obtain the first item from the result
  event := persistence.Event{}
  if len(result.Items) > 0 {
    err = dynamodbattribute.UnmarshalMap(result.Items[0], &event)
  } else {
    err = errors.New("No results found")
  }
  return event, err
}
```

Queries in DynamoDB is an important topic. I recommend that you read the AWS docs explaining queries, which can be found at `http://docs.aws.amazon.com/amazondynamodb/latest/developerguide/Query.html` to properly understand how queries work in DynamoDB.

The last `DatabaseHandler` interface method we will discuss in this chapter is the `FindAllAvailableEvents()` method. This method retrieves all the items of the 'events' table in DynamoDB. Here is what we need to know before diving into the code:

- `FindAllAvailableEvents()` needs to utilize an AWS SDK method called `Scan()`. This method performs a scan operation. A scan operation can be simply defined as a read that goes through every single item in a table or in a secondary index.
- The `Scan()` method requires an argument of the type `ScanInput` struct.
- The `ScanInput` type needs to know the table name in order to perform the scan operation.
- The `Scan()` method returns an object of the `ScanOutput` struct type. The `ScanOutput` struct contains a field called `Items` of the `[]map[string]*AttributeValue` type. This is where the results of the scan operation will go.
- The `Items` struct field can be converted to a slice of `Event` types via the `dynamodbattribute.UnmarshalListofMaps()` function.

The code looks as follows:

```
func (dynamoLayer *DynamoDBLayer) FindAllAvailableEvents()
([]persistence.Event, error) {
  // Create the ScanInput object with the table name
  input := &dynamodb.ScanInput{
    TableName: aws.String("events"),
  }

  // Perform the scan operation
  result, err := dynamoLayer.service.Scan(input)
  if err != nil {
    return nil, err
  }

  // Obtain the results via the unmarshalListofMaps function
  events := []persistence.Event{}
  err = dynamodbattribute.UnmarshalListOfMaps(result.Items, &events)
  return events, err
}
```

One important remark to mention about scan operations is that since in a production environment, a scan operation can return a massive number of results, it is sometimes advised to utilize the pagination feature of the AWS SDK that we mentioned in the preceding chapter with the scans. The pagination feature allows the results of your operations to come in multiple pages, which you can then iterate through. Scan pagination can be performed via the `ScanPages()` method.

Summary

In this chapter, we took a practical dive into some of the most popular services in the AWS world. By now, we have covered enough knowledge to build production-level Go applications that are capable of utilizing some of the key features that AWS provides for cloud native applications.

In the next chapter, we'll take another step to learn more about building Go cloud native applications by covering the topic of continuous delivery.

9
Continuous Delivery

In the previous three chapters, you learned about modern container technologies and cloud environments, how to create container images from your application (or, more precisely, the MyEvents application), and how to deploy them into these environments.

In this chapter, you will learn how to adopt **continuous integration** (**CI**) and **continuous delivery** (**CD**) for anjhalocvhurty your application. CI describes a practice in which you continuously build and verify your software project (ideally, on each and every change made to your software). CD extends this approach by also continually deploying your application in very short release cycles (in this case, of course, into a cloud environment).

Both of these approaches require a high degree of automation to work reliably, both concerning your application's build and deployment processes. In previous chapters, we have already looked at how you can use container technologies to deploy your application. Since technologies such as Docker and Kubernetes are easily automated, they usually integrate very well with CD.

In the course of this chapter, you will learn how to set up your project for adopting CI and CD (for example, by setting up proper version control and dependency management). We will also introduce a few popular tools that you can use to trigger new builds and releases automatically whenever your application's code changes.

We will cover the following topics in this chapter:

- Managing a Go project in version control
- Using dependency vendoring for reproducible builds
- Using Travis CI and/or GitLab to automatically build your application
- Automatically deploying your application to a Kubernetes cluster

Setting up your project

Before actually implementing continuous delivery for our project, let's start by making some preparations. Later, these will make it easier for the tools that we will use to easily build and deploy your application in an automated way.

Setting up version control

Before automatically building your application, you will need a place to store your application's source code. This is typically the job of a **version control system** (**VCS**). Often, the tools that enable you to do continuous delivery are tightly integrated with version control systems, for example, by triggering a new build and deployment of your application whenever the source code is changed.

If you did not do this already on your own, your first step should now be to put your existing code base into a VCS. In this example, we will be working with the current de facto standard VCS, Git. Although there are many other version control systems, Git is the most widely adopted; you will find many providers and tools that offer you Git repositories as a managed service or for self-hosting. Also, many (if not most) CD tools are integrated with Git.

For the remainder of this chapter, we will assume that you are familiar with the basic workings of Git. If you wish to read up on how to work with Git, we recommend the book *Git: Mastering Version Control* by *Ferdinando Santacroce et al.*, also published by Packt.

We will also assume that you have two remote Git repositories available where you can push your Go application source code and the frontend application source code. For the first continuous delivery tool that we will be working with, we will assume that your repositories are hosted at GitHub at the following URLs:

- `git+ssh://git@github.com/<user>/myevents.git`
- `git+ssh://git@github.com/<user>/myevents-frontend.git`

Of course, the actual repository URLs will vary according to your username. In the following examples, we will use `<user>` consistently as a placeholder for your GitHub username, so remember to replace it with your actual username whenever necessary.

You can start by setting up a local Git repository to track changes to your source code on your local machine. To initialize a new Git repository, run the following command in your Go project's root directory (typically, `todo.com/myevents` in your GOPATH directory):

```
$ git init .
```

This will set up a new Git repository, but not add any files to version control, yet. Before actually adding any files to your repository, configure a `.gitignore` file that prevents Git from adding your compiled files to version control:

```
/eventservice/eventservice
/bookingservice/bookingservice
```

After having created the `.gitignore` file, run the following commands to add your current code base to the version control system:

```
$ git add .
$ git commit -m "Initial commit"
```

Next, configure your remote repository using the `git remote` command and push your source code using `git push`:

```
$ git remote add origin ssh://git@github.com/<user>/myevents.git
$ git push origin master
```

Having a working source code repository is the first step to building a continuous integration/delivery pipeline. In the following steps, we will configure CI/CD tools to build and deploy your application whenever you push new code into the master branch of your remote Git repository.

Use the same Git commands to create a new Git repository for your frontend application, and to push it to a remote repository on GitHub.

Vendoring your dependencies

Up until now, we have simply installed Go libraries that we needed for the MyEvents application (such as the `gopkg.in/mgo.v2` or the `github.com/gorilla/mux` packages) using the `go get` command. Although this works reasonably well for development, installing dependencies using `go get` has one significant disadvantage, that is, each time you run `go get` on a package that has not yet been downloaded, it will get the most recent version of that library (technically, the latest *master* branch of the respective source code repository). This can have nasty consequences; imagine that you have cloned your repository at one point in time and installed all dependencies using `go get ./...`. A week later, you repeat these steps, but may now wind up with completely different versions of your dependencies (libraries that are actively maintained and developed may get dozens of new commits to its master branch each day). This is especially critical if one of these changes changed the libraries' API, which may result in your code not compiling anymore from one day to the next.

To solve this issue, Go 1.6 introduced the concept of **vendoring**. Using vendoring allows you to copy libraries that your project requires into a `vendor/` directory within your package (so, in our case, `todo.com/myevents/vendor/` will contain directories such as `todo.com/myevents/vendor/github.com/gorilla/mux/`). When running `go build` to compile a package, libraries from the `vendor/` directory will be favored over libraries in your GOPATH. You can then simply put the `vendor/` directory into version control alongside your application code and have reproducible builds when cloning your source code repository.

Of course, manually copying libraries into your package's `vendor/` directory quickly becomes tedious. Typically, this work is being done by **dependency managers**. Currently, there are multiple dependency managers for Go, the most popular being **Godep** and **Glide**. These are both community projects; an official dependency manager, simply called **dep**, is currently in development and already considered safe for production use, but was, at the time of writing this book, still designated as an experiment.

 You can find more information on dep at `https://github.com/golang/dep`.

In this case, we will populate our application's `vendor/` directory using Glide. First of all, install Glide by running the following command:

```
$ curl https://glide.sh/get | sh
```

This will place a glide executable in your `$GOPATH/bin` directory. If you want to use glide globally, you can copy it from there into your path as follows:

```
$ cp $GOPATH/bin/glide /usr/local/bin/glide
```

Glide works similar to package managers that you might know from other programming languages (for example, npm for Node.js or Compose for PHP). It operates by reading a `glide.yaml` file from your package directory. In this file, you declare all dependencies that your application has and can optionally provide specific versions of these libraries that Glide should install for you. To create a `glide.yaml` file from an existing application, run the `glide init .` command in your package directory:

```
$ glide init .
```

While initializing your project, Glide will inspect the libraries used by your application and try to automatically optimize your dependency declaration. For example, if Glide finds a library that provides stable versions (usually, Git tags), it will prompt you whether you would prefer using the latest of these stable versions instead of the (potentially more unstable) master branch of a dependency.

When running `glide init`, it will produce an output similar to this:

The `glide init` command will create a `glide.yaml` file in your application's root directory in which all required dependencies are declared. For the MyEvents application, this file should look similar to this:

```
package: todo.com/myevents
import:
- package: github.com/Shopify/sarama
  version: ^1.11.0
- package: github.com/aws/aws-sdk-go
  version: ^1.8.17
  subpackages:
  - service/dynamodb
- package: github.com/gorilla/handlers
  version: ^1.2.0
# ...
```

The `glide.yaml` file declares which dependencies your project requires. After creating this file, you can run the `glide update` command to actually resolve the declared dependencies and download them into your `vendor/` directory.

As you can see in the preceding screenshot, `glide update` will not only download the dependencies declared in your `glide.yaml` file into the `vendor/` directory, but also their dependencies. In the end, Glide will recursively download the entire dependency tree of your application and place it in the `vendor/` directory:

For each package it downloaded, Glide will write the exact version into a new file, glide.lock (you can take a look at this file by opening it, but it is really not meant to be edited manually). The glide.lock file allows you to reconstruct this exact set of dependencies with their exact versions at any later moment in time by running glide install. You can verify this behavior by deleting your vendor/ directory and then running glide install.

Having a vendor/ directory and the Glide configuration files leaves you with the following two options:

- You can place your entire vendor/ directory into version control alongside your actual application files. The upside of this is that now anyone can clone your repository (anyone, in this case, includes CI/CD tools that want to build and deploy your code) and have all dependencies in their exact required versions readily available. This way, building your application from scratch is literally nothing more than a git clone or go build command. On the downside, your source code repository grows larger and may take more disk space to store and more time to clone.

- Alternatively, you can just place the glide.yaml and glide.lock files into version control and exclude the vendor/ directory from version control by adding it to the .gitignore file. On the upside, this makes your repository smaller and faster to clone. However, after cloning your repository, users will now need to explicitly run glide install to download the dependencies specified in your glide.lock file from the internet.

Both of these options work reasonably well, so ultimately this is a matter of personal taste. Since repository size and disk space are rarely a consideration these days, and because it makes the build process significantly easier, my personal preference is to put my entire vendor/ directory into version control:

```
$ git add vendor
$ git commit -m"Add dependencies"
$ git push
```

This takes care of our backend services, but there is also still the frontend application that we need to consider. Since we have been using npm to install our dependencies in Chapter 5, *Building a Frontend with React*, most of the work has been already done for us. Interestingly, the exact same argument about whether to put dependencies into version control or not (in this case, the node_modules/ directory instead of vendor/) also applies to npm. Also, yes, just as with Go's vendor/ directory, I prefer to put my entire node_modules/ directory in version control:

```
$ git add node_modules
$ git commit -m "Add dependencies"
$ git push
```

Explicitly declaring your project's dependencies (including the used versions) is a big step to ensure reproducible builds. Depending on whether you chose to include your dependencies into version control or not, users have either the entire application source code (including dependencies) readily available directly after cloning the source code repository or can at least easily reconstruct it by running glide install or npm install, respectively.

Now that we have our project put in version control and have explicitly declared dependencies, we can take a look at some of the most popular CI/CD tools that you can use to continuously build and deploy your application.

Using Travis CI

Travis CI is a hosted service for continuous integration. It is very tightly coupled to GitHub (which is why you will need a Git repository on GitHub to actually use Travis CI). It is free to use for open source projects, which, together with its good GitHub integration, makes it the go-to choice for many popular projects. For building private GitHub projects, there is a paid usage model.

The configuration of your Travis build is done by a .travis.yml file that needs to be present at the root level of your repository. Basically, this file can look like this:

```
language: go
go:
  - 1.6
  - 1.7
  - 1.8
  - 1.9
env:
  - CGO_ENABLED=0
```

```
install: true
script:
  - go build
```

The `language` property describes which programming language your project is written in. Depending on whichever language you provide here, you will have different tools available in your build environment. The `go` property describes for which versions of Go your application should be built. Testing your code for multiple versions of Go is especially important for libraries that might be used by a multitude of users in potentially very different environments. The `env` property contains environment variables that should be passed into the built environment. Note that we have used the `CGO_ENABLED` environment variable before in `Chapter 6`, *Deploying Your Application in Containers*, to instruct the Go compiler to produce statically linked binaries.

The `install` property describes the steps necessary to set up your application's dependencies. If left out entirely, Travis will automatically run `go get ./...` to download the latest versions of all our dependencies (which is exactly what we do not want). The `install: true` property actually instructs Travis not to do anything to set up our dependencies, which is exactly the way to go if your dependencies have been already included in your source code repository.

If you decided not to include your `vendor/` directory in version control, the install step needs to contain instructions for Travis to download Glide and then use it to install your project's dependencies:

```
install:
  - go get -v github.com/Masterminds/glide
  - glide install
```

The `script` property then contains the commands that Travis should run to actually build your project. The most obvious step to build your application is, of course, the `go build` command. Of course, you can add additional steps here. For example, you could use the `go vet` command to check your source code for common errors:

```
scripts:
  - go vet $(go list ./... | grep -v vendor)
  - cd eventservice && go build
  - cd bookingservice && go build
```

The `$(go list ./... | grep -v vendor)` command is a special hack used to instruct `go vet` not to analyze the `vendor/` source code in your package directory. Otherwise, `go vet` would probably complain about a lot of issues in your project's dependencies that you would not want to (or even can not) fix, anyway.

After creating the `.travis.yml` file, add it to version control and push it into the remote repository:

```
$ git add .travis.yml
$ git commit -m "Configure Travis CI"
$ git push
```

Now that you have a *.travis.yml* file in your repository, you can enable the Travis build for this repository. For this, sign in to Travis CI on `https://travis-ci.org` (or `https://travis-ci.com` if you are planning to use the paid tier) using your GitHub credentials. After signing in, you will find a list of your publicly available GitHub repositories, alongside a switch that allows you to enable Travis builds for each repository (just as in the following screenshot):

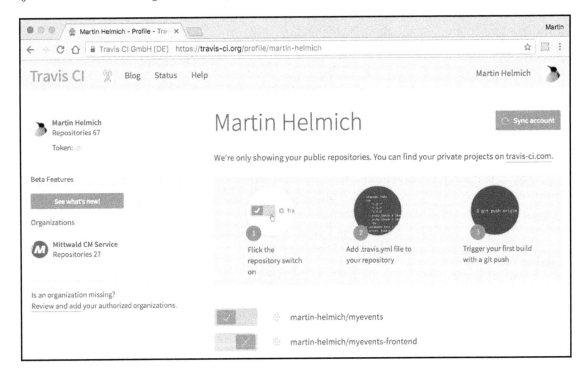

Go ahead and enable both the `myevents` and `myevents-frontend` repositories (it's not that bad if there's no `.travis.yml` file in one of these repositories, yet).

After enabling your project in the Travis user interface, the next Git push into your repository will automatically trigger a build on Travis. You can test this, for example, by making a small change to your code or by just adding a new empty text file somewhere and pushing it to GitHub. In the Travis user interface, you will note a new build popping up for your project quickly.

The build will run for a while (it may take a while from the build being scheduled to the actual execution). After that, you will see whether the build was completed successfully or whether errors occurred (you will also receive a notification via email in the latter case), as follows:

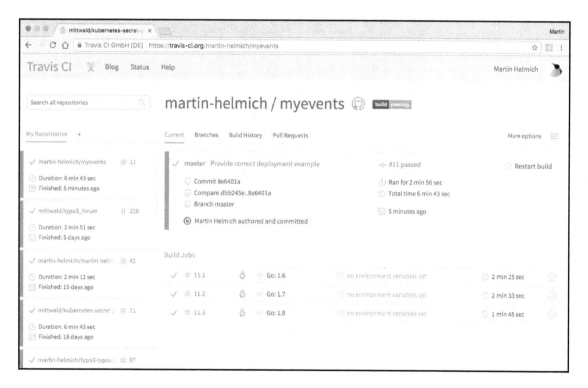

If you have specified multiple Go versions to test against, you will note multiple build jobs for each commit (just like in the preceding screenshot). Click on any one of them to receive a detailed build output. This is especially useful if your build should fail for any reason (which is entirely possible when you push code that does not pass `go vet` or does not even compile).

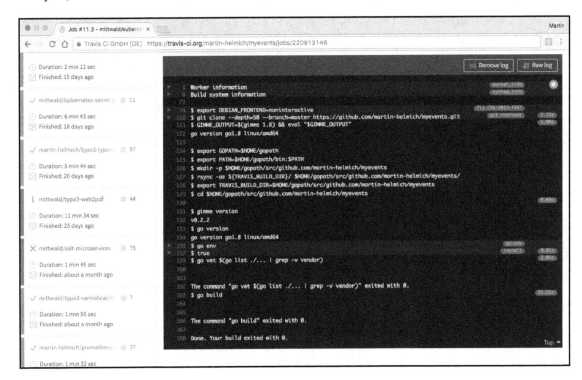

In general, Travis integrates with GitHub really well. In the GitHub UI, you will also see the current build status of each commit and can also use Travis to verify pull requests before they are being merged into the master branch.

So far, we have used Travis to verify that the code in the repository does not contain any errors and compiles (which is typically the goal of continuous integration). However, we have not yet configured any actual deployment of your application. This is what we'll be doing in the following steps.

Within a Travis build, you can use Docker to build and run container images. To enable Docker support, add the following properties to the top of your `.travis.yml` file:

```
sudo: required
services:
  - docker
language: go
go:
  - 1.9
```

Since we do not actually want to build Docker images for multiple different versions of Go, it is also completely alright to remove the Go versions 1.6 to 1.8 from the Travis file.

As our project actually consists of two deployment artifacts (event service and booking service), there is another optimization that we can make: we can use a build matrix to build both of these services in parallel. For this, add an `env` property to your `.travis.yml` file and adjust the `script` property, as follows:

```
sudo: required
services:
  - docker
language: go
go: 1.9
env:
  global:
    - CGO_ENABLED=0
  matrix:
    - SERVICE=eventservice
    - SERVICE=bookingservice
 install: true
script:
  - go vet $(go list ./... | grep -v vendor)
  - cd $SERVICE && go build
```

With this configuration, Travis will start two build jobs for each change in your code repository, each of those building one of the two services contained in that repository.

After that, you can add a `docker image build` command to the `script` property to build a container image from the compiled service:

```
script:
  - go vet $(go list ./... | grep -v vendor)
  - cd $SERVICE && go build
  - docker image build -t myevents/$SERVICE:$TRAVIS_BRANCH $SERVICE
```

The preceding command builds a Docker image named either myevents/eventservice or myevents/bookingservice (dependent on the current value of $SERVICE). The Docker image is built with the current branch (or Git tag) name as the tag. This means that a new push to the *master* branch will result in a myevents/eventservice:master image being built. When a Git tag named *v1.2.3* is pushed, a myevents/eventservice:v1.2.3 image will be created.

Lastly, you will need to push the new Docker image to a registry. For this, add a new property, after_success, to your .travis.yml file:

```
after_success:
  - if [ -n "${TRAVIS_TAG}" ] ; then
      docker login -u="${DOCKER_USERNAME}" -p="${DOCKER_PASSWORD}";
      docker push myevents/$SERVICE:$TRAVIS_BRANCH;
    fi
```

The commands specified in after_success will be run after all commands in scripts have successfully been completed. In this case, we are checking the content of the $TRAVIS_TAG environment variable; as a consequence, only Docker images built for Git tags will actually be pushed to the remote registry.

If you are using a different Docker Image Registry than the Docker Hub, remember to specify the registry's URL in the docker login command. For example, when using quay.io as registry, the command should look as follows: docker login -u="${DOCKER_USERNAME}" -p"${DOCKER_PASSWORD}" quay.io.

For this command to work, you will need to have the environment variables $DOCKER_USERNAME and $DOCKER_PASSWORD defined. In theory, you could define these in the env section of your .travis.yml file. However, for sensitive data such as passwords, it would be a massively stupid idea to define them in a publicly available file for everyone to see. Instead, you should use the Travis user interface to configure these variables for your build. For this, go to the **Settings** page of your project, which you will find when clicking on the **More options** button on your project overview page:

In the project settings, you will find a section labeled **Environment Variables**. Configure your Docker Registry credentials here by specifying the DOCKER_USERNAME and DOCKER_PASSWORD variables:

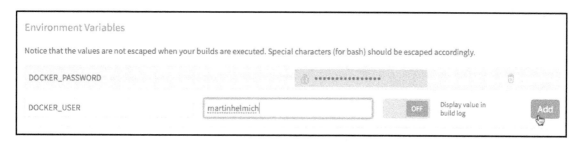

Alternatively, you can add secret variables to your .travis.yml file by encrypting them before placing them in version control. For this, you will need the Travis command-line client CLI. Travis CLI is a Ruby tool that you can install via the Ruby package manager, gem:

```
$ gem install travis
```

After that, you can use the Travis CLI to encrypt a variable and automatically add it to your .travis.yml file:

```
$ travis encrypt DOCKER_PASSWORD="my-super-secret-password" --add
```

This will add a new variable to your .travis.yml file that looks like this:

```
...
env:
  global:
    - secure: <encrypted value>
```

Both adding your secret variables via the Travis UI and encrypting and adding them to your .travis.yml file are valid approaches for handling sensitive data in Travis builds.

Save the new build configuration in .travis.yml and push it to GitHub. To build and publish a new Docker image, you can now push a new git tag:

```
$ git tag v1.0.0
$ git push --tags
```

At this point, Travis CI will pull your code, compile all your Go binaries, and publish two Docker images for the two backend services to the Docker registry configured in your build configuration.

We will still need to add a similar build configuration for the frontend application. Actually, the steps for building the Docker image are exactly identical; however, instead of go build, we will need to run the Webpack module bundler. The following is a .travis.yml file that should cover the entire frontend build:

```
language: node_js
node_js:
  - 6
env:
  - SERVICE=frontend
install:
  - npm install -g webpack typescript
  - npm install
script:
  - webpack
after_success:
  - if [ -n "${TRAVIS_TAG}" ] ; then
    docker login -u="${DOCKER_USERNAME}" -p="${DOCKER_PASSWORD}";
    docker push myevents/${SERVICE}:${TRAVIS_BRANCH};
    fi
```

Deploying to Kubernetes

Using GitHub and Travis, we have now automated the entire workflow from changing the application's source code over building new binaries to creating new Docker images and pushing them to a container registry. That is great, but we are still missing one crucial step, that is, getting the new container images to run in your production environment.

In the previous chapters, you have already worked with Kubernetes and deployed your containerized applications into a Minikube environment. For this section, we will assume that you already have a publicly accessible Kubernetes environment up and running (for example, using a `kops`-provisioned cluster in AWS or the Azure Container Service).

First of all, Travis CI will need to access your Kubernetes cluster. For this, you can create a **service account** in your Kubernetes cluster. This Service Account will then receive an API token that you can configure as a secret environment variable in your Travis build. To create a service account, run the following command on your local machine (assuming that you have `kubectl` set up to communicate with your Kubernetes cluster):

```
$ kubectl create serviceaccount travis-ci
```

The preceding command will create a new service account named `travis-ci` and a new secret object that contains that account's API token. To determine the secret, now run the `kubectl describe serviceaccount travis-ci` command:

```
$ kubectl describe serviceaccount travis-ci
Name:           travis-ci
Namespace:      default
Labels:         <none>
Annotations:    <none>

Image pull secrets:  <none>
Mountable secrets:   travis-ci-token-mtxrh
Tokens:              travis-ci-token-mtxrh
```

Use the token secret name (in this case, `travis-ci-token-mtxrh`) to access the actual API token:

```
$ kubectl get secret travis-ci-token-mtxrh -o=yaml
apiVersion: v1
kind: Secret
data:
  ca.crt: ...
  namespace: ZGVmYXVsdA==
  token: ...
# ...
```

You will need both the `ca.crt` and the `token` properties. Both of these values are BASE64-encoded, so you will need to pipe both values through `base64 --decode` to access the actual values:

```
$ echo "<token from above>" | base64 --decode
$ echo "<ca.crt from above>" | base64 --decode
```

Together with the API server's URL, these two values can be used to authenticate against a Kubernetes cluster from Travis CI (or other CI/CD tools).

To actually configure the Kubernetes deployment in your Travis CI build, start by setting up `kubectl` in your builds by adding the following commands to your `install` section:

```
install:
  - curl -LO https://storage.googleapis.com/kubernetes-
release/release/v1.6.1/bin/linux/amd64/kubectl && chmod +x kubectl
  - echo "${KUBE_CA_CERT}" > ./ca.crt
  - ./kubectl config set-credentials travis-ci --token="${KUBE_TOKEN}"
  - ./kubectl config set-cluster your-cluster --
server=https://your-kubernetes-cluster --certificate-authority=ca.crt
  - ./kubectl config set-context your-cluster --cluster=your-cluster --
user=travis-ci --namespace=default
  - ./kubectl config use-context your-cluster
```

For these steps to work, you will need to have the environment variables `$KUBE_CA_CERT` and `$KUBE_TOKEN` configured as secret environment variables in your Travis CI settings with the values that you took from the preceding `kubectl get secret` command.

After having `kubectl` configured, you can now add an additional step to the `after_success` command of both your projects:

```
after_success:
  - if [ -n "${TRAVIS_TAG}" ] ; then
    docker login -u="${DOCKER_USERNAME}" -p="${DOCKER_PASSWORD}";
    docker push myevents/${SERVICE}:$TRAVIS_BRANCH;
    ./kubectl set image deployment/${SERVICE}
api=myevents/${SERVICE}:${TRAVIS_BRANCH};
    fi
```

The `kubectl set image` command will change the container image that should be used for a given Deployment object (in this case, assuming that you have deployments named `eventservice` and `bookingservice`). The Kubernetes deployment controller will then proceed to create new Pods with the new container image and shut down the Pods running the old image.

Using GitLab

GitHub and Travis are excellent tools for building and deploying open source projects (and also private projects if you do not mind paying for their services). However, in some cases, you might want to host your source code management and CI/CD systems in your own environment instead of relying on an external service provider.

This is where GitLab comes into play. GitLab is a software that offers a service similar to GitHub and Travis combined (meaning source code management and CI) that you can host on your own infrastructure. In the following section, we will show you how to set up your own GitLab instance and build a build and deployment pipeline similar to the one built in the preceding section using GitLab and its CI features.

GitLab offers both an open source **Community Edition** (**CE**) and a paid-for **Enterprise Edition** (**EE**) that offers some additional features. For our purposes, the CE will do just fine.

Setting up GitLab

You can set up your own GitLab instance easily using the Docker images provided by the vendor. To start a GitLab CE server, run the following command:

```
$ docker container run --detach \
  -e GITLAB_OMNIBUS_CONFIG="external_url 'http://192.168.2.125/';" \
  --name gitlab \
  -p 80:80 \
  -p 22:22 \
  gitlab/gitlab-ce:9.1.1-ce.0
```

Note the GITLAB_OMNIBUS_CONFIG environment variable that is passed into the container. This variable can be used to inject configuration code (written in Ruby) into the container; in this case, it is used to configure the GitLab instance's public HTTP address. When starting GitLab on your local machine, it is usually easiest to use your machine's public IP address for this (on Linux or macOS, use the ifconfig command to find it).

If you are setting up GitLab on a server for production usage (as opposed to on your local machine for experimentation), you might want to create two data volumes for configuration and repository data that you can then use in your container. This will allow you to easily upgrade your GitLab installation to a newer version later:

```
$ docker volume create gitlab-config
$ docker volume create gitlab-data
```

After creating the volumes, use the `-v gitlab-config:/etc/gitlab` and `-v gitlab-data:/var/opt/gitlab` flags in your `docker container run` command to actually use these volumes for your Gitlab instance.

The GitLab server running in the newly created container will probably take a few minutes to start up entirely. After that, you can access your GitLab instance at `http://localhost:`

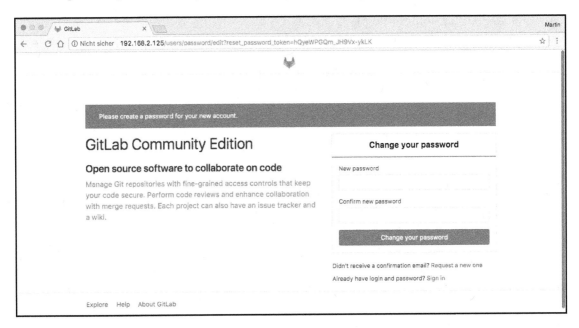

When opening GitLab for the first time in your browser, you will be prompted to set a new password for the initial user. After setting the password, you can sign in with the username `root` and the password that you set previously. If you are setting up a production instance of GitLab, your next step would now be to set up a new user that you can sign in as instead of root. For demo purposes, it is also alright to continue working as root.

After logging in for the first time, you will see a Start page on which you can create new groups and a new project. A GitLab project is (usually) always associated with a Git source code repository. In order to set up a CI/CD pipeline for the MyEvents application, proceed to create two new projects called `myevents` and `myevents-frontend`, as follows:

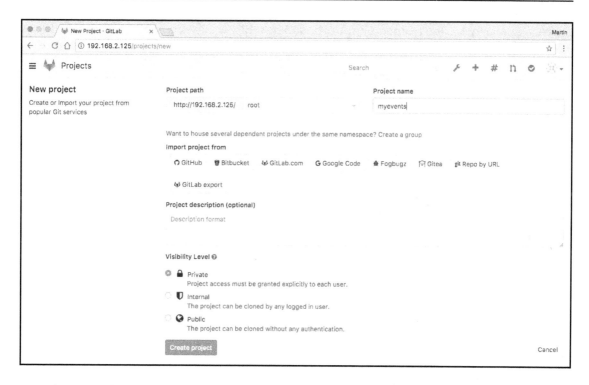

In order to push code into your new GitLab instance, you will need to provide an SSH public key for authentication. For this, click on your user icon in the upper-right corner, select **Settings**, and then the **SSH Keys** tab. Paste your SSH public key into the input field and save it.

Next, add your new GitLab repositories as remotes to your existing MyEvents repositories and push your code:

```
$ git remote add gitlab ssh://git@localhost/root/myevents.git
$ git push gitlab master:master
```

Proceed similarly for the frontend application. After this, you will be able to find your files in the GitLab web UI:

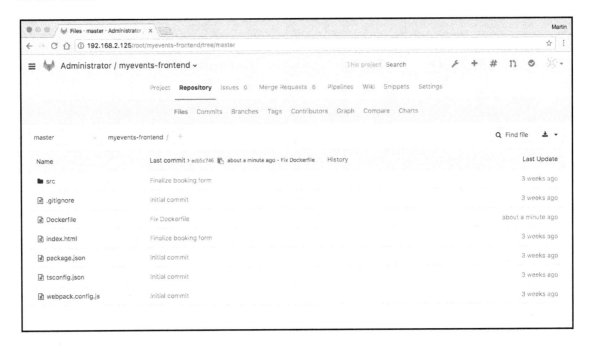

Setting up GitLab CI

In order to use GitLab's CI feature, you will need to set up one additional component: the GitLab CI Runner. While GitLab itself is responsible for managing your application's source code and deciding when to trigger a new CI build, the CI Runner is the component that is responsible for actually executing these jobs. Separating the actual GitLab container from the CI Runner allows you to distribute your CI infrastructure and have, for example, multiple runners on separate machines.

The GitLab CI Runner can also be set up using a Docker image. To set up the CI Runner, run the following command:

```
$ docker container run --detach \
    --name gitlab-runner \
    --link gitlab:gitlab \
    -v /var/run/docker.sock:/var/run/docker.sock \
    gitlab/gitlab-runner:v1.11.4
```

After starting the GitLab CI Runner, you will need to register it at the main GitLab instance. For this, you will need the runners registration token. You can find this token in the Admin Area of the GitLab UI. Access the **Admin Area** via the wrench icon in the upper-right corner, then select **Runners**. You will find the runners registration token in the first text paragraph:

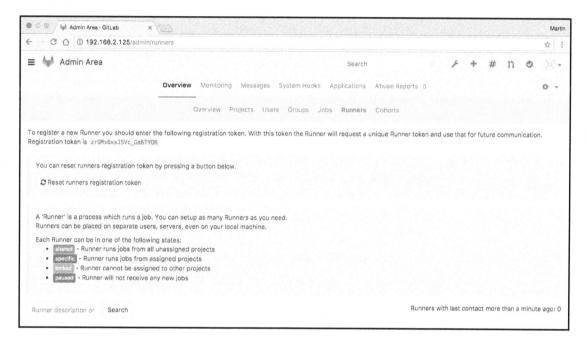

To register your runner, run the following command:

```
$ docker container exec \
    -it gitlab-runner \
    gitlab-runner register -n \
      --url http://gitlab \
      --registration-token <TOKEN> \
      --executor docker \
      --docker-image ubuntu:16.04 \
      --docker-volumes /var/run/docker.sock:/var/run/docker.sock \
      --description "Gitlab CI Runner"
```

This command registers the previously started GitLab CI Runner at the main GitLab instance. The `--url` flag configures the URL that the main GitLab instance is reachable at (usually, this can be `http://gitlab` when your runner is on the same container network as your main Gitlab instance; alternatively, you can use your host machine's public IP address here, which in my case is `http://192.168.2.125/`). Next, copy and paste the registration token for the `--registration-token` flag. The `--executor` flag configures the GitLab CI Runner to run each build job in its own isolated Docker container. The `--docker-image` flag configures the Docker image that should be used as a build environment by default. The `--docker-volumes` flag ensures that you can use the Docker Engine from within your builds (this is especially important since we will be building our own Docker images within these builds).

 Mounting the `/var/run/docker.sock` socket into your Gitlab Runner exposes the Docker engine that is running on your host to the users of your CI system. This might pose a security risk if you do not trust these users. Alternatively, you can set up a new Docker engine that itself runs in a container (called Docker-in-Docker). Refer to the GitLab documentation at `https://docs.gitlab.com/ce/ci/docker/using_docker_build.html#use-docker-in-docker-executor` for detailed setup instructions.

The `docker exec` command should produce an output similar to the one in the following screenshot:

```
● ● ●                    1. mhelmich@mhelmich-macbook: ~ (zsh)
mhelmich@mhelmich-macbook  ➤  docker container exec gitlab-runner gitlab-runner register -
n --url http://192.168.2.125 --registration-token zrGMs6xxJSVc_Ga6TYQR --executor docker --de
scription "GitLab CI Runner" --docker-image ubuntu:16.04
Running in system-mode.

Registering runner... succeeded                      runner=zrGMs6xx
Runner registered successfully. Feel free to start it, but if it's running already the config
 should be automatically reloaded!
mhelmich@mhelmich-macbook  ➤  █
```

After the runner has been successfully registered, you should be able to find it in the GitLab administration UI:

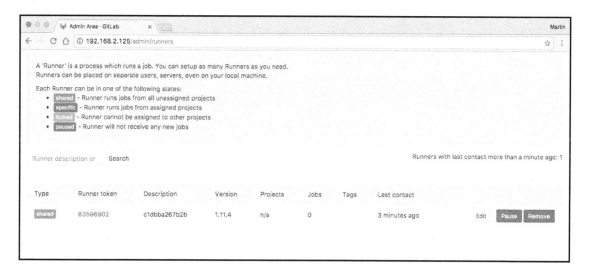

Now that you have a working CI Runner, you can start configuring your actual CI jobs. Similarly to Travis CI, GitLab CI jobs are configured via a configuration file that is placed within the source code repository. Similarly to the already known `.travis.yml`, this file is named `.gitlab-ci.yml`. Although they are similarly named, their format is a little bit different.

Each GitLab CI configuration consists of multiple **Stages** (by default, build, test, and deploy, although this is completely customizable). Each stage can consist of an arbitrary number of **Jobs**. All stages together form a **Pipeline**. Each job of a pipeline is run in its own isolated Docker container.

Let's start with the MyEvents backend services. Place a new file, `.gitlab-ci.yml`, in the root directory of your project:

```
build:eventservice:
  image: golang:1.9.2
  stage: build
  before_script:
    - mkdir -p $GOPATH/src/todo.com
    - ln -nfs $PWD $GOPATH/src/todo.com/myevents
    - cd $GOPATH/src/todo.com/myevents/eventservice
  script:
    - CGO_ENABLED=0 go build
  artifacts:
    paths:
      - ./eventservice/eventservice
```

So, what does this code snippet actually do? First, it instructs the GitLab CI Runner to start this build within a Docker container based on the `golang:1.9.2` image. This ensures that you have access to the latest Go SDK in your build environment. The three commands in the `before_script` section take care of setting up a `$GOPATH`, and the one command in the `script` section is the actual compilation step.

> Note that this build configuration assumes that your project has all its dependencies vendored in version control. If you have just a `glide.yaml` file in your project, you will also need to set up Glide and run `glide install` before actually running `go build`.

Finally, the artifacts property defines that the `eventservice` executable that was created by Go `build` should be archived as a build artifact. This will allow users to download this build artifact later. Also, the artifact will be available in later jobs of the same pipeline.

Now, add the `.gitlab-ci.yml` file to your source code repository and push it to the GitLab server:

```
$ git add .gitlab-ci.yml
$ git commit -m "Configure GitLab CI"
$ git push gitlab
```

When you have pushed the configuration file, head to your project page in the GitLab web UI and go to the **Pipelines** tab. You will find an overview of all build pipelines that were started for your project, and also their success:

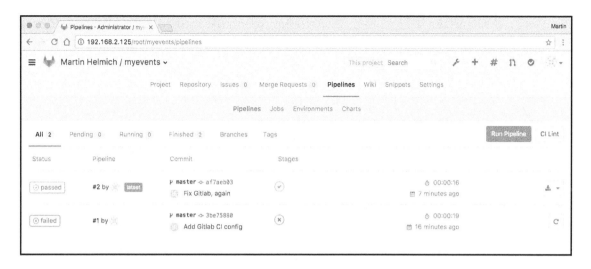

Right now, our pipeline consists of only one stage (`build`) with one job
(`build:eventservice`). You can see this in the **Stages** column of the `Pipelines`
overview. To inspect the exact output of the `build:eventservice` job, click on the
pipeline status icon and then on the `build:eventservice` job:

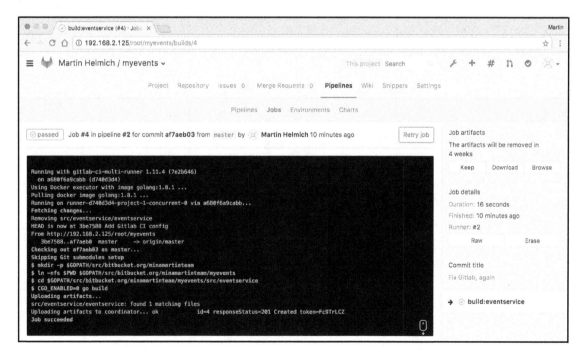

Next, we can extend our `.gitlab-ci.yml` configuration file to also include the build for the booking service:

```
build:eventservice: # ...

build:bookingservice:
  image: golang:1.9.2
  stage: build
  before_script:
    - mkdir -p $GOPATH/src/todo.com
    - ln -nfs $PWD $GOPATH/src/todo.com/myevents
    - cd $GOPATH/src/todo.com/myevents/bookingservice
  script:
    - CGO_ENABLED=0 go build
  artifacts:
    paths:
      - ./bookingservice/bookingservice
```

When you push your code again, you will note that the next **Pipeline** started for your project consists of two jobs that run in parallel (more or less, depending on the configuration of the GitLab CI Runner and its current workload):

Next, we can add two jobs that build the actual Docker images. These jobs need to be executed after the already configured build steps, because we will need the compiled Go binaries to create the Docker images. Owing to this, we cannot configure the docker build steps to run in the build stage (all jobs within one stage are executed in parallel—at least, potentially—and cannot be dependent on each other). For this reason, we will start by reconfiguring the build stages for our project. This is also done on a per-project basis in the .gitlab-ci.yml file:

```
stages:
  - build
  - dockerbuild
  - publish
  - deploy

build:eventservice: # ...
```

Next, we can use these new stages in our actual build jobs:

```
dockerbuild:eventservice:
  image: docker:17.04.0-ce
  stage: dockerbuild
  dependencies:
    - build:eventservice
  script:
    - docker container build -t myevents/eventservice:$CI_COMMIT_REF_NAME
eventservice
  only:
    - tags
```

The dependencies property declares that this step requires the build:eventservice job to complete first. It also makes the build artifacts of that job available within this job. The script consists of just the docker container build command ($CI_COMMIT_REF_NAME) that contains the name of the current Git branch or tag. The only property ensures that the Docker image is only built when a new Git tag is pushed.

Add a corresponding build job for building the booking service container image:

```
dockerbuild:bookingservice:
  image: docker:17.04.0-ce
  stage: dockerbuild
  dependencies:
    - build:bookingservice
  script:
    - docker container build -t myevents/bookingservice:$CI_COMMIT_REF_NAME
bookingservice
  only:
    - tags
```

Add the modified `.gitlab-ci.yml` file to version control, and also, create a new Git tag to test the new build pipeline:

```
$ git add .gitlab-ci.yml
$ git commit -m"Configure Docker builds"
$ git push gitlab

$ git tag v1.0.1
$ git push gitlab --tags
```

In the **Pipeline** overview, you will now find four build jobs:

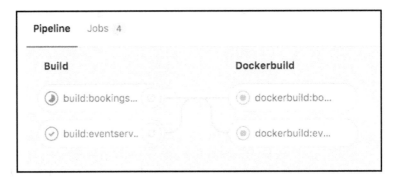

After building the Docker images, we can now add a fifth build step for publishing the created registries into a Docker registry:

```
publish:
  image: docker:17.04.0-ce
  stage: publish
  dependencies:
    - dockerbuild:eventservice
    - dockerbuild:bookingservice
  before_script:
```

```
    - docker login -u ${DOCKER_USERNAME} -p ${DOCKER_PASSWORD}
script:
    - docker push myevents/eventservice:${CI_COMMIT_REF_NAME}
    - docker push myevents/bookingservice:${CI_COMMIT_REF_NAME}
only:
    - tags
```

Similar to our preceding Travis CI build, this build job relies on the environment variables `$DOCKER_USERNAME` and `$DOCKER_PASSWORD`. Luckily, GitLab CI offers a similar feature to Travis CI's secret environment variables. For this, open the project's **Settings** tab in the GitLab web UI, then select the **CI/CD Pipelines** tab and search for the **Secret Variables** section:

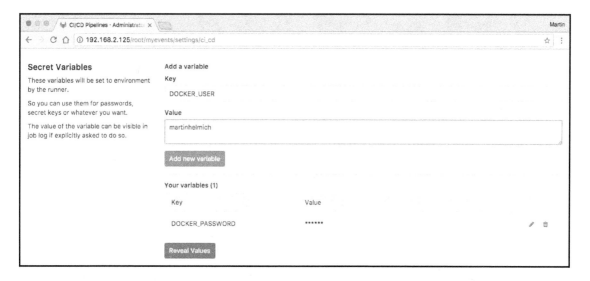

Use this feature to configure the credentials for the container registry of your choice (remember to adjust the `docker login` command in the preceding build job accordingly if you are using a registry other than Docker Hub).

Finally, let's add the final build step for actually deploying our application into a Kubernetes cluster:

```
deploy:
  image: alpine:3.5
  stage: deploy
  environment: production
  before_script:
    - apk add --update openssl
    - wget -O /usr/local/bin/kubectl
https://storage.googleapis.com/kubernetes-
release/release/v1.6.1/bin/linux/amd64/kubectl && chmod +x
/usr/local/bin/kubectl
    - echo "${KUBE_CA_CERT}" > ./ca.crt
    - kubectl config set-credentials gitlab-ci --token="${KUBE_TOKEN}"
    - kubectl config set-cluster your-cluster --
server=https://your-kubernetes-cluster.example --certificate-
authority=ca.crt
    - kubectl config set-context your-cluster --cluster=your-cluster --
user=gitlab-ci --namespace=default
    - kubectl config use-context your-cluster
  script:
    - kubectl set image deployment/eventservice
api=myevents/eventservice:${CI_COMMIT_REF_NAME}
    - kubectl set image deployment/bookingservice
api=myevents/eventservice:${CI_COMMIT_REF_NAME}
  only:
    - tags
```

This build step uses the `alpine:3.5` base image (a minimalist Linux distribution with a very small image size), in which we first download and then configure the `kubectl` binary. These steps are similar to our Travis CI deployment, which we configured in the preceding section, and require the environment variables $KUBE_CA_CERT and $KUBE_TOKEN to be configured as secret variables in the GitLab UI.

Note that, in this example, we are using a Kubernetes Service Account named `gitlab-ci` (previously, we created an account named `travis-ci`). So, for this example to work, you will need to create an additional service account using the commands that have already been used in the preceding section.

At this point, our GitLab-based build and deployment pipeline is complete. Take another look at the Pipelines view in the GitLab UI to have a last look at our pipeline in all its glory:

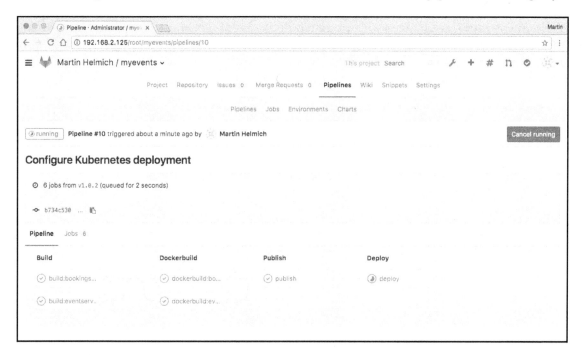

GitLab's pipeline feature is a nearly perfect solution for implementing complex build and deployment pipelines. While other CI/CD tools constrain you into a single build job with one environment, GitLab pipelines allow you to use an isolated environment for each step of your build, and to even run these in parallel if possible.

Summary

In this chapter, you learned how to easily automate your application's build and deployment workflow. Having an automated deployment workflow is especially important in microservice architectures where you have many different components that are deployed often. Without automation, deploying complex distributed application would become increasingly tedious and would eat away your productivity.

Now that the deployment problem of our application is solved (in short, containers + continuous delivery), we can direct our attention to other matters. That our application is running where we deployed it does not mean that it is actually doing what it is supposed to do. This is why we need to monitor applications that are run in production environments. Monitoring enables you to track your application's behavior at runtime and note errors quickly, which is why the focus of the next chapter will be on monitoring your application.

10
Monitoring Your Application

In the previous chapters, you learned how to build a Microservice application with the Go programming language and how to (continuously) deploy it into various environments.

However, our work is not yet complete. When you have an application running in a production environment, you will need to ensure that it stays up and running and behaves the way that you as a developer intended. This is what monitoring is for.

In this chapter, we will introduce you to **Prometheus**, an open source monitoring software that has quickly gained popularity for monitoring cloud-based distributed applications. It is often used together with **Grafana**, a frontend for visualizing metrics data collected by Prometheus. Both applications are licensed under the Apache license. You will learn how to set up Prometheus and Grafana and how to integrate them into your own applications.

In this chapter, we will cover the following topics:

- Installing and using Prometheus
- Installing Grafana
- Exporting metrics to Prometheus from your own application

Setting up Prometheus and Grafana

Before using Prometheus and Grafana in our own application, let's take a look at how Prometheus works in principle.

Prometheus's basics

Unlike other monitoring solutions, Prometheus works by pulling data (called **metrics** in Prometheus jargon) from clients at regular intervals. This process is called **scraping**. Clients monitored by Prometheus have to implement an HTTP endpoint that can be scraped by Prometheus in a regular interval (by default, 1 minute). These metrics endpoints can then return application-specific metrics in a predefined format.

For example, an application could offer an HTTP endpoint at /metrics that responds to GET requests and returns the following body:

```
memory_consumption_bytes 6168432
http_requests_count{path="/events",method="get"} 241
http_requests_count{path="/events",method="post"} 5
http_requests_count{path="/events/:id",method="get"} 125
```

This document exposes two metrics—memory_consumption_bytes and http_requests_count. Each metric is associated with a value (for example, the current memory consumption of 6,168,432 bytes). Since Prometheus scrapes these metrics from your application at fixed intervals, it can use these point-in-time values to build a time series of this metric.

Prometheus metrics can also have labels. In the preceding example, you may note that the http_request_count metric actually has three different values for different combinations of the path and method labels. Later, you will be able to use these labels to query data from Prometheus using a custom query language, **PromQL**.

Metrics exported to Prometheus by applications can get quite complex. For example, using labels and different metrics names, a client could export a histogram where data is aggregated in different buckets:

```
http_request_duration_seconds_bucket{le="0.1"} 6835
http_request_duration_seconds_bucket{le="0.5"} 79447
http_request_duration_seconds_bucket{le="1"} 80700
http_request_duration_seconds_bucket{le="+Inf"} 80953
http_request_duration_seconds_sum 46135
http_request_duration_seconds_count 80953
```

The preceding metrics describe a histogram of your application's HTTP response times. In this case, 6,835 requests were processed with a response time of less than 0.1 seconds; 79,447 requests with a response time of less than 0.5 seconds (which includes the previous 6,835 requests); and so on. The last two metrics export the total amount of processed HTTP requests and the sum of time needed to process these requests. Both of these values together can be used to compute the average request duration.

Do not worry, you will not need to build these complex histogram metrics by yourself; that's what the Prometheus client library is for. However, first, let's get started by actually setting up a Prometheus instance.

Creating an initial Prometheus configuration file

Before using Prometheus and Grafana in our own application, we will need to set it up first. Luckily, you can find Docker images for both applications on the Docker Hub. Before starting our own Prometheus container, we just need to create a configuration file that we can then inject into the container.

Start by creating a new directory somewhere on your local machine and placing a new `prometheus.yml` file in it:

```
global:
  scrape_interval: 15s

scrape_configs:
  - job_name: prometheus
    static_configs:
      - targets: ["localhost:9090"]
```

This configuration defines a global scraping interval of 15 seconds (the default is 1 minute) and already configures the first scraping target, which is Prometheus itself (yes, you have read correctly; Prometheus exports Prometheus metrics that you can then monitor with Prometheus).

Later, we will add more configuration items to the `scape_configs` property. For the time being, it will suffice.

Running Prometheus on Docker

After having created the configuration file, we can use a volume mount to inject this configuration file into the Docker containers we are about to start.

For this example, we will assume that you have the MyEvents application running in Docker containers on your local machine and that the containers are attached to a container network named myevents (whether you created the containers manually or via Docker Compose does not really matter).

For this reason, starting both applications is easy enough. We'll start by defining a separate container network for the monitoring components:

```
$ docker network create monitoring
```

Next, create a new volume in which the Prometheus server can store its data:

```
$ docker volume create prometheus-data
```

Now, you can use both the newly created network and volume to create a Prometheus container:

```
$ docker container run \
    --name prometheus \
    --network monitoring \
    --network myevents \
    -v $PWD/prometheus.yml:/etc/prometheus/prometheus.yml
    -v prometheus-data:/prometheus
    -p 9090:9090
    prom/prometheus:v1.6.1
```

Note that in the preceding example, we are attaching the prometheus container to both the myevents and monitoring networks. This is because later, the Prometheus server will need to access the MyEvents service via the network to scrape metrics from them.

After starting the Prometheus container, you will be able to open the Prometheus web UI in your browser by navigating to `http://localhost:9090`:

Prometheus web UI

In our configuration file, we have already configured our first scraping target—the Prometheus server itself. You will find an overview of all configured scraping targets by selecting the **Status** menu item and then the **Targets** item:

Targets item in Prometheus web UI

As you can see in the preceding screenshot, Prometheus reports the current state of the scrape target (**UP**, in this case) and when it was last scraped.

You can now use the **Graph** menu item to inspect the metrics that Prometheus has already collected about itself. There, enter `go_memstats_alloc_bytes` into the **Expression** input field and click on **Execute**. After that, switch to the **Graph** tab. Prometheus will now print its own memory usage over the past 1 hour. You can change the observation period using the controls above the graph. By default, Prometheus will keep its time series data for 2 weeks:

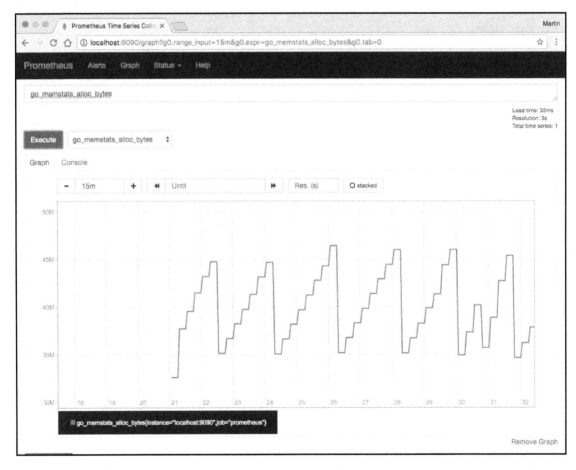

Prometheus web UI graph

Prometheus also supports more complex expressions. For example, consider the `process_cpu_seconds_total` metric. When displaying it as a graph, you will note that it is monotonically increasing. This is because that specific metric describes the sum of all CPU seconds that the program used over its entire lifetime (which, by definition, must always be increasing). However, for monitoring purposes, it is often more interesting to know the current CPU usage of a process. For this, PromQL offers the `rate()` method that calculates the per-second average increase of a time series. Try this out using the following expression:

```
rate(process_cpu_seconds_total[1m])
```

In the graph view, you will now find the 1-minute average CPU usage per second (which is probably a more comprehensible metric than the total sum of all used CPU seconds ever):

The Prometheus web UI is good for quick analyses and ad-hoc queries. However, Prometheus does not support saving queries for later use or presenting more than one graph on the same page. This is where Grafana comes into play.

Running Grafana on Docker

Running Grafana is equally as easy as running Prometheus. Start by setting up a volume for persistent storage:

```
$ docker volume create grafana-data
```

Then, start the actual container and attach it to the `monitoring` network (not the `myevents` network; Grafana needs to communicate with the Prometheus server, but it will not have any need to communicate with your backend services directly):

```
$ docker container run \
    -v grafana-data \
    -p 3000:3000 \
    --name grafana \
    --network monitoring \
    grafana/grafana:4.2.0
```

After this, you will be able to access Grafana in your browser on `http://localhost:3000`. The default credentials are the username `admin` and the password `admin`.

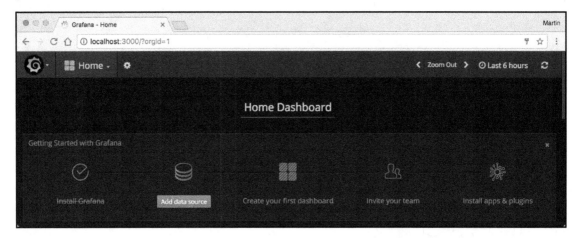

Gafana home page

On your first access, you will be prompted to configure a data source for your Grafana instance. Click on the **Add data source** button and configure access to your Prometheus server on the next page. There, select **Prometheus** as **Type**, enter `http://prometheus:9090` as **URL**, and select **Proxy** *as* **Access mode**.

After adding your Data Source, continue by creating a dashboard (select the Button in the top-left corner, select **Dashboards**, and then **New**). Then, add a new Graph to the dashboard by clicking on the respective button. After adding the graph panel, edit the panel by clicking on the **Panel Title** and selecting **Edit**:

Panel

Then, in the **Metrics** tab, enter the CPU usage query from before into the **Query input** field. To further customize the panel, you might want to enter `{{ job }}` as a legend to make the graph legend more comprehensible and change the Y axis format (in the **Axes tab**, **Left Y** section, and **Unit** field) to **Percent (0.0-1.0)**:

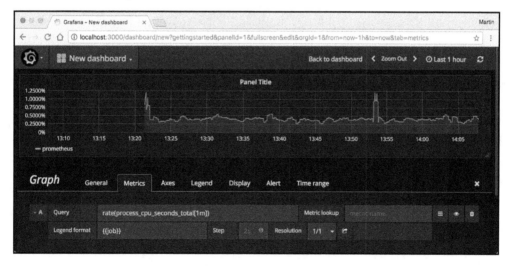

Gafana new dashboard

Close the editing panel and save your dashboard by clicking on the **Save** button or pressing *Ctrl + S*. Your dashboard is now saved. You can view it again at a later point in time with updated metrics or share this dashboard with other users.

You can also experiment by adding more panels to your dashboard in which you visualize other metrics (by default, Prometheus already exports a boatload of metrics about itself that you can experiment with). For a detailed reference on the Prometheus Query Language, you can also take a look at the official documentation at the following URL: `https:// prometheus.io/docs/querying/basics/`.

Now that we have a working Prometheus and Grafana setup up and running, we can take a look at how to get metrics from your own application into Prometheus.

Exporting metrics

As already shown, exporting metrics from your own application is easy, at least in principle. All your application needs to do is offer an HTTP endpoint that returns arbitrary metrics that can then be saved in Prometheus. In practice, this gets more difficult, especially when you care about the status of the Go runtime (for example, CPU and memory usage, Goroutine count, and so on). For this reason, it is usually a good idea to use the Prometheus client library for Go, which takes care of collecting all possible Go runtime metrics.

As a matter of fact, Prometheus is itself written in Go and also uses its own client library to export metrics about the Go runtime (for example, the `go_memstats_alloc_bytes` or `process_cpu_seconds_total` metrics that you have worked with before).

Using the Prometheus client in your Go application

You can get the Prometheus client library using `go get`, as follows:

```
$ go get -u github.com/prometheus/client_golang
```

In case your application uses a dependency management tool (such as Glide, which we introduced in the preceding chapter), you will also probably want to declare this new dependency in your `glide.yaml` file and add a stable release to your application's `vendor/` directory. To do all this in one step, simply run `glide get` instead of `go get` within your application directory:

```
$ glide get github.com/prometheus/client_golang
$ glide update
```

For security reasons, we will expose our metrics API on a different TCP port than the event service's and booking service's REST APIs. Otherwise, it would be too easy to accidentally expose the metrics API to the outside world.

Let's start with the event service. Setting up the metrics APIs does not require much code, so we will do this directly in the `main.go` file. Add the following code to the main function before the `rest.ServeAPI` method is called:

```
import "net/http"
import "github.com/prometheus/client_golang/prometheus/promhttp"
// ...

func main() {
  // ...

  go func() {
    fmt.Println("Serving metrics API")

    h := http.NewServeMux()
    h.Handle("/metrics", promhttp.Handler())

    http.ListenAndServe(":9100", h)
  }()

  fmt.Println("Serving API")
  // ...
}
```

Now, compile your application and run it. Try opening the address at `http://localhost:9100/metrics` in your browser, and you should see a large number of metrics being returned by the new endpoint:

```
# TYPE go_goroutines gauge
go_goroutines 11
# HELP go_memstats_alloc_bytes Number of bytes allocated and still in use.
# TYPE go_memstats_alloc_bytes gauge
go_memstats_alloc_bytes 975448
# HELP go_memstats_alloc_bytes_total Total number of bytes allocated, even if freed.
# TYPE go_memstats_alloc_bytes_total counter
go_memstats_alloc_bytes_total 975448
# HELP go_memstats_buck_hash_sys_bytes Number of bytes used by the profiling bucket hash table.
# TYPE go_memstats_buck_hash_sys_bytes gauge
go_memstats_buck_hash_sys_bytes 2483
# HELP go_memstats_frees_total Total number of frees.
# TYPE go_memstats_frees_total counter
go_memstats_frees_total 1412
# HELP go_memstats_gc_sys_bytes Number of bytes used for garbage collection system metadata.
# TYPE go_memstats_gc_sys_bytes gauge
go_memstats_gc_sys_bytes 131072
# HELP go_memstats_heap_alloc_bytes Number of heap bytes allocated and still in use.
# TYPE go_memstats_heap_alloc_bytes gauge
go_memstats_heap_alloc_bytes 975448
# HELP go_memstats_heap_idle_bytes Number of heap bytes waiting to be used.
# TYPE go_memstats_heap_idle_bytes gauge
go_memstats_heap_idle_bytes 319488
# HELP go_memstats_heap_inuse_bytes Number of heap bytes that are in use.
# TYPE go_memstats_heap_inuse_bytes gauge
go_memstats_heap_inuse_bytes 1.384448e+06
# HELP go_memstats_heap_objects Number of allocated objects.
# TYPE go_memstats_heap_objects gauge
go_memstats_heap_objects 11073
```

Page shown at localhost:9100/metrics

Now, make the same adjustment to the booking service. Also, remember to add an EXPOSE 9100 statement to both service's Dockerfiles and to recreate any containers with an updated image and the `-p 9100:9100` flag (or `-p 9101:9100` to prevent port conflicts).

Configuring Prometheus scrape targets

Now that we have two services up and running that expose Prometheus metrics, we can configure Prometheus to scrape these services. For this, we can modify the `prometheus.yml` file that you created earlier. Add the following sections to the `scrape_configs` property:

```
global:
  scrape_interval: 15s

scrape_configs:
  - job_name: prometheus
    static_configs:
      - targets: ["localhost:9090"]
```

```
  - job_name: eventservice
    static_configs:
      - targets: ["events:9090"]
  - job_name: bookingservice
    static_configs:
        - targets: ["bookings:9090"]
```

After adding the new scraping targets, restart the Prometheus container by running `docker container restart prometheus`. After that, the two new scraping targets should show up in the Prometheus web UI:

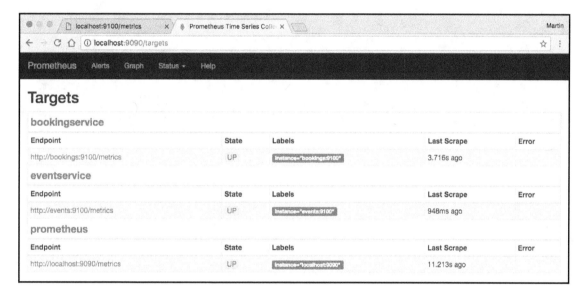

Prometheus web UI targets

Now, for the best part—remember the Grafana dashboard that you have created a few sections earlier? Now that you have added two new services to be scraped by Prometheus, take another look at it:

Gafana

As you can see, Grafana and Prometheus pick up metrics from the new services instantly. This is because the `process_cpu_seconds_total` and `go_memstats_alloc_bytes` metrics that we have worked with until now are actually exported by all three of our services since they're all using the Prometheus Go client library. However, Prometheus adds an additional job label to each metrics that is scraped; this allows Prometheus and Grafana to distinguish the same metrics coming from different scraping targets and present them accordingly.

Exporting custom metrics

Of course, you can also use the Prometheus client library to export your own metrics. These do not need to be technical metrics that reflect some aspect of the Go runtime (such as CPU usage and memory allocation), but it could also be business metrics. One possible example could be the amount of booked tickets with different labels per event.

For example, within the `todo.com/myevents/bookingservice/rest` package, you could add a new file—let's call it `metrics.go`—that declares and registers a new Prometheus metrics:

```
package rest

import "github.com/prometheus/client_golang/prometheus"

var bookingCount = prometheus.NewCounterVec(
  prometheus.CounterOpts{
    Name:      "bookings_count",
    Namespace: "myevents",
    Help:      "Amount of booked tickets",
  },
  []string{"eventID", "eventName"},
)

func init() {
  prometheus.MustRegister(bookingCount)
}
```

The Prometheus client library tracks all created metric objects in a package, a global registry that is automatically initialized. By calling the `prometheus.MustRegister` function, you can add new metrics to this registry. All registered metrics will automatically be exposed when a Prometheus server scrapes the `/metrics` endpoint.

The `NewCounterVec` function used creates a collection of metrics that are all named `myevents_bookings_count` but are differentiated by two labels, `eventID` and `eventName` (in reality, these are functionally dependent and you wouldn't really need both; but having the event name as a label comes in handy when visualizing this metric in Grafana). When scraped, these metrics might look like this:

```
myevents_bookings_count{eventID="507...",eventName="Foo"} 251
myevents_bookings_count{eventID="508...",eventName="Bar} 51
```

The Prometheus client library knows different types of metrics. The Counter that we used in the preceding code is one of the simpler ones. In one of the previous sections, you saw how a complex histogram was represented as a number of different metrics. This is also possible with the Prometheus client library. Just to demonstrate, let's add another metric—this time, a histogram:

```
var seatsPerBooking = prometheus.NewHistogram(
  prometheus.HistogramOpts{
    Name: "seats_per_booking",
    Namespace: "myevents",
```

```
      Help: "Amount of seats per booking",
      Buckets: []float64{1,2,3,4}
   }
)

func init() {
  prometheus.MustRegister(bookingCount)
  prometheus.MustRegister(seatsPerBooking)
}
```

When being scraped, this histogram will be exported as seven individual metrics: you will get five histogram buckets (*Number of bookings with one seat or less* up to *Four seats or less* and *Infinitely many seats or less*), and one metric for the sum of all seats and sum of all observations, respectively:

```
myevents_seats_per_booking_bucket{le="1"} 1
myevents_seats_per_booking_bucket{le="2"} 8
myevents_seats_per_booking_bucket{le="3"} 18
myevents_seats_per_booking_bucket{le="4"} 20
myevents_seats_per_booking_bucket{le="+Inf"} 22
myevents_seats_per_booking_sum 72
myevents_seats_per_booking_count 22
```

Of course, we will need to tell the Prometheus library the values that should be exported for these metrics when scraped by the Prometheus server. Since both metrics (amount of bookings and amount of seats per booking) can only change when a new booking is made, we can add this code to the REST handler function that handles POST requests on the /events/{id}/bookings route.

In the booking_create.go file, add the following code somewhere after the original request has been processed (for example, after the EventBooked event is emitted on the event emitter):

```
h.eventEmitter.emit(&msg)

bookingCount.
  WithLabelValues(eventID, event.Name).
  Add(float64(request.Seats))
seatsPerBooking.
  Observe(float64(bookingRequest.Seats))

h.database.AddBookingForUser(
  // ...
```

The first statement adds the amount of booked seats (`request.Seats`) to the counter metric. Since you defined one label named `event` in the `CounterVec` declaration, you will need to call the `WithLabelValues` method with the respective label values (if the metric declaration consisted of two labels, you would need to pass two parameters into `WithLabelValues`).

The second statement adds a new `observation` to the histogram. It will automatically find the correct bucket and increment it by one (for example if three seats are added with the same booking, the `myevents_seats_per_booking_bucket{le="3"}` metric will be increased by one).

Now, start your application and make sure that Prometheus is scraping it at regular intervals. Take the time and add a few example records to your application. Also, add a few event bookings at the booking service; ensure that you do not create them all at once. After that, you can use the `myevents_bookings_count` metric to create a new graph in your Grafana dashboard:

Gafana graph

By default, Prometheus will create one time series per scraped instance. This means that when you have multiple instances of the booking service, you will get multiple time series, each with a different `job` label:

```
myevents_bookings_count{eventName="Foo",job="bookingservice-0"} 1
myevents_bookings_count{eventName="Foo",job="bookingservice-1"} 3
myevents_bookings_count{eventName="Bar",job="bookingservice-0"} 2
myevents_bookings_count{eventName="Bar",job="bookingservice-1"} 1
```

When displaying a business metric (for example, the number of tickets sold), you may not actually care at which instance each particular booking was placed and prefer an aggregated time series over all instances, instead. For this, you can use the PromQL function `sum()` when building your dashboard:

```
sum(myevents_bookings_count) by (eventName)
```

Running Prometheus on Kubernetes

Up until now, we have configured all scraping targets for Prometheus manually by adding them to the `prometheus.yml` configuration file. This works well for testing, but becomes tedious quickly in larger production setups (and completely pointless as soon as you introduce feature such as autoscaling).

When running your application within a Kubernetes cluster, Prometheus offers a turn-key solution for this—using the `prometheus.yml` configuration file, you can actually configure Prometheus to automatically load its scraping targets from the Kubernetes API. For example, if you have a Deployment defined for your booking service, Prometheus can automatically find all Pods that are managed by this Deployment and scrape them all. If the Deployment is scaled up, the additional instances will be automatically added to Prometheus.

For the following examples, we will assume that you have either a Minikube VM running on your local machine or a Kubernetes cluster somewhere in a cloud environment. We'll start by deploying the Prometheus server first. To manage the Prometheus configuration file, we will be using a Kubernetes resource that we have not used before—a `ConfigMap`. A `ConfigMap` is basically just an arbitrary key-value map that you can save in Kubernetes. When creating a Pod (or Deployment or StatefulSet), you can mount these values into your container as files, which makes `ConfigMaps` ideal for managing configuration files:

```
apiVersion: v1
kind: ConfigMap
name: prometheus-config
```

```
data:
  prometheus.yml: |
    global:
      scrape_config: 15s

    scrape_configs:
    - job_name: prometheus
      static_configs:
      - targets: ["localhost:9090"]
```

You can create the `ConfigMap` just like any other resource by saving it to a `.yaml` file and then calling `kubectl apply -f` on that file. You can also use the same command to update the `ConfigMap` when you have modified the `.yaml` file.

With the `ConfigMap` created, let's deploy the actual Prometheus server. Since Prometheus is a stateful application, we will deploy it as a `StatefulSet`:

```
apiVersion: apps/v1beta1
kind: StatefulSet
metadata:
  name: prometheus
spec:
  serviceName: prometheus
  replicas: 1
  template:
    metadata:
      labels:
        app: prometheus
    spec:
      containers:
      - name: prometheus
        image: prom/prometheus:v1.6.1
        ports:
        - containerPort: 9090
          name: http
        volumeMounts:
        - name: data
          mountPath: /prometheus
        - name: config
          mountPath: /etc/prometheus
      volumes:
      - name: config
        configMap:
          name: prometheus-config
  volumeClaimTemplates:
  - metadata:
      name: data
```

```
      annotations:
        volume.alpha.kubernetes.io/storage-class: standard
    spec:
      accessModes: ["ReadWriteOnce"]
      resources:
        requests:
          storage: 5Gi
```

Also, create the associated `Service`:

```
apiVersion: v1
kind: Service
metadata:
  name: prometheus
spec:
  clusterIP: None
  selector:
    app: prometheus
  ports:
  - port: 9090
    name: http
```

Now, you have a Prometheus server running inside your Kubernetes cluster; however, at the moment, that server only scrapes its own metrics endpoint, and not yet any of the other pods running in your cluster.

To enable the automatic scraping of Pods, add the following section to the `scrape_configs` section of your `prometheus.yml` file in your `ConfigMap`:

```
scrape_configs:
  # ...
  - job_name: kubernetes-pods
    kubernetes_sd_configs:
    - role: pod
  relabel_configs:
  - source_labels: [__meta_kubernetes_pod_annotation_prometheus_io_scrape]
    action: keep
    regex: true
  - source_labels: [__meta_kubernetes_pod_annotation_prometheus_io_path]
    action: replace
    target_label: __metrics_path__
    regex: (.+)
  - source_labels: [__address__,
__meta_kubernetes_pod_annotation_prometheus_io_port]
    action: replace
    regex: ([^:]+)(?::\d+)?;(\d+)
    replacement: $1:$2
```

```
    target_label: __address__
  - action: labelmap
    regex: __meta_kubernetes_pod_label_(.+)
  - source_labels: [__meta_kubernetes_namespace]
    action: replace
    target_label: kubernetes_namespace
  - source_labels: [__meta_kubernetes_pod_name]
    action: replace
    target_label: kubernetes_pod_name
```

Yes, this is quite a lot of configuration, but do not panic. Most of these configurations is for mapping the properties of known Kubernetes pods (such as the Pod names and labels defined by users) to Prometheus labels that will be attached to all metrics that are scraped from these Pods.

Note that after updating the `ConfigMap`, you may need to destroy your Prometheus Pod for the updated configuration to become active. Do not worry; even if you delete the Pod, the `StatefulSet` controller will create a new one almost immediately:

`$ kubectl delete pod -l app=prometheus`

This configuration also defines that Prometheus will scrape all Pods found in the cluster that have an annotation named `prometheus.io/scrape`. This annotation can be set when defining a Pod template, for example, in a Deployment. Also, you can now adjust your event service deployment as follows (remember to add the TCP port `9100` to the list of exposed ports):

```
apiVersion: apps/v1beta1
kind: Deployment
metadata:
  name: eventservice
spec:
  replicas: 2
  template:
    metadata:
      labels:
        myevents/app: events
        myevents/tier: api
      annotations:
        prometheus.io/scrape: true
        prometheus.io/port: 9100
    spec:
      containers:
      - name: api
        image: myevents/eventservice
        imagePullPolicy: Never
```

```
        ports:
        - containerPort: 8181
          name: http
        - containerPort: 9100
          name: metrics
        # ...
```

After updating the Deployment, Kubernetes should automatically start recreating the event service Pods. As soon as new Pods with the `prometheus.io/scrape` annotation are created, Prometheus will automatically pick them up and scrape them for metrics. If they are deleted again (for example, after updating or downscaling a Deployment), Prometheus will keep the metrics collected from these pods, but stop scraping them.

By having Prometheus pick up new scraping targets automatically based on annotations, managing the Prometheus server becomes very easy; after the initial setup, you probably will not need to edit the configuration file again.

Summary

In this chapter, you learned how to use Prometheus and Grafana to set up a monitoring stack to monitor both your application's health on a technical level (by keeping an eye on system metrics, such as RAM and CPU usage) and custom, application-specific metrics, such as, in this case, the amount of booked tickets.

Over the course of this book, we have covered almost the entire lifecycle of a typical Go cloud application, starting at architecture and the actual programming, building container images, continuously deploying them in various cloud environments, and monitoring your applications.

In the following chapter, we will take the opportunity to look back in detail at what we have achieved so far and also point out where to go from here.

11
Migration

Welcome to chapter 11 of our journey to learn the world of cloud native programming and the Go language. In this chapter, we'll cover some practical techniques to migrate applications from monolithic architectures to microservice architectures. We have already covered monolithic and microservice architectures in `Chapter 2`, *Building Microservices Using Rest APIs*. However, we will start this chapter by covering the practical definitions of monolithic and microservice architectures, in case you are reading this chapter separately.

In this chapter, we'll cover the following topics:

- A review on monolithic applications and microservices architectures
- Techniques for migrating from monolithic applications to microservices applications
- Advanced microservices design patterns
- Data consistency in microservices architectures

What is a monolithic application?

A **monolithic application** is simply a single piece of software that undertakes several independent tasks at once. Let's take an online store application as an example. In a monolithic architecture, we'd have a single piece of software that would handle the customers, their orders, the database connections, the website, the inventory, and any other tasks needed for the online store to be successful.

A single piece of software doing everything might seem like an inefficient approach for software design, which is the case in some scenarios. However, it is important to mention that monolithic applications are not always bad. There are some scenarios where a single software service doing all the work is an acceptable idea. This includes minimum viable products or MVPs where we try to build something fast to get it out for test users to try. It also includes use cases where not a lot of data load or traffic is expected, such as an online store for legacy board game hobbyists.

What are microservices?

A **microservice architecture** takes a different approach to building software as compared to monolithic applications. In a microservice architecture, the tasks are distributed among multiple smaller software services, which are known as microservices. In a well-designed microservice architecture, each microservice should be self-contained, deployable, and scalable. Well-designed microservices also enjoy clean APIs that allow other microservices to communicate with them. The concept of independent software services working together to reach a common goal is not new; it existed in the past as **service-oriented architectures** (**SOA**). However, modern microservices architectures take the idea a bit further by insisting on the software services being relatively small, independent, and fully self-contained.

Let's go back to the online store example. In the case of a microservice architecture, we would have a microservice for customer handling, a microservice for inventory handling, and so on.

A typical microservice contains multiple essential layers in the inside to handle logging, configuration, APIs to communicate with other microservices, and persistence. There is also the core code of the microservice, which covers the main task the service is supposed to do. The following is what a microservice should internally look like:

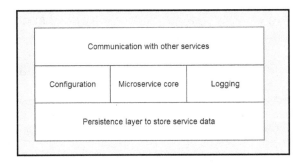

Internal look of microservice

Microservice architectures have major advantages over monolithic applications when it comes to scalability and flexibility. Microservices allow you to scale indefinitely, utilize the power of more than one programming language, and gracefully tolerate failures.

Migrating from monolithic applications to microservices

So, now, let's say that you have a monolithic application, your business is growing, your customers are demanding more features, and you need to migrate to an architecture that is both flexible and scalable. It's time to use microservices. The first key rule of thumb to have in mind when migrating is that there is no golden set of steps we need to follow to perform a successful migration from monolithic applications to microservices. The steps we need to follow differ from one situation to another and from one organization to another. Having said that, there are some very helpful concepts and ideas that we can cover in this chapter, which will help you make informed decisions on how to go about the migration.

Humans and technology

One of the most overlooked aspects when transitioning from monolithic applications to microservices is the **people factor**. We typically think of technology and architecture, but what about teams who write the code, manage the projects, and redesign the application? Moving from a monolithic application to a microservice is a paradigm shift that needs to be properly planned for in an organization.

The first thing we need to consider right after making the decision to move to microservices is the structures of teams involved with the development process. Typically, the following comprises the team that works on monolithic applications:

- Developers who are used to working in very specific pieces of the application in a single programming language and nothing else
- IT infrastructure teams who are used to deployments being nothing more than updating a few number of servers hosting the monolithic application and its databases
- Team leads who own a piece of an application as opposed to an entire software service from A to Z

As mentioned before, microservices migration represents a paradigm shift. This means that when transitioning to a microservice architecture, a new way of thinking needs to get engaged in the organization. Consider the following :

- Developers will need to be divided into smaller teams, where each team should be in charge of one or more microservices. Developers will need to be comfortable being in charge of an entire software service as opposed to a bunch of software modules or classes. Of course, if the organization is large enough, you can still have developers being responsible for specific modules within the microservice. However, it pays off if the developers are trained to think of their product as the entire microservice, as this will produce a better-designed microservice. Developers will also need to be comfortable with using the right programming language for the job. For example, Java is important for data processing and pipelining, Go is very good for building fast reliable microservices, C# is good for Windows services, and so on.
- IT infrastructure teams will need to learn about horizontal scaling, redundancy, expandable cloud platforms, and the planning process involved with deploying a massive number of services distributed among numerous servers.
- Team leads will carry the responsibility of an entire software service from A to Z. They will need to consider implementation details such as how to scale the service, whether to share a database with other services or have its own database, and how the service would communicate with other service.

Cutting a monolithic application to pieces

Now that we discussed the people aspect of the migration, let's take a dive into the technical details. One golden rule that virtually everyone agrees on is that writing everything from scratch and ignoring all the code in the existing monolithic application (also known as the big bang rewrite) is not a good idea. Instead, the best approach to migrate from a monolithic application to microservices is to cut the monolithic application piece by piece over time. Each detached piece becomes a microservice. For every new microservice, we will need to ensure that it can still communicate with the monlithic application, as well as other new microservices. If this approach goes well, the monolithic application will keep shrinking overtime till it becomes a microservice.

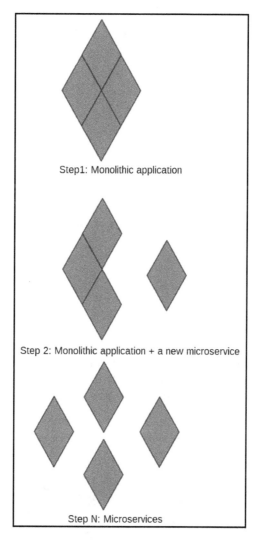

Monolithic application shrinking overtime

This sounds simple; however, in real life, it is typically not that straightforward. Let's cover some planning strategies to make the piece-by-piece approach more executable.

How do we break the code?

One key technical question we will need to ask is how exactly should we break the monolithic application's code? Here are some important points to keep in mind:

- If an application is well-written, there will be clean and obvious separations between the different classes or software modules. This makes cutting up the code an easier task.
- On the other hand, if there are no clean separations in the code, we'll need to do some refactoring to the existing code before we can start moving pieces of code to new microservices.
- It is typically preferred not to add new code or features to the monolithic application without trying to separate the new feature into a new microservice.

Glue code

In order for the new microservice to fit into the original application without breaking its functionality, the microservice needs to be capable of exchanging information with the original application. To make this happen, we may need to write some glue code that will link the new with the old. The glue code typically includes some API interfaces that would act as the communication channel between the original application and the microservice. The glue code will also include any code necessary to make the new microservice work with the existing application:

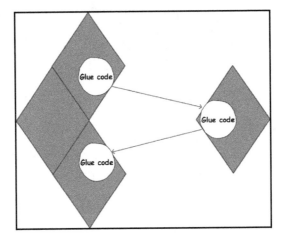

Glue code

The glue code might be temporary or permanent, depending on our application. Sometimes, the glue code might need to do some data modeling translation or communicate with an old database to make things work.

If your application is a web application, the glue code may include a temporary web HTTP API that can connect your newly separated microservice with your viewing layer.

Microservices design patterns

In this section, we will discuss some important design patterns and architectural approaches that can help us build robust and effective cloud-ready microservices. Let's get started.

Sacrificial architecture

Sacrificial architecture is an important design approach that doesn't typically get the attention it deserves. It was mentioned by Martin Folwer in 2014 and can be found at https://martinfowler.com/bliki/SacrificialArchitecture.html.

The core idea of sacrificial architecture is that we should write our software in a way where it is easily replaceable in the future. To understand the previous statement better, let's consider an example scenario. Let's say that a couple of years ago, we had built a computer networking application that utilizes custom data serialization formats designed by our developers. Today, we need to rewrite the application in a more modern programming language that can handle a lot more data load and user requests. This task will not be fun or easy by any measure because our application relies on custom serialization and communications protocols that can only be understood by the original developers of the application.

Now, what if we had used a more standardized serialization format such as protocol buffers? The task of rewriting or updating the application will be much easier and more efficient because protocol buffers are supported by a wide range of programming languages and frameworks. Building our application with a standard serialization format instead of a custom one is what sacrificial architecture is about.

When we design our software with sacrificial architecture in mind, the tasks of upgrading, refactoring, and/or evolving our application become much more straightforward. If our monolithic application gets designed with sacrificial architecture in mind, separating pieces of the application into microservices becomes easy.

If we write our glue code with sacrificial architecture in mind, evolving the glue code in the future or getting rid of it altogether and replacing it with something else becomes much easier. If we build our new microservices with sacrificial architecture in mind, we give ourselves the capability to grow and evolve our microservices quickly, painlessly, and efficiently.

A four-tier engagement platform

A **four-tier engagement platform** is an architectural approach that targets the application as a whole. It was described by Forrester research at ;https://go.forrester.com/blogs/13-11-20-mobile_needs_a_four_tier_engagement_platform/. This architecture is very suited for modern applications targeting the mobile and web age. The architecture allows scalability, flexibility, and performance. It also makes integrating cloud services and internal microservices quite easy and efficient.

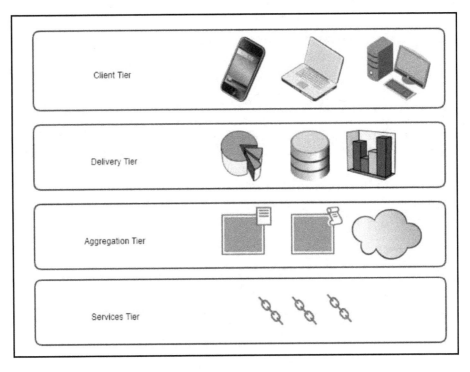

Four-tier engagement architecture

The main idea behind this architecture is that the overall application should be divided into four main layers or tiers:

- **The client layer**: This layer is responsible for the user experience; it tailors the user experience based on the user's context environment. A context environment includes the user device type, the user's location, the time of day, among other things. For example, if the user of your product is using a smart watch, then the client layer should render content suitable for a smart watch. If they are using a tablet, a user interface that is perfect for a tablet greets the user. If the user is viewing data from China, the client layer needs to show the information in Chinese. If the user is viewing the data from Canada, the information needs to be shown in English.

- **The delivery layer**: The delivery layer is responsible for delivering optimized data to the users as requested by the client layer. This is achieved by doing on-the-fly optimizations, such as image compression or bandwidth reduction. The layer can make use of monitoring tools to track user activity, then utilize algorithms to use this information to deliver better customer experience. This layer is also where we would using caching algorithms and techniques to ensure better performance for our customers.

- **The aggregation layer**: This layer is where data from different sources is aggregated to form stable and uniform data models, which can then be handed over to the preceding layers. Tasks undertaken by this layer include the following:
  - Acting as an API hub between layer, providing service discoverability, and data access to the preceding layers.
  - Integrating outputs from internal services such as in-house microservices and external services such as AWS cloud services.
  - Merging data from different source types—for example, reading a base64-encoded message from one source and a JSON-encoded message from another source and then linking them together to form a unified data model.
  - Encoding data to formats suitable for delivery to the users.
  - Specifying role-based access to the data.

- **The services layer:** This layer is composed of our external and internal services. It provides the raw data and functionality to the layers. These layers are composed of a set of deployable internal and external services. The services layer is where we would communicate with databases such as MySQL or DynamoDB; it's where we would use third-party services such as AWS S3 or Twilio. This layer should be designed to be pluggable, meaning that we could easily add or remove services to it as we please.

If we design our modern applications with the preceding architectural pattern, we will gain endless flexibility and scalability. For example, we can target new user device types in the client layer without needing to change much code in other layers. We can add or remove microservices or cloud services in the services layer without needing to change much code in the layers above it. We can support new encoding formats in the aggregation layer such as Thrift or protocol buffers without needing to change much code on the other layers. The four-tier engagement platform is currently being utilized by companies such as Netflix and Uber.

Bounded contexts in domain-driven designs

Domain-driven design (DDD) is a popular design pattern that we can use to internally design microservices. Domain-driven design typically targets complex applications that are likely to grow exponentially over time. If your monolithic application was already designed via DDD, migrating to microservices architecture will be straightforward. Otherwise, if you are expecting the new microservices to grow in scope and complexity, then considering DDD may be a good idea.

Domain-driven design is a massive topic. The wikipedia article can be found at `https://en.wikipedia.org/wiki/Domain-driven_design`. However, for the purpose of this section, we will cover some brief concepts that can help us obtain practical understanding of DDD. Then, from there, you'll learn why this design approach is good for complex microservices architectures.

The idea of domain-driven design is that a complex application should be considered to be functioning within a *domain*. A domain is simply defined as a sphere of knowledge or activity. The domain of our software application can be described as everything related to the purpose of the software. So, for example, if our software application's main goal is to facilitate planning social events, then planning social events becomes our domain.

A domain contains *contexts*; each context would represent a logical piece of the domain, where people talk the same language. Language used within a context can only be understood based on the context from which it belongs.

From my experience, it is difficult to understand what a context is without an example. So, let's take a simple example. Assume that the organization that is behind the social events application is a large organization, with a sales department, a marketing department, and a support department. This means that the domain-driven design of this organization may need to include the following three main contexts: a sales context, a marketing context, and a support context.

Some of the language used by the sales people will only be relevant to the sales people. For example, the concepts of sales funnel, sales opportunity, or sales pipeline are very important to sales, but may not be relevant to the support department. That is why, a sales context can include the concept of a sales funnel, but you won't find that language or concept in the support context much.

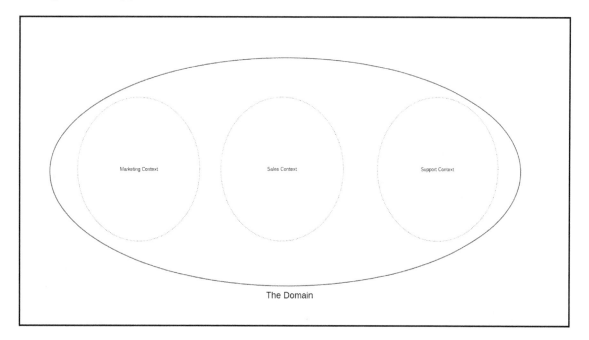

The Domain

Domains also contain models. Each model is an abstraction that describes an independent concept in the domain. Models are what end up getting transformed into software modules or objects. Models typically live inside contexts. For example, in a sales context, we will need models to represent a sales contract, a sales funnel, a sales opportunity, the sales pipeline, and the customers among others, whereas in the support context, we need models to show tickets, customers, and defects. The following is a simple diagram showing some models inside the sales context and the support context:

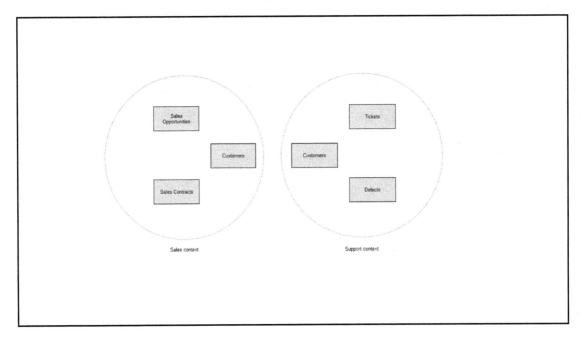

Sales and support contact

Different contexts can share the same language or concept, but focus on a different aspect of it. In our huge organization example, a word used by the sales people might not always mean the same word for the support people. For example, the word *customer* for sales represents a customer who is likely to buy a product from the organization, but hasn't done so just, yet. On the other hand, a customer for the support department is probably a customer who already bought the product, bought a support contract, and is suffering from some kind of issue with the product. So, both contexts share the concept of a customer; however, they care about different things when it comes to that concept.

The fact that the same language might mean different things in different contexts introduces one of the key ideas in the world of DDD, which is bounded contexts. Bounded contexts are contexts that share a concept, but then they implement their own models of that concept. For example, the concept of *customers* is represented by a model in the sales context, which reflects the version of customer that the sales department cares about. The concept of customers is also modeled in the support context according to their version of it. Although they are two models, they are still linked. That is because, at the end of the day, they both represent a customer for the social events planning company. The following is a simple diagram that shows what this would look like:

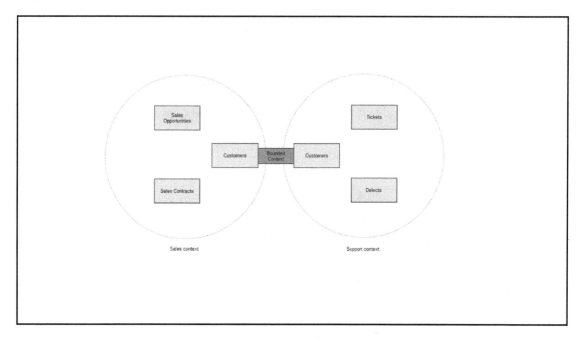

Bounded sales and support contact

Contexts and Bounded contexts is where the worlds of domain-driver design and microservices start to meet. It is a key design factor when it comes to complex modern microservices, because contexts can map easily to microservices. If you try to define bounded contexts, you will find yourself not only defining what a microservice should be in practice, but also what information should be shared between microservices to form the overall application. A simple definition for a bounded context is that it's a self-contained logical block that is part of a bigger application. This same definition can be applied with no additions to describe a well-designed microservice. Sometimes, a bounded context can be divided into more than one service, but that typically depends on the level of complexity of the application.

In our example here, we would then end up with a microservice that handles sales operations and a microservice that handles support operations.

If your monolithic application has been already designed with the DDD principles in mind, migrating to a microservices architecture gets easier. That is because transitioning from code that form the bounded contexts to self-containing microservices would make sense.

If, on the other hand, your monolithic application is not designed this way, but the application is complex and growing, then DDD principles can be utilized to build future microservices.

Data consistency

The database that powers an application is a vital block that must be handled with extreme care and respect when migrating to a microservice architecture. In the world of monolithic applications, you would likely deal with a small number of databases (one or maybe two) that connects to your monolithic application through a fat data handling layer, as follows:

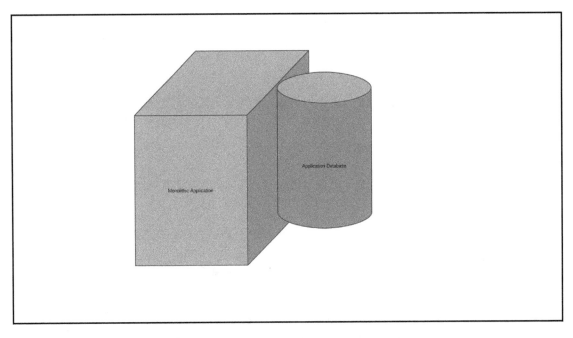

Monolithic application with database

However, in the case of microservices and distributed cloud architectures, things can get wildly different. That is because the architecture will likely include a wider range of data models and database engines to serve the needs of the distributed microservices. Microservices can have their own databases, share databases with other applications, or make use of multiple databases at once. Data consistency and modeling in a modern microservices architecture are a nontrivial challenge that we need to tackle with good applications design before it gets out of control.

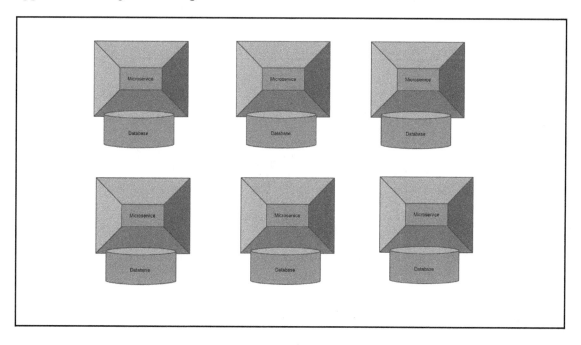

In the following section, we'll discuss some strategies to keep in mind when breaking the data models from a monolithic application paradigm to microservices.

Event-driven architecture for data consistency

A key design patterns that we can utilize to protect data consistency in a microservices architecture is an event-driven design. The reason why data consistency is difficult to maintain with microservices is that each microservice is typically responsible for a piece of data from the overall application. The sum of the data stores handled by the application's microservices represent the total state of the application. So, that means when a microservice updates its database, other microservices that are affected by this data change need to know about it so that they can take appropriate actions and update their own states.

Let's take the sales and support microservices example from the bounded context section of this chapter. In the event that a new customer buys a product, the sales microservice will need to update its own database to reflect the new customer status as an actual paying customer instead of just a potential customer. This event will also need to be communicated to the support microservice so that it can update its own database to reflect the fact that there is a new paying customer who deserves customer or technical support whenever needed.

This kind of event communication between microservices is what event-driven design is about in the world of microservices. A message queue or a message broker between the microservices can be utilized to communicate event messages between microservices. Message brokers were discussed in detail in Chapter 4, *Asynchronous Microservice Architectures Using Message Queues*. Microservices that need to be notified whenever a certain event happens will have to subscribe to those events.

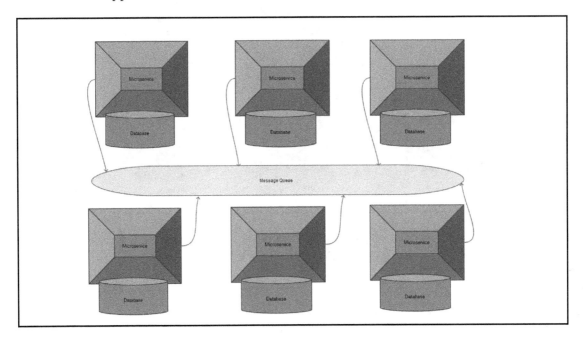

For example, the support service will need to subscribe to the event topic on the message queue that represents a customer buying the product. The sales microservice then triggers this event whenever a customer buys the product. Since the support service is subscribed to that event, it will receive the notification of the event shortly after, which will include the new customer's information. From there, the support service will be able to carry out its own logic to ensure that the support organization is ready for that customer whenever help is needed or even maybe trigger a welcome email for the new customer.

Now, this all sounds good, but what if the support microservice fails before it can receive the new customer event? This means that the support service will end up not knowing about the new customer, and hence it will not apply any logic to add the relevant information about the new customer into the support database. Does that mean when the customer calls later for help, the support team won't help because they don't see the customer in their system? Obviously, we don't want that to happen. One approach would be to have a central database that stores customer data, which would be shared between different microservices, but what if we seek a flexible design where each microservice is fully responsible for it's entire state. This is where the concepts of event sourcing and CQRS come into the picture.

Events sourcing

The basic idea behind event sourcing is that instead of fully relying on a local database to read the state, we need to make use of a recorded stream of events to form the state. To make that work, we will need to store all current and past events so that we can retrieve them at a later time.

We need an example to solidify this theoretical definition. Let's say that the support service had failed and crashed before it could receive the new customer event. If the support service doesn't use event sourcing, then when it restarts, it will not find the customer information in its own database and will never know about the customer. However, if it uses event sourcing, then instead of only looking at its local database, it will look at an event store which is shared with all the other microservices. The event store will record any event that was ever triggered between our microservices. In that event store, the support service will be able to replay the new customer event that got triggered recently and will see that this customer doesn't currently exist in the local support microservice database. The support service can then take this information and process it as normal.

Again, a key trick for this design to work is to never discard any events, past or new. This is achieved by saving them in an event store; here is what this would look like:

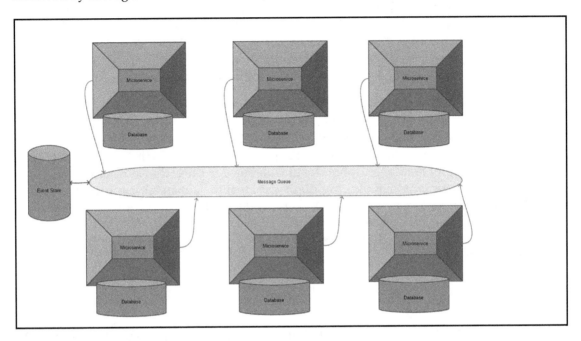

There are multiple ways to implement an event store; it can be a SQL database, a NoSQL database, or even a message queue that supports having events saved forever. Kafka is an example of a message queue that claims to also be a good engine for event sourcing.

There are multiple approaches to tackling event sourcing; the scenario that we covered in this section represented an approach where we use event stores with snapshots. A snapshot in this case was the support microservice local database, which also tried to keep a snapshot state. However, the ultimate state was still expected to be in the event store.

There are other approaches to implementing event sourcing, where no snapshots are used and the entire state always has to be derived from the event store.

The disadvantage of event sourcing is that it can grow exponentially in complexity. That is because in some environments, we may need to replay tons of events in order to build the current state of the system, which requires a lot of processing and complexity. The queries we need to run in order to form data models that join data from different replay events can easily become painful.

A popular approach to control the complexity of event sourcing is CQRS.

CQRS

The basic idea behind **Command Query Responsibility Segregation (CQRS)** is that commands—which means any operations related to changing data such as add, updates, or deletes—should be separated from queries—which are any operations related to reading data. In a microservices architecture, that may mean that some services should be responsible for commands, whereas others are responsible for querying.

A key advantage of CQRS is separation of concerns. That is because we separate write concerns from read concerns and allow them to scale independently. For example, let's say that we work with a complex application where we need different view models of our data to be available. We would like to store all customer data in an elastic search cluster in order to be able to efficiently search for them and retrieve their information. At the same time, we would like to store all the customer data in a graph database because we would like a graph view of the data.

In this case, we will create micrservices that are responsible for querying the customer events from the events stream (message queue) and then updating elastic search and the graph database whenever a new customer event is received via event sourcing. Those services will be the querying part of CQRS. On the other hand, we'll have other microservices that are responsible for triggering new events whenever needed. Those services will end up being the command part of CQRS.

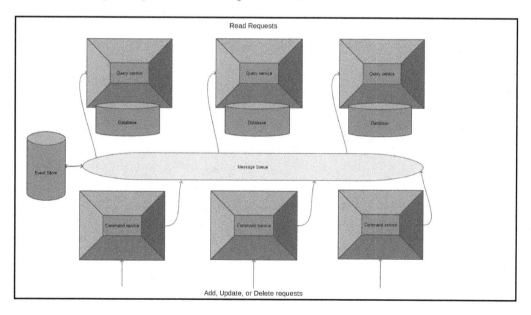

Those read and write microservices can then work with the rest of our services to form our application.

Summary

In this chapter, we dove deeper into the practical aspects of migrating from monolithic applications to microservices applications. We had a close look at some advanced design patterns and architectures that we can utilize to our benefit in order to switch from monolithic applications to microservices applications. This chapter concludes our learning journey for this book.

In the next chapter, we'll discuss some technologies and topics that you can start exploring after acquiring the knowledge contained within this book.

12
Where to Go from Here?

Welcome to the last chapter in our journey to learning cloud native programming in the Go language. By now, you should have enough knowledge to build production grade microservices, design complex distributed architectures, utilize the power of key Amazon web services, empower your software with containers, among other things.

However, the subject of cloud native programming is a very deep and massive one. This means that there are topics that you can still learn to enrich your knowledge and skills in that area. The purpose of this chapter is to light a path for you from where this book leaves off, by providing some practical overviews of topics not covered in this book that are strong avenues to pursue after you absorb the knowledge contained in this book.

In this chapter, we will cover the following topics:

- Additional microservice communication patterns and protocols, such as Protocol Buffers and GRPC
- More useful features offered by cloud providers
- Other cloud providers (Azure, GCP, and OpenStack)
- Serverless Computing

Microservices communications

In this book, we covered two approaches for microservices to communicate with each other:

- The first approach was via RESTful APIs, where a web HTTP layer would be built into a microservice, effectively allowing the microservice to communicate with any web client, whether the web client is another microservice or a web browser. One advantage to this approach is that it empowers microservices to communicate with the outside world when needed, since HTTP is now a universal protocol that is supported by all software stacks out there. The disadvantage of this approach, however, is the fact that HTTP can be a heavy protocol with multiple layers, which may not be the best choice when the requirement is fast efficient communications between internal microservices.
- The second approach is via message queues, where a message broker software such as RabbitMQ or Kafka will facilitate the exchange of messages between microservices. Message brokers receive messages from sending microservices, queue the messages, and then deliver them to microservices that previously indicated their interests in those messages. One major advantage of this approach is the fact that it can solidify data consistency in large-scale distributed microservices architectures, as explained in Chapter 11, *Migration*. This approach enables event-driven distributed architectures, such as event sourcing and CQRS. However, if our scaling requirements are relatively simple in scope, this approach may be too complex for our needs. This is because it requires us to maintain a message broker software with all its configurations and backends. In those cases, direct microservice to microservice communication may be all what we need.

If you haven't noted already, one obvious disadvantage for either of those approaches is the fact that they don't offer direct efficient microservice to microservice communications. There are two popular choices for technologies that we can employ for direct microservices communications: Protocol buffers and GRPC.

Protocol buffers

In their official documentations, protocol buffers are defined as a language-neutral, platform-neutral mechanism for serializing structured data. Let's take a look at an example to help build a clear picture of what protocol buffers are.

Assume that you have two microservices in your application; the first microservice (service 1) has collected information about a new customer and would like to send it to the second microservice (service 2). This data is considered structured data because it contains structured information such as the customer name, age, job, and phone numbers. One way to send this data is to send it as a JSON document (our data format) over HTTP from service 1 to service 2. However, what if we want to send this data faster and in a smaller form? This is where protocol buffers come into the picture. Inside service 1, protocol buffers will take the customer object, then serialize it into a compact form. From there, we can take this encoded compact piece of data and send it to service 2 via an efficient communications protocol such as TCP or UDP.

Note that we described protocol buffers as inside the service in the preceding example. This is true because protocol buffers come as software libraries that we can import and include in our code. There are protocol buffer packages for a wide selection of programming languages (Go, Java, C#, C++, Ruby, Python, and more).

The way how protocol buffers work is as follows:

1. You define your data in a special file, known as the `proto` file.
2. You use a piece of software known as the protocol buffer compiler to compile the proto file into code files written in the programming language of your choice.
3. You use the generated code files combined with the protocol buffer software package in your language of choice to build your software.

This is protocol buffers in a nutshell. In order to obtain more deep understanding of protocol buffers, go to `https://developers.google.com/protocol-buffers/`, where you will find good documentation to get you started with the technology.

There are currently two commonly used versions for protocol buffers: protocol buffers 2 and protocol buffers 3. A lot of the current training resources available online cover the newest version, Protocol Buffers 3. If you are looking for a resource to help with protocol buffers version 2, you can check this article in my website at `http://www.minaandrawos.com/2014/05/27/practical-guide-protocol-buffers-protobuf-go-golang/`.

GRPC

One key feature missing from the protocol buffers technology is the communications part. Protocol buffers excel at encoding and serializing data into compact forms that we can share with other microservices. However, when the concept of Protocol buffers was initially conceived, only serialization was considered, but not the part where we actually send the data elsewhere. For that, developers used to roll their sleeves and implement their own TCP or UDP application layer to exchange the encoded data between services. However, what if we can't spare the time and effort to worry about an efficient communication layer? This is where GRPC comes into picture.

GRPC can simply be described as protocol buffers combined with an RPC layer on top. A **Remote Procedure Call (RPC)** layer is a software layer that allows different piece of software such as microservices to interact via an efficient communications protocol such as TCP. With GRPC, your microservice can serialize your structured data via protocol buffers version 3 and then will be able to communicate this data with other microservices without you having to worry about implementing a communications layer.

If your application architecture needs efficient and fast interactions between your microservices, and at the same time you can't use message queues or Web APIs, then consider GRPC for your next application.

To get started with GRPC, visit `https://grpc.io/`. Similar to protocol buffers, GRPC is supported by a wide range of programming languages.

More on AWS

In this book, we dedicated two chapters to providing a practical dive into AWS fundamentals, with a focus on how to write Go microservices that would site comfortably on Amazon's cloud. However, AWS is a very deep topic that deserves an entire book to cover it as opposed to just a few chapters. In this section, we will provide brief overviews on some useful AWS technologies that we didn't get a chance to cover in this book. You can use the following section as an introduction for your next steps in learning AWS.

DynamoDB streams

In Chapter 8, *AWS II - S3, SQS, API Gateway, and DynamoDB*, we covered the popular AWS DynamoDB service. We learned what DynamoDB is, how it models data, and how to write Go applications that can harness DynamoDB's power.

There is one powerful feature of DynamoDB that we didn't get a chance to cover in this book, which is known as DynamoDB streams. DynamoDB streams allow us to capture changes that happen to items in a DynamoDB table, at the same time the change occurs. In practice, this means that we can react to data changes that happen to the database in real time. As usual, let's take an example to solidify the meaning.

Assume that we are building the cloud native distributed microservices application that powers a large multiplayer game. Let's say that we use DynamoDB as the database backend for our application and that one of our microservices added a new player to the database. If we are utilizing DynamoDB streams in our application, other interested microservices will be able to capture the new player information shortly after it gets added. This allows the other microservices to act accordingly with this new information. For instance, if one of the other microservices is responsible for locating players in the game map, it will then attach the new player to a start location on the game map.

The way DynamoDB streams work is simple. They capture changes that happen to a DynamoDB table item in order. The information gets stored in a log that goes up to 24 hours. Other applications written by us can then access this log and capture the data changes.

In other words, if an item gets created, deleted, or updated, DynamoDB streams would store the item primary key and the data modification that occurred.

DynamoDB streams need to be enabled on tables that need monitoring. We can also disable DynamoDB streams on existing tables, if, for any reason, the tables don't need any more monitoring. DynamoDB streams operate in parallel to the DynamoDB tables, which basically means that there are no performance impact to using them.

To get started with DynamoDB streams, check out http://docs.aws.amazon.com/amazondynamodb/latest/developerguide/Streams.html.

To get started with DynamoDB streams support in the Go programming language, check out https://docs.aws.amazon.com/sdk-for-go/api/service/dynamodbstreams/.

Autoscaling on AWS

Due to the fact that AWS is designed from the grounds up to be utilized with massively distributed microservices applications, AWS comes with built-in features to allow developers of these huge applications to autoscale their applications in the cloud with the least manual intervention possible.

In the world of AWS, the word autoscaling means three main things:

- The ability to automatically replace unhealthy applications or bad EC2 instances without your intervention.
- The ability to automatically create new EC2 instances to handle increased loads on your microservices application without your intervention. Then, the ability to shut down EC2 instances when the application loads decrease.
- The ability to automatically increase cloud service resources available for your application, when the application loads increase. AWS cloud resources here go beyond just EC2. An example of a cloud service resource that can go automatically up or down according to your need is DynamoDB read and write throughput.

To serve this broad definition of autoscaling, the AWS autoscaling service offers three main features:

- **Fleet management for EC2 instances**: This feature allows you to monitor the health of running EC2 instances, automatically replaces bad instances without manual intervention, and balances Ec2 instances across multiple zones when multiple zones are configured.
- **Dynamic Scaling**: This feature allows you to first configure tracking policies to engage the amount of load on your applications. For example, monitor CPU utilization or capture the number of incoming requests. Then, the dynamic scaling feature can automatically add or remove EC2 instances based on your configured target limits.
- **Application Auto Scaling**: This feature allows you to dynamically scale resources on AWS services that go beyond EC2, based on your application's needs.

To get started with the AWS autoscaling services, visit `https://aws.amazon.com/autoscaling/`.

Amazon Relational Database Service

In `Chapter 8`, *AWS II - S3, SQS, API Gateway, and DynamoDB*, when we covered the database service in the AWS world, we covered DynamoDB exclusively. DynamoDB is a managed NoSQL database service that is offered by Amazon on AWS. If you have enough technical expertise with database engines, you would probably ask the obvious question: what about relational databases? Shouldn't there be a managed AWS service for that as well?

The answer for the previous two questions is yes, there is, and it's called **Amazon Relational Database Service** (**RDS**). AWS RDS allows developers to easily configure, operate, scale, and deploy a relational database engine on the cloud.

Amazon RDS supports a collection of well-known relational database engines that a lot of developers use and love. This includes PostgreSQL, MySQL, MariaDB, Oracle, and Microsoft SQL server. In addition to RDS, Amazon offers a service known as Database Migration service that allows you to easily migrate or replicate your existing database to Amazon RDS.

To get started on AWS RDS, visit `https://aws.amazon.com/rds/`. To build Go applications capable of interacting with RDS, visit `https://docs.aws.amazon.com/sdk-for-go/api/service/rds/`.

Other cloud providers

Up until now, we have focused on AWS as a cloud provider. Of course, there are other providers that offer similar services, the two biggest being the Microsoft Azure Cloud and the Google Cloud Platform. Besides these, there are many other providers that also offer IaaS solutions, more often than not based on the open source platform OpenStack.

All cloud providers employ similar concepts, so if you have experience with one of them, you will probably find your way around others. For this reason, we decided not to cover each of them in depth within this book, but instead focus on AWS and give you a short outlook on other providers and how they are different.

Microsoft Azure

You can sign up for the Azure cloud on `https://azure.microsoft.com/en-us/free/`. Like AWS, Azure offers multiple regions and availability zones in which you can run your services. Also, most of the Azure core services work similar to AWS, although they often are named differently:

- The service managing virtual machines (EC2 in AWS terms) is called just that, **virtual machines**. When creating a virtual machine, you will need to select an image (both Linux and Windows images are supported), provide an SSH public key, and choose a machine size. Other core concepts are named similarly. You can configure network access rules using **Network Security Groups**, loadbalance traffic using **Azure Load Balancers** (named Elastic Load Balancer in AWS), and manage automatic scaling using **VM Scale Sets**.
- Relational databases (managed by the Relational Database Service in AWS) are managed by **Azure SQL Databases**. However, at the time of writing this book, only Microsoft SQL databases are supported. Support for MySQL and PostgreSQL databases is available as a preview service only.
- NoSQL databases, similar to DynamoDB, are available in the form of the **Azure Cosmos DB**.
- Message Queues similar to the Simple Queue Service are provided by the **Queue Storage** service.
- Access to APIs provided by your services is possible using the **Application Gateway**.

To consume Azure services from within your Go application, you can use the **Azure SDK for Go**, which is available at `https://github.com/Azure/azure-sdk-for-go`. You can install it using the usual `go get` command:

```
$ go get -u github.com/Azure/azure-sdk-for-go/...
```

The Azure SDK for Go is currently still under heavy development and should be used with caution. To not be surprised by any breaking changes in the SDK, ensure that you use a dependency management tool such as *Glide* to put a version of this library into your vendor/directory (as you learned in `Chapter 9`, *Continuous Delivery*).

Google Cloud Platform

The **Google Cloud Platform** (**GCP**) is the IaaS offering by Google. You can sign up at `https://console.cloud.google.com/freetrial`. Just as with the Azure cloud, you will recognize many core features, although differently named:

- You can manage virtual instances using the **Google Compute Engine**. As usual, each instance is created from an image, a selected machine type, and an SSH public key. Instead of Security Groups, you have **Firewall Rules**, and autoscaling groups are called **Managed Instance Groups**.
- Relational databases are provided by the **Cloud SQL** service. GCP supports both MySQL and PostgreSQL instances.
- For NoSQL databases, you can use the **Cloud Datastore** service.
- The **Cloud Pub/Sub** service offers the possibility to implement complex publish/subscribe architectures (in fact, superceding the possibilities that AWS offers with SQS).

Since both come from Google, it goes without saying that GCP and Go go hand in hand (pun intended). You can install the Go SDK via the usual `go get` command:

```
$ go get -u cloud.google.com/go
```

OpenStack

There are also many cloud providers that build their products on the open source cloud management software, OpenStack (`https://www.openstack.org`). OpenStack is a highly modular software, and clouds built on it may vary significantly in their setup, so it's difficult to make any universally valid statements about them. Typical OpenStack installations might consist of the following services:

- **Nova** manages virtual machine instances and Neutron to manage networking. In the management console, you will find this under the **Instances** and **Networks** labels.
- **Zun** and **Kuryr** manage containers. Since these are relatively young components, it will probably be more common to find managed Kubernetes clusters in OpenStack clouds, though.
- **Trove** provides database services for both relational and nonrelational databases, such as MySQL or MongoDB.
- **Zaqar** provides messaging services similar to SQS.

If you want to access OpenStack features from a Go application, there are multiple libraries that you can choose from. First of all, there is the official client library—`github.com/openstack/golang-client`—which, however, is not yet recommended for production use. At the time of writing this book, the most mature Go client library for OpenStack is the `github.com/gophercloud/gophercloud` library.

Running containers in the cloud

In `Chapter 6`, *Deploying Your Application in Containers*, we got a thorough look at how to deploy a Go application using modern container technologies. When it comes to deploying these containers into a cloud environment, you have a variety of different ways to do that.

One possibility to deploy containerized applications is using an orchestration engine such as **Kubernetes**. This is especially easy when you are using the Microsoft Azure cloud or the Google Cloud Platform. Both providers offer Kubernetes as a managed service, although not under that name; look for the **Azure Container Service (AKS)** or **Google Container Engine (GKE)**.

Although AWS does not offer a managed Kubernetes service, they have a similar offering called **EC2 Container Service (ECS)**. Since ECS is a service available exclusively on AWS, it is very tightly integrated with other AWS core services, which can be both an advantage and disadvantage. Of course, you can set up your own Kubernetes cluster on AWS using the building blocks provided in the form of VMs, networking, and storage. Doing this is incredibly complex work, but do not despair. You can use third-party tools to set up a Kubernetes cluster on AWS automatically. One of these tools is **kops**.

You can download kops at `https://github.com/kubernetes/kops`. After that, follow the setup instructions for AWS that you can find in the project documentation at `https://github.com/kubernetes/kops/blob/master/docs/aws.md`.

Kops itself is also written in Go and uses the very same AWS SDK that you have already come across in `Chapters 7`, *AWS I–Fundamentals, AWS SDK for Go, and EC2*, and `Chapter 8`, *AWS II - S3, SQS, API Gateway, and DynamoDB*. Take a look at the source code to see a real-life example of some very sophisticated usage of the AWS client library.

Serverless architectures

When consuming a traditional Infrastructure-as-a-Service offering, you are provided a number of virtual machines along with the respective infrastructure (such as storage and networking). You typically need to operate everything running within these virtual machines yourself. This usually means not only your compiled application, but also the entire operating system, including the kernel of each and every system service of a full-blown Linux (or Windows) system. You are also responsible for the capacity planning of your infrastructure (which means estimating your application's resource requirements and defining sensible boundaries for your autoscaling groups).

All of this means **Operational Overhead** that keeps you from your actual job, that is, building and deploying software that drives your business. To reduce this overhead, you can instead use a Platform-as-a-Service offering instead of an IaaS one. One common form of PaaS hosting is using container technologies, where the developer simply provides a container image, and the provider takes care of running (and optionally, scaling) the application and managing the underlying infrastructure. Typical container-based PaaS offerings include the EC2 Container Service by AWS or any Kubernetes cluster, such as the Azure Container Service or the Google Container Engine. Noncontainer-based PaaS offerings might include AWS Elastic Beanstalk or Google App Engine.

Recently, another approach has arisen that strives to eliminate even more operational overhead than PaaS offerings: **Serverless Computing**. Of course, that name is wildly misleading, as applications being run on a serverless architecture obviously still require servers. The key difference is that the existence of these servers is completely hidden from the developer. The developer only provides the application to be executed, and the provider takes care of provisioning infrastructure for this application and deploying and running it. This approach works well with Microservice Architectures, as it becomes incredibly easy to deploy small pieces of code that communicate with each other using web services, message queues, or other means. Taken to the extreme, this often results in single functions being deployed as services, resulting in the alternate term for serverless computing: **Functions-as-a-Service (FaaS)**.

Many cloud providers offer FaaS functionalities as part of their services, the most prominent example being **AWS Lambda**. At the time of writing this book, AWS Lambda does not officially support Go as a programming language (supported languages are JavaScript, Python, Java, and C#), and running Go functions is only possible using third-party wrappers such as `https://github.com/eawsy/aws-lambda-go`.

Other cloud providers offer similar services. Azure offers **Azure Functions** (supporting JavaScript, C#, F#, PHP, Bash, Batch, and PowerShell) and GCP offers **Cloud Functions** as a Beta product (supporting only JavaScript). If you are running a Kubernetes cluster, you can use the Fission framework (`https://github.com/fission/fission`) to run your own FaaS platform (which even supports Go). However, Fission is a product in an early alpha development stage and not yet recommended for production use.

As you may have noticed, support for the Go language is not yet far spread among the popular FaaS offerings. However, given the popularity of both Go as a programming language and Serverless Architecture, not all hope is lost.

Summary

With this, we reach the end of our book. By now, you should have enough knowledge to build sophisticated microservices cloud native applications that are resilient, distributed, and scalable. With this chapter, you should also develop ideas of where to go next to take your newly acquired knowledge to the next level. We thank you for giving us the chance to guide you through this learning journey and look forward to being part of your future journeys.

Index

A

Advanced Message Queueing Protocol (AMQP) 85
Amazon Machine Image (AMI) 224, 231
Amazon Relational Database Service (RDS)
  about 377
  reference link 377
Amazon Web Services (AWS)
  about 201, 374
  Amazon API Gateway 202
  AWS SDK for Go 203
  command-line interface (CLI) 204
  console 203
  DynamoDB 203
  DynamoDB streams 375
  Elastic Beanstalk 205
  Elastic Compute Cloud (EC2) 202
  fundamentals 202
  RDS 377
  regions 204
  Simple Queue Service (SQS) 202
  Simple Storage Service (S3) 202
  tags 205
  zones 204
AmazonS3FullAccess 209
Apache ActiveMQ
  URL 87
Apache Kafka
  about 79
  connecting, with Go 113
  messages, consuming 117, 119, 122
  messages, publishing 114
  principles 110
  used, for implementing event sourcing 109
  used, for implementing publish/subscribe 109
  with Docker 110
Apache Mesos 18

Apache QPID
  URL 87
Application Gateway 378
application
  deploying, to cloud 178
asymmetrical cryptography
  about 64
  in HTTPS 66, 67
asynchronous messaging 18
auto-scaling 12
AWS API gateway 265, 274
AWS autoscaling
  application autoscaling 376
  dynamic scaling 376
  features 376
  fleet management, for EC2 instances 376
  reference link 376
AWS CLI
  URL 204
AWS console
  URL 265
AWS identity and access management (IAM) 207
AWS Lambda
  about 381
  reference link 381
AWS SDK Go SQS package
  URL 254
AWS services
  about 206
  AWS region, configuring 206
  AWS SDK authentication, configuring 207
  AWS SDK fundamentals, for Go 215
  AWS SDK, for Go 206
  Elastic Compute Cloud (EC2) 221
  errors, handling 220
  IAM Roles, creating 212
  IAM users, creating 207

native datatypes 217
pagination methods 218
service clients 216
sessions 215
shared configuration 218
waiters 220
Azure Container Service 18, 180
Azure Container Service (AKS) 380
Azure Cosmos DB 378
Azure Functions 382
Azure Load Balancers 378
Azure SDK for Go
   about 378
   reference link 378
Azure SQL Databases 378

B

basic design goals
   about 11
   easy deployment 13
   resiliency 13
   statelessness 12
Binary JSON
   reference link 45
bindings 85
booking process
   implementing 145, 146, 149, 153
booking service
   about 22, 82, 83
   building 105
bounded contexts
   in DDD 360

C

CA (certificate authority) 67
certificate authority providers
   reference link 68
certificate
   generate_cert.go 70, 72
   obtaining 68
   OpenSSL 69
cloud application architecture patterns
   about 14
   asynchronous messaging 18

microservices 17
microservices, deploying 17
REST web services 18
twelve-factor app 15
Cloud Datastore service 379
Cloud Functions
   about 382
   reference link 382
cloud providers
   about 377
   GCP 379
   Microsoft Azure 378
   OpenStack 379
Cloud Pub/Sub service 379
cloud service models
   about 13
   IaaS 13
   PaaS 14
   SaaS 14
cloud
   application, deploying 178
   containers, executing 380
Command Query Responsibility Segregation
   (CQRS) 369
Community Edition (CE) 313
component 127
container images 156
containers
   about 156
   building 165
   executing, in cloud 380
continuous delivery (CD) 295
continuous integration (CI) 295
control groups (cgroups) 156
Cross-Origin Resource Sharing (CORS)
   about 140
   enabling, in backend services 140
custom metrics
   exporting 342, 346

D

data consistency
   about 364
   CQRS 369
   event sourcing 368

event-driven architecture 365
  events sourcing 367
data types
  document types 276
  scalar Types 275
  set types 276
decryption key 62
dependency managers 298
destructuring assignment 151
digital certificate 66
Docker Compose
  about 172
  application, deploying 172, 176
  URL 172
Docker Swarm 18
Docker
  about 10, 155, 157
  containers, executing 157
  containers, networking 162
  Grafana, executing 336
  images, building 160
  Prometheus, executing 332
  URL 157, 178
  using, in RabbitMQ 87
Dockerfile 160
domain-driven design (DDD)
  bounded contexts 360
  reference link 360
DynamoDB streams
  about 375
  reference link 375
DynamoDB
  about 22, 274, 283
  attribute value data types 275
  attributes 275
  components 274
  items 275
  primary keys 276
  secondary indexes 277
  tables 274
  tables, creating 278
  URL 291

E

EC2 Container Service (ECS) 380
Elastic Beanstalk
  about 205
  URL 206
Elastic Block Store (EBS) 224
Elastic Compute Cloud (EC2) 202
  about 221
  accessing, from Windows 233, 239
  instances, accessing 229
  instances, accessing from Linux 231
  instances, accessing from macOS machine 231
  instances, creating 222, 226, 228
  security groups 240, 244
Elastic Container Service 18
Elastic Load Balancer 198
encryption key 62
endpoint 73
event collaboration 83
event list components
  booking process, implementing 145, 146, 149, 151, 153
  building 134, 136, 138
  CORS, enabling in backend services 140
  navigation layer, adding 142, 144
  responsibilities 135
  route layer, adding 142, 144
event list
  client 134
  implementing 133
  testing 142
event Service 22
event sourcing
  about 108
  implementing, with Apache Kafka 109
event subscriber
  building 101
EventList component 135
EventListContainer component 135
EventListItem component 135
EventService 83
exchange type 85
exchanges
  about 85

direct exchanges 85
fanout exchanges 85
topic exchanges 85

F

Firewall Rules 379
four-tier engagement platform
  about 358
  aggregation layer 359
  client layer 359
  delivery layer 359
  reference link 358
  services layer 360
Functions-as-a-Service (FaaS) 381

G

generate_cert.go 70
GitLab
  CI feature, setting up 316, 320, 326, 327
  setting up 313, 316
  using 313
Glide 298
Go application
  Prometheus client, using 338
Go language
  about 283
  URL 284
Go
  HTTPS server, building 72
  Kafka, connecting 113
  need for 10
  RabbitMQ, connecting 89
Godep 298
golang-client
  reference link 380
Google Cloud Platform (GCP)
  about 379
  reference link 379
Google Container Engine 180
Google Container Engine (GKE) 18, 380
Gorilla web toolkit 32
Grafana
  about 329
  executing, on Docker 336

setting up 329
GRPC
  about 374
  URL 374

H

handshake 66
horizontal scaling 11
HTTPS server
  building, in Go 72, 73, 76, 78
HTTPS
  about 62
  asymmetric cryptography 64, 66
  asymmetrical cryptography 67
  symmetric cryptography 62
  symmetric-key algorithms 63

I

IaaS (Infrastructure as a Service) 13
images
  publishing 177
immutable 157
Ingress 198
Internet of Things (IOT) 9

J

JSX 127

K

Kafka 22
kops
  about 380
  references 380
kubectl 181
Kubelet 180
Kubernetes
  about 18, 179
  core concepts 182, 185
  deploying to 310
  GitLab, using 313
  HTTP Ingress, configuring 198
  images availability 194
  local Kubernetes, setting up with Minikube 180
  MongoDB containers, creating 193

MyEvents components, deploying 195
MyEvents, deploying 190
persistent volumes 188
Prometheus, executing 346
RabbitMQ broker, creating 190
services 186

M

Managed Instance Groups 379
message attributes 255
message body 255
messages
  consuming, from Apache Kafka 117, 119, 122
metrics
  about 330
  custom metrics, exporting 342, 346
  exporting 338
  Prometheus client, using in Go application 339
  Prometheus scrape targets, configuring 340
mgo
  about 45
  reference link 45, 47
microservice architecture 352
microservices communications
  about 372
  GRPC 374
  protocol buffers 373
microservices design patterns
  about 357
  bounded contexts, in DDD 360
  data consistency 364
  four-tier engagement platform 358
  sacrificial architecture 357
microservices
  about 17, 23, 26, 352
  deploying 17
  internals 27
  monolithic applications, migrating from 353
  reference link 17
Microsoft Azure
  reference link 378
Minikube
  local Kubernetes, setting up 180
  URL 181
MongoDB 22, 39, 45

monolithic applications
  about 23, 351
  code, breaking 356
  dividing 354
  glue code 356
  migrating, to microservices 353
  people factor 353
  technology 353
Mozilla Public License 87
MyEvents application
  about 24
  booking, processing 24
  deploying, to Kubernetes 190
  events, handling 24
  handle, searching 24
MyEvents platform 20

N

namespaces 156
navigation layer
  adding 142, 144
Network Security Groups 378
NGINX 159
Node Package Manager (npm) 124
Node.js
  setting up 124
NodePort services 198

O

OpenSSL
  about 69
  arguments 69
  reference link 69
  URL 69
OpenStack
  about 379
  Kuryr 379
  Nova 379
  Trove 379
  URL 379
  Zaqar 379
  Zun 379
Operational Overhead 381

P

PaaS (Platform as a Service) 14
pagination 218
people factor 353
Pivotal 87
primary key
  composite key 277
primary keys
  about 276
  partition keys 276
project
  dependencies, vendoring 298
  setting up 296
  version control, setting up 296
Prometheus Query Language
  reference link 338
Prometheus
  about 22, 329
  basics 330
  client, using in Go application 338
  configuration file, creating 331
  executing, on Docker 332
  executing, on Kubernetes 346
  scrape targets, configuring 340
  setting up 329
PromQL 330
protocol buffers
  about 373
  references 373
  working 373
publish/subscribe pattern
  about 80
  advantages 81
publish/subscribe
  implementing, with Apache Kafka 109
  implementing, with RabbitMQ 85
PuTTY tool
  URL 230, 233

Q

Quay
  URL 177
Queue Storage service 378
Queues 85

R

RabbitMQ broker
  creating 190
RabbitMQ cluster
  URL 89
RabbitMQ
  about 22, 79
  Advanced Message Queueing Protocol (AMQP)
    85
  advanced setups 89
  AMQP messages, publishing 91
  AMQP messages, subscribing 91
  booking service, building 105
  connecting, with Go 89
  event emitter, building 94
  event subscriber, building 101
  used, for implementing publish/subscribe 85
  with Docker 87
React principles
  about 127, 130
  event list, implementing 133
  MyEvents frontend 130, 132, 133
React
  Node.js, setting up 124
  project, initializing 124, 127
  starting with 124
  TypeScript, setting up 124
regions, AWS
  URL 204
Remote Procedure Call (RPC) 374
Representational State Transfer (REST) 28
REST web services 18
RESTful Web APIs
  about 28
  DELEETE method 32
  GET method 31
  Go language 45, 51
  Gorilla web toolkit 32
  handler functions, implementing 52, 55, 56, 58,
    59
  implementing 33, 36
  MongoDB 39, 45, 51
  persistence layer 38
  POST method 31

PUT method 32
  reference link 31
RKT 155
route layer, adding 142
route layer
  adding 144
routing key 85

S

SaaS (Software as a Service) 14
sacrificial architecture
  about 357
  reference link 357
scalability 11
scale out 11
scale up 11
scrapping 330
secondary indexes
  about 277
  base table 277
  global secondary index 277
  local secondary indexes 278
  projected attributes 277
Secure Shell (SSH) 230
secure web services
  about 68
  certificate, obtaining 68, 69
  HTTPS server, building 73, 76, 78
  HTTPS server, building in Go 72
self-signing 67
serverless architectures 381
Serverless Computing 381
service account 311
service-oriented architectures (SOA) 17, 352
sessions 215
Simple Queue Service (SQS) 82, 217, 252, 265
Simple Storage Service (S3)
  about 249
  configuring 249

single-responsibility principle 135
SQS 22
symmetric cryptography 62

T

TLS (Transport Layer Security) 61
TLS protocol
  about 62
  asymmetric cryptography 64
  symmetric cryptography 62
topic-based 81
Travis CI
  URL 304
  using 302
TSX 128
twelve-factor app
  about 13, 15
  backing services 16
  configuration 15
  dependencies 15
  disposability 16
  processes 16
  URL 15
TypeScript
  setting up 124

V

vendoring 298
version control system (VCS) 296
vertical scaling 11
virtual machines 378
VirtualBox
  URL 180
visibility timeout 257
volumes
  containers, building 165
  containers, building for backend services 165
  containers, building for frontend 170
  static compilation, using for smaller images 168
  working with 164